TABLE OF CONTENT

PART I   1

THE ESSENTIAL 500 WORDS

THE
INSIDER'S
COMPLETE GUIDE
TO

SAT
VOCABULARY:
THE
ESSENTIAL
500
WORDS

LARRY KRIEGER
WITH CONTRIBUTIONS BY
VINAY BHASKARA

The Insider's Complete Guide To
SAT VOCABULARY:
The Essential 500 Words

LARRY KRIEGER
WITH CONTRIBUTIONS BY
VINAY BHASKARA

ISBN: 978-0985291211

An INSIDER TEST PREP publication of Larry Prep LLC

Art Direction & Design by Station16 Creative (Station16 LLC)

For more Insider resources visit
www.InsiderTestPrep.com

PART II   195
THE ESSENTIAL GUIDE TO SENTENCE COMPLETIONS

PART III   235

THE ESSENTIAL GUIDE TO PASSAGE-BASED VOCABULARY QUESTIONS

THE TOP 30 SAT ROOTS

1. ACRI AND ACER; 2. AMICUS; 3. BELLI; 4. CHRON; 5. CLUD AND CLUS; 6. CRED; 7. DEMOS; 8. FID; 9. FLU; 10. GREG; 11. LOQU; 12. LUC AND LUMEN; 13. MORI; 14. MORPH; 15. MUT; 16. NOV; 17. ONUS; 18. PACIS; 19. PAR; 20. PATHOS; 21. PLAC; 22. POTEN; 23. PUG; 24. QUIESCERE; 25. SCRIB; 26. SEMIN; 27. SPEC AND SPIC; 28. TEN; 29. TURB; 30. VIVERE:

ABOUT THE ESSENTIAL 500 WORDS

NO WIND FAVORS A SHIP WITHOUT A DESTINATION

When I was your age, my guidance counselor asked me to describe my goals. When I said that I didn't know, my counselor admonished me by saying, "Larry, no wind favors a ship without a destination." My counselor was right – goals are important. So I'd like to begin by asking you an important question: What score are you trying to achieve on the Critical Reading portion of the SAT? As you think about your answer, keep in mind that the average Critical Reading score is 500 and that only about 10 percent of all test-takers score above a 650.

I'm guessing that the overwhelming majority of you are striving for a score above a 600. Congratulations! *The Essential 500 Words* is designed to help you achieve your goal.

FIVE LEVELS OF QUESTIONS
IT IS VERY IMPORTANT TO UNDERSTAND THAT SAT TEST QUESTIONS ARE DIVIDED INTO THE FOLLOWING FIVE LEVELS OF DIFFICULTY:

<u>LEVEL 1:</u> These questions are easy. About 80 percent of all test takers correctly answer the Level 1 questions. If you answer all of the Level 1 questions correctly, your score will be about a 340.

<u>LEVEL 2:</u> These questions are a bit more challenging. About 65 percent of all test takers correctly answer Level 2 questions. If you answer all of the Level 2 questions correctly, your score will be about a 440.

<u>LEVEL 3:</u> These questions are average to above average in difficulty. About 50 percent of all test takers correctly answer Level 3 questions. If you answer all of the Level 3 questions correctly, your score will be about a 580.

<u>LEVEL 4:</u> These questions are challenging. Only about 35 percent of all test takers correctly answer Level 4 questions. If you answer all of the Level 4 questions correctly, your score will be about a 680.

<u>LEVEL 5:</u> These questions are very challenging. Only about 20 percent of all students correctly answer Level 5 questions. If you answer all of the Level 5 questions correctly your score will soar into the 700s!

VOCABULARY! VOCABULARY!! VOCABULARY!!!

Answering Level 4 and Level 5 questions correctly is crucial to achieving a critical reading score above a 600. My students often ask me, "What can we do to correctly answer the Level 4 and Level 5 questions?" I always respond with a simple answer: "Vocabulary! Vocabulary!! Vocabulary!!!"

It is important to understand that challenging vocabulary words are the defining characteristic of most Level 4 and Level 5 questions. This brings us to an important paradox: the hard questions are actually easy if you know the words. You read correctly. The most challenging Level 5 questions can usually be answered very quickly if you have a strong SAT vocabulary.

WHY THE ESSENTIAL 500 WORDS IS THE BEST SAT VOCABULARY BOOK

There are a number of vocabulary books all claiming to be the best. So why is *The Essential 500 Words* the best vocabulary book?

Each of the 500 words is the answer to a real SAT question. Each SAT is a link in an overlapping chain of tests stretching back over half a century. As a result, test writers continually repeat key words. *The Essential 500 Words* takes advantage of this often neglected fact by focusing on words that have been repeatedly used on real SATs.

The Essential 500 Words is divided into chapters based upon types of SAT questions. For example, critical reading questions often test your ability to identify an author's tone and spot rhetorical devices such as figurative language and personification. *The Essential 500 Words* devotes three full chapters to attitude, tone, and mood words and two full chapters to rhetorical device words.

The Essential 500 Words focuses particular attention on the Level 4 and 5 words you will need to score above a 600. We define and illustrate 100 Level 5 words and 100 Level 4 words.

Each of the 500 words is illustrated by a vivid example designed to promote your ability to recall and use the word. My examples are drawn from an eclectic range of topics. You will find examples from popular songs and movies, from AP courses, from current events, from the experiences of my students, and even from my own life and teaching career. In addition, many of my examples focus on topics such as the college admission process that are relevant to your life.

Many of the words include a heading labeled "Insider Info." These sections are designed to share my knowledge of how a word has typically been used in real SAT questions.

The Essential 500 Words is more than just a vocabulary book. In order to achieve a high score on the SAT it is not enough to simply learn these words. You must also know how to apply them to sentence completion and passage-based questions. Chapters 48 – 53 provide a detailed discussion of the key types of sentence completion questions. These chapters contain over 100 practice sentence completions. Chapters 54 – 59 provide a detailed discussion of four key types of vocabulary passage-based questions. These chapters contain over 60 practice passages.

The Essential 500 Words includes a special Appendix that identifies the Top 30 SAT roots and defines 94 key words derived from these roots.

I hope you enjoy using *The Essential 500 Words*. Be sure to check out InsiderTestPrep.com for additional insights and materials! Good luck!

ABOUT LARRY KRIEGER

Larry Krieger was born and raised in western North Carolina. He earned his Bachelor of Arts and Master of Arts in Teaching from the University of North Carolina at Chapel Hill and his Master of Arts degree in Sociology from Wake Forest University.

Larry's teaching career began in 1970 at Olympic High School in Charlotte, North Carolina. During the next 35 years Larry taught urban, rural, and suburban students in North Carolina and New Jersey. Larry taught a variety of AP subjects including American History, World History, European History, American Government, and Art History. His popular courses were renowned for their energetic presentations, commitment to scholarship, and dedication to excellence. All of Larry's AP students scored above a 3, with most scoring a 4 or a 5. In 2004 and 2005, the College Board recognized Larry as one of the nation's foremost AP teachers.

Larry is also widely known as one of America's top SAT coaches. In 2005 Larry led Montgomery High School to a Number 1 ranking in New Jersey. His students achieved a public school record national average score of 629 on the Critical Reading section of the SAT. Larry has conducted SAT workshops across the United States in a variety of cities including Denver, Louisville, Atlanta, and Minneapolis.

Larry's success has extended far beyond the classroom. He is the author of widely known Sociology, American History, and World History textbooks and a number of AP and SAT prep books. Larry founded InsiderTestPrep.com to share his SAT and AP materials with students around the world. *The Essential 500 Words* joins the *AP US History: The Essential Content* as the company's second major book. Insider Test Prep expects to publish a series of innovative SAT and AP books and eBooks in the near future.

ABOUT VINAY BHASKARA

Vinay is one of Larry's finest SAT students. He scored a 2400 on his SAT and a 5 on nearly a dozen AP exams. Vinay's academic achievements extend beyond standardized tests. He is an avid student of aviation and has published a highly regarded book entitled *Delta Airlines' Widebody Operations*. Vinay's eclectic background includes a love of movies, TV shows and other aspects of popular culture. Vinay will be a student at the University of Chicago. You can learn more about Vinay by reading Words 56, 93, 94, 159-160, and 268.

ACKNOWLEDGEMENTS

Books do not write themselves. They require the help of a number of dedicated and creative people.

First and foremost, I would like to thank my wife Susan. Every chapter benefited from Susan's "close reads." Susan and I also had a lot of fun recalling anecdotes about the students we taught at Jordan-Matthews High School in North Carolina.

I would also like to thank Jan Altman for her help and encouragement. Jan is a tireless researcher and an inspiring SAT and ACT tutor.

I have been blessed with an exceptional number of outstanding students who have made significant contributions to this book. I would like to thank Akash Bagaria and Abha Kulkarni for suggesting a number of outstanding popular culture examples. I would also like to thank Sanjana Mehta for her close reads, Dhara Patel for her great examples, Nikita Kachroo for spontaneously creating the first of the popular "Meet My Students" examples, Anid Laoui for suggesting that I take a look at the film *Ratatouille*, Emily Cai for being a great host and superb writer, Nicole Lorenzi for encouraging me to add a feature on K-Stew and R-Pattz, and Kavin and Pranay for being great critical readers. And finally, special thanks to the parents of all my students. We have all benefited from your support and encouragement.

I would like to thank the creative team at Station16 in Atlanta for their hard work and dedication to producing a quality product. I would especially like to thank Annie Smith for her meticulous editing and fine eye for details.

THE PERFECT SCORE CLUB

The materials in this book have helped my students achieve outstanding PSAT and SAT scores. Several dozen students have achieved an 800 on Critical Reading and overall scores above a 2300. I would especially like to recognize the following members of our Perfect Score Club. These students achieved either a 2400 on the SAT or a 240 on the PSAT:

VINAY BHASKARA	2400 SAT
ROBBIE BHATTACHARJEE	2400 SAT
HRID BISWAS	2400 SAT
LINDSAY EPSTEIN	240 PSAT
RISHI KANERIYA	2400 SAT
PRANAY NADELLA	2400 SAT
KEVIN SHEN	2400 SAT
CODY SHENG	240 PSAT
ZACK PERKINS	2400 SAT
JOHAN ZHANG	2400 SAT

THE BOARD OF STUDENT ADVISORS

VIJAY APPASAMY
Montgomery High School
Montgomery, New Jersey

JAYAN ARIYAWANSA
Montgomery High School
Montgomery, New Jersey

AKASH BAGARIA
Lawrenceville School
Lawrenceville, New Jersey

DHRUV BAGGA
West Windsor Plainsboro High School
West Windsor, New Jersey

ANCHAL BATRA
West Windsor Plainsboro High School
West Windsor, New Jersey

ARCHANA BEERAM
Montgomery High School
Montgomery, New Jersey

MUKHI BHUPATIRAJU
Montgomery High School
Montgomery, New Jersey

EMILY CAI
Montgomery High School
Montgomery, New Jersey

NIVE CHALAM
Hillsborough High School
Hillsborough, New Jersey

ARVIND CHANDAK
Hillsborough High School
Hillsborough, New Jersey

AKHIL CHHUGANI
Montgomery High School
Montgomery, New Jersey

THE BOARD OF STUDENT ADVISORS (cont...)

THE BOARD OF STUDENT ADVISORS (cont...)

THE BOARD OF STUDENT ADVISORS (cont…)

PART I

THE ESSENTIAL 500 WORDS

CHAPTER 1
THE TOP TWENTY WORDS
PART 1

Each SAT is a link in an overlapping chain of tests that stretches back over half a century. As a result, test writers use key vocabulary words repeatedly. This chapter defines and illustrates ten of the twenty most frequently used words on the SAT. You'll find other high-frequency words such as *ANECDOTE*, *SKEPTICAL*, and *AMBIVALENT* in our chapters on Rhetorical Devices (Chapters 3–4) and the Author's Tone (Chapters 6–8).

1. AESTHETIC
- *characterized by a sensitivity to beauty in art and taste*

INSIDER INFO
AESTHETIC is the Number 1 word on the SAT. There is a fifty percent chance you will see it on your test. Be alert for sentence completion questions that contrast *AESTHETIC*, meaning "beauty," with *UTILITARIAN*, meaning "useful or functional." Of course, it is possible for an object to be both *AESTHETICALLY* pleasing and functional. For example, Steve Jobs and his Apple design team created iPhones and iMac computers that are praised for their *AESTHETIC* design and also for their *UTILITARIAN* features.

2. CONVENTIONAL
- *customary; conforming to established practices*

INSIDER INFO
The CONVENTIONAL approach to critical reading is first to read the entire passage and then to answer all the questions. I advocate a new and UNCONVENTIONAL approach. It is important to remember that almost all critical reading questions are anchored in a specific paragraph. So use a back-and-forth strategy in which you read a paragraph and then answer all the questions that pertain to that paragraph.

3. MITIGATE

- *to make less severe or harsh; to moderate; to lessen; to relieve*

INSIDER INFO

MITIGATE is one of the most frequently used correct answers for sentence completion questions. For example, Arctic animals use fur, feathers, and blubber to MITIGATE or lessen the effects of bitterly cold weather. *MITIGATE* is part of a very important synonym cluster that includes *ASSUAGE, MOLLIFY, ALLEVIATE, and PALLIATE.* All of these words mean "to lessen or make less severe."

4. PRAGMATIC

- *practical; realistic; down to earth*

IN YOUR LIFE

A PRAGMATIC person is a realist who does what is practical and what works best. In contrast, an IDEALISTIC person dreams of perfection. For example, let's say that you are a top math student who made a single careless mistake on your first SAT. Most students would be EUPHORIC (jubilant) to score a 770. But your goal is to score an 800. Should you take the SAT again? A PRAGMATIC student would realize that few if any colleges would reject a student for missing just one math question. An IDEALISTIC student, however, would strive for perfection. What would you do? Would you be a PRAGMATIST or an IDEALIST?

5. ALTRUISTIC

- *characterized by unselfish concern for the welfare of others; not egotistical*

POP CULTURE

In the movie *The Hunger Games*, Katniss and Prim Everdeen are sisters who are both eligible to become tributes in the 74th annual Hunger Games, a gruesome fight to the death on live TV. Prim is a sweet and innocent girl who is just twelve years old. Although the odds are seemingly in her favor, Effie Trinket unexpectedly draws Prim's name out of a huge glass bowl. Stunned by what has happened, Katniss pushes through the crowd of onlookers and shouts, "I volunteer! I volunteer as tribute!" Katniss's ALTRUISTIC act saves Prim's life but places Katniss in mortal danger.

6. DIFFIDENT

- *timid; lacking self-confidence; shy and reserved,*
  especially in social gatherings; SELF-EFFACING

INSIDER INFO

The Latin root *fid*, meaning "faith or trust," is central to the meaning of the SAT word *DIFFIDENT*. People who are DIFFIDENT lack faith in themselves. So a DIFFIDENT person would almost certainly not aspire to be a talk-show host. On SAT sentence completion questions, DIFFIDENT people are often mistaken for being ALOOF and therefore distant and detached.

7. FRANK

- *open and honest; CANDID*

MEET MY STUDENTS: MEGHA

FRANK is a very tricky word. Most students associate it with a common male name. Megha recently found a clever way to help everyone remember the SAT meaning of *FRANK*. She pointed out that Frank Ocean is a popular hip hop singer and song writer. Ocean recently released a statement acknowledging that he is gay. His FRANK admission enabled Ocean to declare openly, "Now I don't have any secrets." As noted by Megha, "Frank was FRANK."

8. REVERE

- *to show great respect for a person, idea, or symbol; to VENERATE*

IN MY LIFE

When I travel around the country, I always ask my students to name a REVERED local figure. In Charlottesville, Virginia, the students named Thomas Jefferson; in Louisville the students named Muhammad Ali; and in New Jersey the students named Bruce Springsteen. When I asked students in Boston to name a REVERED local figure they cleverly replied "Paul Revere, of course!"

9. SUBTLE

- *gradual and therefore not obvious*

IN YOUR LIFE

The signs that a relationship is in trouble can sometimes be very SUBTLE. For example, a decrease in the number of text messages and the use of last-minute excuses to change long-planned activities can be SUBTLE signs that your boyfriend or girlfriend is beginning to lose interest in the relationship. So be vigilant and look out for SUBTLE changes that seem innocent at first but PORTEND (indicate) future problems.

10. RETICENT

- *reluctant to publicly discuss one's thoughts, feelings, and personal affairs; restrained and RESERVED in style; not outspoken*

INSIDER INFO

RETICENT is a high-frequency word that is often used as an answer in Level 5 sentence completion questions. Test writers typically use *RETICENT* in contrast sentences that include key antonyms such as *outspoken*, *talkative*, and *FLAMBOYANT*. For example, the acclaimed novelist Harper Lee is privately engaging but publicly RETICENT to express her views. Despite the success of *To Kill a Mockingbird*, Lee has granted just one interview in the last forty years.

CHAPTER 2
THE TOP TWENTY WORDS
PART 2

Each SAT is a link in an overlapping chain of tests that stretches back over half a century. As a result, test writers use key vocabulary words repeatedly. This chapter defines and illustrates the next ten of the twenty most frequently used words on the SAT. You'll find other high-frequency words such as *ANECDOTE*, *SKEPTICAL*, and *AMBIVALENT* in our chapters on Rhetorical Devices (Chapters 3–4) and the Author's Tone (Chapters 6–8).

11. ANTITHETICAL
• *characterized by an extreme contrast or POLAR opposites*
POP CULTURE
In her song "You Belong with Me," Taylor Swift draws a sharp contrast between herself and her rival. According to Taylor, "She wears high heels, I wear sneakers. She's Cheer Captain and I'm on the bleachers." And to make the contrast even greater, her rival wears short skirts, and Taylor wears t-shirts. In short, the two girls have totally ANTITHETICAL personalities. They are POLAR opposites.

12. PRESCIENT
• *perceiving the significance of events before they occur; showing foresight*
AP U.S. HISTORY
The Missouri Compromise of 1820 temporarily defused the political crisis over the expansion of slavery; however, the settlement foreshadowed the increasingly bitter sectional struggles that lay ahead. Thomas Jefferson sensed the future peril when he PRESCIENTLY wrote, "This momentous question, like a fire bell in the night, awakened and filled me with terror … It is hushed for the moment, but this is a reprieve only."

13. NOSTALGIA

- *a bittersweet longing for something in the past*

INSIDER INFO

SAT critical reading sections often include passages in which a person revisits a childhood home. The visit inevitably triggers feelings of NOSTALGIA for home-cooked meals and beloved childhood pets. Feelings of NOSTALGIA are not limited to adults revisiting their childhood homes. Over the years I have noticed that many of my graduating seniors become very NOSTALGIC when they view pictures and video clips of themselves and their friends performing in elementary school plays.

14. BEGUILE

- *to trick or captivate someone, either with deception or with irresistible charm*

POP CULTURE

In his classic song "She Looks Like an Angel," Elvis Presley fell for a girl who looked, walked, and talked like an angel. BEGUILED by this seemingly perfect girl, Elvis briefly thought that he was in heaven. But Elvis finally got wise and realized that his girlfriend was actually a BEGUILING "devil in disguise" who cheated, schemed, and fooled him with her irresistible charm. Don't expect College Board test writers to BEGUILE you with lyrics from a pop song. Instead, be prepared to see *BEGUILE* in Level 5 sentence completion questions. For example, on a recent test rebellious intellectuals were BEGUILED by provocative political doctrines.

15. OMINOUS

- *menacing and threatening; foreshadowing ill-fortune*

INSIDER INFO

The word *OMINOUS* has become a very popular wrong answer choice. Many students incorrectly believe that *OMINOUS* means "all," because they confuse the letters *omin* with the prefix *omni*, which does mean "all." Don't make this mistake! *OMINOUS* refers to something that is menacing and threatens danger. For example, in the *Harry Potter* saga the Dark Mark is an OMINOUS symbol of the danger posed by Lord Voldemort and his Death Eaters.

16. SUCCINCT

- *brief and to the point; concise*

INSIDER INFO

SUCCINCT is a very popular answer for Level 4 and 5 sentence completion questions. Test writers typically use the phrases "remarkably few words," "notably brief," and "an economy of means" to signal that *SUCCINCT* is the correct answer. It is also important to remember that *RAMBLING* means "long and disjointed" and is thus an antonym of *SUCCINCT*. A writer who is known for a RAMBLING prose style would not be SUCCINCT.

17. DISCERNING

- *demonstrating keen insight and good judgment; able to distinguish good from bad*

POP CULTURE

In the movie *Ratatouille*, Anton Ego is an arrogant but also very DISCERNING French food critic. The haughty Ego has often expressed great DISDAIN (contempt) for Chef Gusteau's famous motto, "Anyone can cook." Ego changes his mind, however, after eating an unforgettable stew prepared by Remy, an ANTHROPOMORPHIC (attributing human characteristics to other animals) rat who is a gifted chef. The DISCERNING critic recognizes that the dish was "an extraordinary meal from a singularly unexpected source." Ego now understands that while "not everyone can become a great artist, a great artist can come from anywhere."

18. BELIE

- *to give a false impression; to misrepresent*

MEET MY STUDENTS: BRENNA

Brenna has a MULTIFACETED (many-sided) personality. In my SAT class he is RESERVED (shy) and studious; however, his shy demeanor BELIES another far more outgoing side of his personality. It turns out that Brenna is an excellent musician, talented singer, and an amazing break dancer. You can see Brenna perform by going to YouTube and searching for the Lemon Brownie Krew. I promise you won't be disappointed.

19. ANOMALY

- *a deviation from a common pattern; a departure from the norm; something that is ATYPICAL and thus ABERRANT*

IN THE NEWS

Everybody knows that high school cheerleading squads are comprised of high school students. Well, not always. The cheerleading squad at St. Ignace High School in Michigan is an ANOMALY. Why? When the students failed to form a team, a group of moms took matters into their own hands by creating their own cheerleading squad. The cheerleader moms have even brought back EXUBERANT (filled with enthusiasm) and ANOMALOUS 1970s-era cheers such as "Hold that line" and "Two bits, four bits, six bits, a dollar, all for the Saints stand up and holler!"

20. PEREMPTORY

- *an order or command that does not allow discussion or refusal; an arbitrary order*

INSIDER INFO

PEREMPTORY has recently become a very popular answer for Level 5 sentence completion questions. Test writers use BRUSQUE (abrupt) officials, overbearing partners, and stern teachers to signal a PEREMPTORY manner. Fans of *The Hunger Games* will recall how the Gamesmakers made sudden and PEREMPTORY announcements that arbitrarily changed the course of the contest.

CHAPTER 3
THE TOP TWENTY RHETORICAL DEVICE WORDS
PART 1

Most SATs now include a question directing you to specific lines in a passage and asking you to identify the rhetorical device used by the author. RHETORIC is the art of speaking or writing. Effective writers employ a variety of rhetorical devices in order to convey meanings in fresh, unexpected ways. This chapter defines and illustrates the first ten of the twenty most frequently tested rhetorical devices on the SAT.

21. ANECDOTE

• *a short story told to illustrate a point*

INSIDER INFO

Many SATs ask you to read a passage and identify an ANECDOTE. Always remember two key points: First, SAT ANECDOTES are short and are never longer than a paragraph. And second, an SAT ANECDOTE illustrates a key point in the passage. For example, John Mercer Langston was a black leader from Virginia who was elected to Congress during the late 19th century. One author used the following ANECDOTE to illustrate that Langston was a fierce defender of equal rights who did not believe in barriers: "During his years in Congress, John Langston rode from his residence near Howard University to the Capitol by a route passing through a particular white neighborhood where residents objected to his twice-daily trips along the street. One day Langston found a wooden barricade there, blocking his passage. The next day, Langston stopped off at a hardware store on Pennsylvania Avenue where he purchased an ax. When his carriage arrived at the barrier he took the ax and proceeded to chop it down."

22. VIGNETTE

* *a brief literary sketch*

INSIDER INFO

Do not confuse a literary VIGNETTE with an SAT ANECDOTE. While SAT ANECDOTES are less than a paragraph in length, a VIGNETTE is a sketch that is typically several paragraphs long. Test writers rarely use the word *VIGNETTE* in critical reading passage questions. Instead, they typically use VIGNETTES in sentence completion questions as a contrast with SAGAS. It is important to remember that a SAGA is a long epic story.

23. SIMILE

* *a figure of speech in which two essentially unlike things are compared, often in a phrase introduced by "like" or "as"*

POP CULTURE

SIMILES are all around us. We use them in everyday speech, read them in novels, and hear them in popular songs. Here are three examples:
* "I love you like a love song, baby." –Selena Gomez, "Love You Like a Love Song"
* "Uhmma's hands are as old as sand." –An Na, "A Step From Heaven"
* "Look into my eyes and I'll own you with the moves like Jagger. I got the moves like Jagger." –Maroon 5, "Moves Like Jagger"

24. METAPHOR

* *a figure of speech in which two unrelated objects are compared*

POP CULTURE

Like SIMILES, METAPHORS are all around us; however, unlike a SIMILE, a METAPHOR does not use either *like* or *as*. It is important to remember that SIMILES and METAPHORS are both figures of speech and are thus examples of FIGURATIVE LANGUAGE. Here are three METAPHORS:
* "Life is a beach. I'm just playin' in the sand." –Lil Wayne
* "My heart's a stereo. It beats for you, so listen close." –Gym Class Heroes
* "Shot me out of the sky. You're my Kryptonite. You keep making me weak." – One Direction, "One Thing"

25. PERSONIFICATION

• *a figure of speech in which inanimate objects are endowed with human characteristics*

INSIDER INFO

Many tests now include a question asking you to identify a rhetorical device used in a paragraph or specific set of lines. In order for *PERSONIFICATION* to be the correct answer, the phrase must meet two tests. First, there must be a specific inanimate object. And second, the object must be given human qualities. For example, in *Darjeeling: A Novel*, the author Bharti Kirschner uses PERSONIFICATION to describe a stack of "final divorce papers" that "stared accusingly from the top of Aloka Gupta's writing desk." This example meets our two criteria because the divorce papers are inanimate objects that have been given the human quality of staring accusingly.

26. PARADOX – CRITICAL READING

• *a seemingly contradictory statement that may nonetheless be true*

INSIDER INFO

A PARADOX always indicates the presence of a contradiction. For example, in their song "What Makes You Beautiful," the boys of One Direction have fallen for a girl who doesn't know she's beautiful. Of course, PARADOXICALLY, that's what makes her so beautiful! Don't expect to see cool lyrics from a One Direction song on your SAT. Instead, expect to see BLAND (colorless, dull) but straightforward PARADOXES in the critical reading passages. For example, in one passage a daughter wrote that at a family reunion her uncle "stood out because he did not stand out."

27. PARADOX – SENTENCE COMPLETIONS

• *a seemingly contradictory statement that may nonetheless be true*

INSIDER INFO

Uses of PARADOX are not limited to critical reading questions. Test writers sometimes begin a sentence completion question with the word *PARADOXICALLY* to signal that the sentence will require contrasting answers. For example, PARADOXICALLY, the poet was outgoing and even GREGARIOUS (sociable) at public readings but reserved and even RETICENT (withdrawn and retiring) in the privacy of her home.

28. VERBAL IRONY

- *saying one thing and implying something else, usually the opposite of the expressed meaning*

INSIDER INFO

SAT test writers focus on VERBAL IRONY, in which the intended meaning of a statement differs from the apparent meaning of the words. For example, in one passage Lewis is a rugged outdoorsman who holds "real estate people" in contempt. He urges his fellow hikers to see a PRISTINE (unspoiled) wilderness area "before the real estate people get hold of it and make it over into one of their heavens." Lewis' use of the word "heavens" is deliberately IRONIC. He actually believes that the realtors will "develop" and therefore ruin the wilderness area.

29. SITUATIONAL IRONY

- *an inconsistency between what is expected or intended and what actually occurs*

INSIDER INFO

Authors use SITUATIONAL IRONY when there is an inconsistency between what is expected or intended and what actually happens. For example, in one recent SAT passage a mother gives her young daughter three gifts—a doll, a doll house, and a book, *The Arabian Nights*. The mother expects that her daughter will treasure the doll and the doll house while ignoring the book. Instead, the daughter is indifferent towards the doll and doll house and prizes the book. This illustrates a SITUATIONAL IRONY since the young girl was influenced most by the gift least valued by her mother.

30. PARALLEL STRUCTURE

- *the repetition of words, phrases, or sentences that are similar in meaning and structure*

INSIDER INFO

PARALLEL STRUCTURE is a rhetorical device that is tested in both the Writing and Critical Reading sections. PARALLEL STRUCTURE is easy to spot in a critical reading passage. For example, in the novel *The Namesake*, Jhumpa Lahiri uses PARALLEL STRUCTURE when she writes, "It is as Nikhil, that first semester, that he grows a goatee and discovers musicians like Brian Eno and Elvis Costello and Charlie Parker. It is as Nikhil that he takes the train into Manhattan with Jonathan. It is as Nikhil that he introduces himself to people he meets." The repetition of the phrase "It is as Nikhil that," in three straight sentences is a particularly vivid example of PARALLEL STRUCTURE. It is important to note that College Board test writers also use the term *REPETITION* to describe PARALLEL STRUCTURE.

CHAPTER 4
THE TOP TWENTY RHETORICAL DEVICE WORDS
PART 2

Most SATs now include a question directing you to specific lines in a passage and asking you to identify the rhetorical device used by the author. RHETORIC is the art of speaking or writing. Effective writers employ a variety of rhetorical devices in order to convey meanings in fresh, unexpected ways. This chapter defines and illustrates the final ten of our twenty most frequently tested rhetorical devices on the SAT.

31. UNDERSTATEMENT

- *a figure of speech in which a writer or speaker deliberately makes a situation seem less important or serious than it is*

AP U.S. HISTORY

Apollo 13 was the seventh manned mission in the American space program and the third intended to land on the Moon. The mission began uneventfully on April 11, 1970; however, two days later an oxygen tank exploded, crippling the service module. In what is now recognized as a classic UNDERSTATEMENT, Commander James Lovell reported the emergency to the Houston command center by calmly saying, "Houston, we have a problem." The crew returned safely home after successfully overcoming the loss of cabin heat, a shortage of potable water, and a disruption of the carbon dioxide removal system.

32. HYPERBOLE

• *the use of exaggerated language for the purpose*
  of emphasis or heightened effect

INSIDER INFO

HYPERBOLE begins with the root word *hyper*, which means "over." So a HYPERBOLE literally means "to overstate a point or go too far." We frequently use HYPERBOLES in everyday speech to dramatize or exaggerate feelings. For example, students often express dissatisfaction with a TEDIOUS (long and boring) lesson by complaining that "This class is lasting forever." It is interesting to note that *HYPERBOLE* is often used as an incorrect answer in rhetorical device questions.

33. ALLUSION

• *a reference to a person, place, or thing, historical or literary,*
  that adds to the reader's understanding of the subject

POP CULTURE

Taylor Swift is well known for her use of ALLUSIONS or references to her former boyfriends. For example, in her song "Better than Revenge," Taylor angrily declares, "She's an actress. She's better known for the things that she does in the mattress." This is a pointed ALLUSION to Camilla Belle, who allegedly stole Joe Jonas from Taylor. Swift's songs also contain a number of LITERARY ALLUSIONS. For example, in "Love Story" the narrator refers to herself as a "Scarlet Letter," a reference to Hawthorne's 1850 novel in which Hester Prynne wore a scarlet *A* on her chest to signify that she is "off limits."

34. PARENTHETICAL EXPRESSION

• *an expression inserted into the flow of thought and set off by parentheses*

INSIDER INFO

On the SAT, PARENTHETICAL EXPRESSIONS are typically used to extend the meaning of a word, phrase, or theme. For example, in one passage an author argued that the popularity of texting is promoting poor writing habits. The author contended that "the usual litany of acronyms and abbreviations (such as "2" for *to* or *two*, or "btw" for *by the way*) is seeping into everyday writing" and "eroding a public sense that the quality of writing matters." In this example, the author's PARENTHETICAL comment provides specific examples that illustrate his point.

35. SATIRE

• *the use of wit, IRONY, and sarcasm to make fun of human follies*

POP CULTURE

Saturday Night Live is a late-night show that SATIRIZES political figures, current events, and social trends. No one is safe from the sly humor and witty barbs of *SNL*'s SATIRISTS. For example, in 2008 *SNL* used Tina Fey to LAMPOON (mock) the speech and manner of vice presidential candidate Sarah Palin. Her SATIRE of Palin was especially humorous because of the close physical resemblance between Fey and Palin. At times it almost felt like Palin was on TV making fun of herself.

36. ANALOGY

• *a comparison of an unfamiliar idea or object to a familiar one*

INSIDER INFO

College Board test writers often write critical reading questions asking students to recognize an ANALOGY. For example, what do small oily fish called *menhaden* have in common with the human liver? On first glance, nothing. But looks are deceiving. The menhaden are filter feeders that consume vast quantities of phytoplankton, thus preventing algae blooms that can devastate coastal fisheries. Similarly, the human liver filters out harmful substances from the blood. So we can make an ANALOGY by saying that menhaden are to a bay as the liver is to the human body. Both filter out harmful substances!

37. ANALOGOUS

• *characterized by a parallel similarity that permits the drawing of an ANALOGY*

INSIDER INFO

Most SATs now include a question asking you to read several lines and then identify a situation that is "most ANALOGOUS" to the one described in the passage. Don't be confused by the phrase "most ANALOGOUS to." It simply means to identify a situation that is "most similar" to the one described in the passage.

38. LAMPOON

• *to ridicule with SATIRE*

AP WORLD HISTORY

Socrates was one of ancient Greece's greatest and most controversial philosophers. In his play *The Clouds*, the SATIRIST Aristophanes ridicules Socrates as the owner of a "Think Shop." The playwright LAMPOONS Socrates by placing him in a basket suspended from the ceiling. His implication is that Socrates can't be bothered with everyday concerns since he is engrossed in deep thoughts.

39. EULOGIZE

- *to praise with eloquent words*

AP WORLD HISTORY

Socrates was both LAMPOONED (ridiculed) for his lofty philosophy and EULOGIZED for his personal integrity. The philosopher Plato deeply mourned Socrates' death. He EULOGIZED his beloved teacher by writing, "of all the men of his time whom I have known, he was the wisest, the justest, and the best."

40. EUPHEMISM

- *a more agreeable or less offensive substitute for a generally unpleasant word or concept*

MEET VINAY

In modern society, we often use EUPHEMISMS to describe things we find distasteful. For example, when we say that someone has "passed away" or is "no longer with us," we are really using EUPHEMISMS instead of directly saying that someone has died. My favorite EUPHEMISM is "sanitation engineer," which is used in place of "garbage man." This phrase comes in handy for me whenever an OVERBEARING (domineering) adult interrogates me about my plans for the future. I simply reply with a straight face that I plan to study sanitation engineering. The adult is usually so confused by the EUPHEMISM (which seems like a scholarly pursuit) that he or she abandons that line of questioning.

CHAPTER 5
THE TOP TEN WORDS USED TO EVALUATE ARGUMENTS

Each SAT includes a long dual passage and a short dual passage. The authors of these passages typically disagree about an idea or issue. As a result, it is very common for test writers to pose questions that ask you to evaluate and compare each author's argument. This chapter defines and illustrates ten words that are frequently used in questions asking you to evaluate arguments.

41. QUALIFY

• *to limit, modify, or restrict*

INSIDER INFO

QUALIFY is a tricky word with two distinct meanings. Most people assume that *QUALIFY* means "to become eligible for something." For example, athletes QUALIFY for a team, and workers QUALIFY for a promotion. *QUALIFY* can also mean "to limit, modify, or restrict." SAT test writers frequently use this secondary meaning of the word when they ask students to recognize how an author QUALIFIES an argument. For example, one historian wrote, "In his discovery of the law of the pendulum, Galileo used—if legend can be believed—his own pulse beat as a test." The phrase "if legend can be believed" serves to QUALIFY or limit the author's assertion that Galileo used "his own pulse beat as a test."

42. CONCEDE

• *to acknowledge or admit; to make concessions*

INSIDER INFO

SAT authors often CONCEDE or acknowledge a contrary point. For example, one author argued that nuclear power is America's best hope for ending our dependence on imported oil. The author CONCEDED, however, that nuclear power plants do have some risks, such as waste disposal and radiation containment.

43. REBUT

- *to attempt to prove that an accusation or theory is false*

POP CULTURE

According to the movie *Anonymous*, the plays and sonnets attributed to William Shakespeare were actually written by Edward de Vere, the Earl of Oxford. Needless to say, Shakespeare's legion of outraged supporters have vigorously attempted to REBUT this theory. They point out that de Vere wrote undistinguished and often PEDESTRIAN (commonplace) verse that never approaches the eloquence and insights found in Shakespeare's plays.

44. REFUTE

- *to disprove an accusation or theory*

AP EUROPEAN HISTORY

For centuries most people believed that the Earth was the unmoving center of the universe; however, Copernicus and Galileo successfully REFUTED this theory by providing IRREFUTABLE evidence that the Earth is in fact a planet orbiting the sun.

45. UNDERMINE

- *to weaken; subvert; hinder*

AP U.S. HISTORY

Look closely at the word *UNDERMINE*. It literally means "to dig under a mine and therefore to weaken it." So when an author undermines an argument or position, he or she weakens or subverts it. For example, the Declaration of Independence was intended to UNDERMINE or weaken belief in the divine right of kings.

46. UNDERSCORE

- *to emphasize; to draw special attention to a fact, idea, or situation*

INSIDER INFO

Has one of your teachers ever written a key term on the board and then EMPHATICALLY drawn a line under it? If so, you have witnessed a dramatic and hopefully effective illustration of the word *UNDERSCORE*. It is important to note that although SAT passages rarely include an underlined word or phrase, they often include italicized words and phrases. Pay close attention to italicized words and to rhetorical questions. They are both often used to UNDERSCORE a key fact or idea.

47. COHERENT

- *marked by an orderly, logical, and clear relationship*

POP CULTURE

In the movie *Clueless*, Mr. Hall asks Cher to present a COHERENT two-minute speech answering this question: "Should all oppressed people be allowed refuge in America?" Cher begins by CONCEDING (admitting) that allowing more refugees to enter America will put a "strain on our resources." She then compares allowing refugees to enter America to allowing more guests to attend a garden party for her father's birthday. Cher ordered more food and the party was a success. Cher therefore concludes that America can certainly make more room for refugees. A clearly confused Mr. Hall believes that Cher's speech lacks COHERENCE, and he gives her a low grade.

48. BIAS

- *a mental tendency or inclination; especially an unfair preference for a person or group; not objective and therefore PARTISAN*

IN YOUR LIFE

Everyone has BIASES. For example, we cheer for our favorite sports teams and vote for our favorite political leaders. It is important to remember always that a BIASED person is not OBJECTIVE.

49. CRITERION

- *a standard of judging something*

INSIDER INFO

Students often ask, "Will I receive a low SAT essay score if the readers don't like my examples?" The answer is that the reader's personal BIASES are not a factor in how they score your essay. Instead, SAT readers follow a scoring guide that contains a set of six clearly defined CRITERIA that are used to evaluate your essay. If you use well-developed examples that illustrate your thesis, you will receive a good score.

50. CONJECTURE

- *a hypothesis formed from incomplete evidence; a deduction*

IN MY LIFE

When I take the SAT, I never speak to the students; however, I broke this rule once, when just before the test began a student discovered that his calculator wouldn't work. Seeing his despair, I offered him my calculator. He turned down my offer saying, "I can't do that. You are a Vietnam veteran who served our country. It wouldn't be right of me to hurt your chance of going back to college and turning your life around." The student made an incorrect CONJECTURE about my life story based upon my age. He assumed that an older looking adult male must be a war veteran taking the SAT to go to college. While I am an older adult, I am not a Vietnam veteran and have several college degrees. So I insisted that he use my calculator. He did and profusely thanked me after the test.

CHAPTER 6
THE TOP THIRTY ATTITUDE, MOOD, AND TONE WORDS
» POSITIVE WORDS

Interpreting a person's mood requires good human relations skills. Interpreting an author's mood requires a good vocabulary and good critical reading skills. Each author has an attitude, or state of mind, toward the subject he or she is writing about. While authors cannot literally frown or smile at the reader, they can reveal their attitudes by the descriptive phrases and examples they use. This chapter defines and illustrates ten of the most frequently used positive words in attitude, tone and mood questions.

51. SANGUINE
- *confidently optimistic and cheerful*

POP CULTURE
In the movie *The Avengers*, the power-hungry Norse god Loki plans to subjugate Earth and rule the planet as a king. Feeling SANGUINE about the prospect of his success, Loki confidently boasts to Tony Stark (Iron Man), "I have an army." But the surprisingly SANGUINE Stark is not intimidated. He feels supremely confident when he reminds Loki, "We have a Hulk."

52. EXUBERANT
- *really happy and enthusiastic; joyously unrestrained*

MEET MY STUDENTS: PALLAVI
One day after class I asked Pallavi to describe the happiest day of her life. "That's easy!" Pallavi exclaimed. "The happiest day of my life was two months ago when my friends and I saw Drake perform at an outdoor concert. It rained the entire evening but we didn't care. Drake was awesome! I was ECSTATIC, ELATED, and very EXUBERANT!"

53. DIDACTIC

* *designed or intended to teach and instruct; serving to enlighten and inform*

INSIDER INFO

Your parents, teachers, coaches and religious leaders are often DIDACTIC because they want to teach and instruct. SAT critical reading authors are also frequently DIDACTIC. For example, in one passage an experienced fiction writer adopted a DIDACTIC tone when she offered her daughter the following advice: "Do not try to puzzle your reader unnecessarily; a puzzled reader is an antagonistic reader."

54. EMPHATIC

* *marked by great conviction; forceful and clear; UNAMBIGUOUS*

INSIDER INFO

Don't be confused by the word *EMPHATIC*. It is simply another form of the familiar word *emphasis*. An EMPHATIC statement is neither neutral nor guarded. It is instead decisive and made with great conviction. SAT test writers often ask you to recognize a statement with an EMPHATIC tone. Here are two examples:
* "Ashoka was classical India's greatest ruler," Abha declared with great conviction.
* The idea that the European era between the fall of the Roman Empire and the Renaissance was a "Dark Age" of cultural barbarism is as widespread as it is wrong.

55. EARNEST

* *marked by deep sincerity and serious intent*

POP CULTURE

In his song "Watcha Say," Jason Derulo sadly CONCEDES (admits) to his girlfriend that he "was so wrong for so long." He readily acknowledges that he should have treated her better. Derulo then EARNESTLY begs his girl to "give me another chance to really be your man."

56. FERVENT

* *very enthusiastic; having or showing great intensity of spirit*

MEET VINAY

While there are many people who are fans of college sports, few if any are as FERVENT as I am about the Texas Longhorns. Growing up in Austin, Texas, I naturally supported the local University of Texas in all of its sports. I became a FERVENT Longhorn fan after watching my first Texas football game in 2001. Since then my FERVENT support for the University of Texas has never wavered. For example, nothing can stop me from watching the annual Texas–Oklahoma football game, the Longhorn equivalent of the Super Bowl. I have overcome a power outage and even an ongoing wedding to cheer for my beloved Horns. As a FERVENT member of Longhorn Nation I just have one final thing to say—"Hook 'em Horns!"

57. JOVIAL

• *describes people who display high-spirited merriment; full of joy; JOCULAR*

POP CULTURE

In the *Harry Potter* saga, Fred and George Weasley are JOVIAL pranksters who were both born on April Fools' Day. When they attended Hogwarts the JOVIAL twins were renowned for such high-spirited pranks as turning a hall into a swamp and transforming unsuspecting students into canaries. After leaving Hogwarts the twins opened Weasley's Wizard Wheezes, a shop that sold magical joke items. J. K. Rowling has said that the JOVIAL brothers are among her favorite characters.

58. SCHOLARLY

• *describes a tone that is academic, learned, and studious*

INSIDER INFO

College Board test writers frequently use *SCHOLARLY* as a tempting but incorrect answer on both sentence completions and critical reading questions. It is important to remember that *SCHOLARLY* is characteristic of a SCHOLAR, who devotes himself or herself to serious academic study. A SCHOLARLY passage would be serious, objective, and filled with well-documented facts and quotations. One way to remember *SCHOLARLY* is to recall that academic SCHOLARSHIPS are awarded to students who study hard and achieve high scores on their SATs.

59. LIGHTHEARTED

• *describes an attitude or mood that is carefree and cheerful*

POP CULTURE

In the movie *The Avengers*, Tony Stark is famous for his LIGHTHEARTED quips. For example, when Hawkeye urgently tells him that Thor is engaged in a desperate fight with an enemy squadron, Stark LIGHTHEARTEDLY quips, "And he didn't invite me."

60. EXHILARATED

• *filled with excitement and enthusiasm; thrilled*

MEET MY STUDENTS: NIKKI

"I'm so EXHILARATED!" Nikki excitedly exclaimed. "I've got a great example for EXHILARATED." Nikki is a member of the Montgomery High School marching band. The band was invited to perform for the Philadelphia Phillies at their Citizens Bank Park stadium. As Nikki and the band settled into their upper deck seats, she had a great idea. Why not start a human wave? At first, the wave fizzled and was a flop. But Nikki and her friends were persistent. After several attempts the wave caught on as 40,000 cheering fans joined the MHS band in an epic mass wave. Needless to say, Nikki and the entire band were totally EXHILARATED!

CHAPTER 7

THE TOP THIRTY ATTITUDE, MOOD, AND TONE WORDS
» NEGATIVE WORDS

Interpreting a person's mood requires good human relations skills. Interpreting an author's mood requires a good vocabulary and good critical reading skills. Each author has an attitude, or state of mind, toward the subject he or she is writing about. While authors cannot literally frown or smile at the reader, they can reveal their attitudes by the descriptive phrases and examples they use. This chapter defines and illustrates ten of the most frequently used negative words in attitude, tone and mood questions.

61. INDIGNANT

- *characterized by outrage caused by something perceived as unjust or wrong*

POP CULTURE

In her song "Take a Bow," Rihanna is INDIGNANT because she has discovered that her boyfriend has been cheating on her. "Don't tell me you're sorry, because you're not," Rihanna INDIGNANTLY insists. "You're only sorry you got caught." Don't expect SAT passages to be quite as direct as Rihanna's song. Even so, INDIGNANT SAT authors do use forceful words to signal their outrage. For example, one author DECRIED (strongly disapproved) chocolate factories as places that "pump out pollution and provide an indulgence that is unconscionable." The key word *unconscionable* signals the author's attitude of INDIGNATION.

62. SARDONIC

- *very sarcastic; scornful, MOCKING, and DERISIVE*

INSIDER INFO

Most students can easily recognize a mocking sarcastic tone. After all, how many times have you playfully mocked a friend or teammate? But while a mocking and even sarcastic tone is relatively common in high school humor, a SARDONIC tone is very unusual. *SARDONIC* takes sarcasm to a new, more DERISIVE level of scorn. For example, in one SAT passage the author was very SKEPTICAL that fortune-tellers could really foretell the future. He SARDONICALLY suggested that if they could really predict the future, fortune-tellers should give up their psychic hotlines and become wealthy by providing stock tips to Wall Street traders.

63. FLIPPANT

- *characterized by a casual disrespectful attitude, especially in situations that call for a serious response*

INSIDER INFO

In the movie *The Avengers*, Tony Stark (Iron Man) is famous for his FLIPPANT remarks. For example, when Nick Fury asks Stark to become part of the Avengers Initiative, he FLIPPANTLY replies, "I thought I didn't qualify. I was considered, what was it… VOLATILE, self-centered, and I don't play well with others." While a FLIPPANT remark is easy to spot in a movie, it can be much harder to recognize in an SAT critical reading passage. The key is to recognize when a person responds to a serious question with a disrespectful or FLIPPANT answer. For example, in one passage a reporter asked an archaeologist why she endured the rigors of a demanding dig. The archaeologist FLIPPANTLY replied, "I'm crazy."

64. SKEPTICAL AND SKEPTICISM

- *characterized by an attitude of doubt and distrust; DUBIOUS; CYNICAL*

INSIDER INFO

The words *SKEPTICAL* and *SKEPTICISM* are among the most frequently used words on the SAT. Although they do occasionally appear in sentence completion questions, they appear most frequently in critical reading questions that ask about an author's tone or attitude. *SKEPTICAL* or *SKEPTICISM* will be the answer if the author raises doubts and questions an accepted truth. For example, in one passage a SKEPTICAL author questions the corporate use of comedy consultants by asking, "But how exactly are funnier employees better for business?"

65. NONCHALANT

- *marked by an air of casual unconcern*

POP CULTURE

In *The Hunger Games* each tribute is given a mentor for guidance and support. When Katniss asks her mentor, Haymitch Abernathy, for advice, he NONCHALANTLY tells her to enjoy a bite to eat and accept the fact that she will soon die. Katniss is justifiably enraged by Haymitch's NONCHALANT attitude towards death and the imminent peril she faces.

66. DISDAIN

- *a feeling of intense dislike and great scorn; contempt*

AP U.S. HISTORY

Between 1890 and 1920 a massive wave of "new immigrants" from southern and eastern Europe entered the United States. The new immigrants spoke unfamiliar languages, practiced different religions, and worked for low wages. Alarmed nativists accused the new immigrants of being a threat to their jobs and way of life. Francis A. Walker, president of Massachusetts Institute of Technology, expressed the nativists' DISDAIN for the newcomers when he described them as "beaten men from beaten races; representing the worst failures in the struggle for existence."

67. VEHEMENT

- *characterized by strong emotions or convictions; very EMPHATIC*

IN MY LIFE

I first invited my mother to meet my future wife Susan at Anderson's, our favorite restaurant in Charlotte, North Carolina. Everything was going really well until Susan asked mom if she would mind if she smoked a cigarette. Mom VEHEMENTLY declared, "I certainly do. Smoking is a filthy, dirty, rotten habit. My son will never marry a woman who smokes!" My mom's VEHEMENT objection stunned Susan. To my surprise and relief Susan said "OK" and never smoked another cigarette. To this day, she and my mother are the best of friends. Don't expect SAT authors to be quite as VEHEMENT as my mother. The key point to remember is that a VEHEMENT statement is characterized by a strongly worded conviction.

68. CAUSTIC

- *characterized by a critical tone and biting words that cause hurt feelings*

INSIDER INFO

On a recent SAT many students confused a VEHEMENT tone with a CAUSTIC tone. It is important to remember that a VEHEMENT tone expresses a strong conviction. In contrast, a CAUSTIC tone uses cutting words that can cause hurt feelings. In the final scene of the movie *Gone With the Wind*, a desperate Scarlett O'Hara rushes down a grand staircase and tearfully beseeches Rhett Butler: "Rhett, Rhett…Rhett, if you go, where shall I go?" But Rhett no longer cares what will happen to Scarlett. He CAUSTICALLY answers, "Frankly my dear, I don't give a damn." The American Film Institute voted this CAUSTIC quotation the number one movie line of all time.

69. WARY

- *marked by caution; a watchful concern that is alert to danger or deception*

POP CULTURE

In the movie *The Dark Knight Rises*, Alfred Pennyworth is Bruce Wayne's trusted butler and confidant. Concerned about Bruce's desire to revive his Batman persona, Alfred warns him to be WARY of the grave risks he would be taking. But Bruce ignores Alfred's warning, forcing his WARY butler to resign from his post. The danger that soon unfolds proves that Alfred's WARINESS was more than justified.

70. POMPOUS

- *characterized by an excessive and elevated sense of self-importance; arrogant and PRETENTIOUS*

POP CULTURE

In the television show *How I Met Your Mother*, Barney Stinson is proud, boastful, and conceited. In short, he is a POMPOUS person with an inflated sense of his own self-worth. Barney's POMPOUS nature is constantly on display. In one episode he POMPOUSLY proclaims, "I have rediscovered how awesome my life is. I'm awesome." In another episode, Barney hurts his girlfriend's feelings and then POMPOUSLY declares, "In my body, where the shame gland should be, there is a second awesome gland. True story."

CHAPTER 8
THE TOP THIRTY ATTITUDE, MOOD, AND TONE WORDS
» NEUTRAL WORDS

Interpreting a person's mood requires good human relations skills. Interpreting an author's mood requires a good vocabulary and good critical reading skills. Each author has an attitude, or state of mind, toward the subject he or she is writing about. While authors cannot literally frown or smile at the reader, they can reveal their attitudes by the descriptive phrases and examples they use. This chapter defines and illustrates ten of the most frequently used neutral words in attitude, tone and mood questions.

71. AMBIVALENT
- *characterized by mixed feelings about a person, object, or course of action*

INSIDER INFO
AMBIVALENT appears on about four of every ten SATs. But watch out! *AMBIVALENT* is often a wrong answer in critical reading questions that ask you to determine an author's attitude or tone. For *AMBIVALENT* to be the correct answer, there must be a clear indication of mixed feelings. For example, if you were chosen to give a commencement address at your high school graduation, you would be proud of the honor but at the same time feel a sense of anxiety about speaking in front of so many people.

72. INDIFFERENT
- *characterized by a lack of interest or concern; APATHETIC*

IN MY LIFE
Many years ago I taught in Siler City, North Carolina, a small town about forty miles from Chapel Hill. I once asked a student named Junior Hicks if he was worried about the threat to global peace posed by nuclear proliferation. Junior promptly responded, "Mr. Krieger, it don't make me no difference." Junior was INDIFFERENT to say the least! Fortunately for Junior, the SAT did not include a writing section at that time!

73. WISTFUL

- *sadly thoughtful; pensively REFLECTIVE*

IN MY LIFE

A few years ago I was sitting on a park bench next to an older woman. As a happy young couple walked by, the older woman looked at me and sadly said, "Once I looked like her. I had long, beautiful hair and a boyfriend who adored me." The older woman's mood was WISTFUL, or sadly thoughtful, as she yearned for a past now gone.

74. WHIMSICAL

- *spontaneously fanciful or playful; given to chance or whims*

POP CULTURE

The 1966 song "Feelin' Groovy" perfectly captures the hippie movement's carefree, WHIMSICAL attitude toward enjoying life. Written by Paul Simon, the song encourages listeners to "slow down" and "make the morning last." Instead of going to a boring job, Simon advises people to spend untroubled days "looking for fun," watching flowers grow, and "feelin' groovy." While College Board test writers will not encourage you to be groovy, they will expect you to know the difference between feeling WHIMSICAL and feeling WISTFUL. Remember, *WHIMSICAL* refers to spontaneous, carefree behavior, while *WISTFUL* refers to a nostalgic mood that is sadly thoughtful.

75. EVENHANDED

- *marked by impartiality; fair to all sides*

INSIDER INFO

SAT dual passages compare and contrast the views of two authors. Recent tests have included Level 5 questions asking students to recognize which author's argument is more or less EVENHANDED. For example, in a dual passage on the electoral college, one author discussed several weaknesses in the current political system. The second author was more EVENHANDED because he talked about both the electoral college's weaknesses and its strengths.

76. PRUDENT

- *characterized by a watchful and careful consideration of all potential consequences; cautious and sensible; CIRCUMSPECT*

MEET MY STUDENTS: MADISON

Would you allow your home to be the site of a party while your parents were out of town? Madison recently faced this problem. She admits that hosting a party would have been "a very cool and popular thing to do." But even a small party would have betrayed her parents' trust. So Madison adopted a PRUDENT attitude, and after weighing all the potential consequences, decided to say no. Madison is now glad that she decided to be PRUDENT. One of her friends was grounded for YIELDING to peer pressure by holding a party that "totally spun out of control."

77. REFLECTIVE

- *taking time to think carefully about things; thoughtful*

INSIDER INFO

In her song "The One Who Got Away," Katy Perry laments the loss of a boyfriend who once meant everything to her. Her tone is REFLECTIVE as she sadly notes, "In another life, I would be your girl." Don't expect SAT test writers to use lyrics from a Katy Perry song to illustrate a REFLECTIVE tone. Critical reading passages instead often feature an author's REFLECTIONS on an academic topic. In one recent passage, a prominent literary critic adopted a REFLECTIVE tone as he offered his thoughts on how art can represent either the concrete external world or the abstract world of art itself.

78. CONVERSATIONAL

- *an informal exchange or presentation of thoughts and feelings*

INSIDER INFO

During a typical day most teenagers participate in conversations with their friends and family members. A CONVERSATIONAL tone describes an informal exchange of thoughts and feelings. SAT authors adopt a CONVERSATIONAL tone when they are informal and chatty. For example, in one passage the famous baseball pitcher Satchel Paige adopts a CONVERSATIONAL tone when he opens a paragraph by writing, "After I hit the top, every couple of months just about I got my name in the papers when those writers played guessing games about when I was born."

79. OBJECTIVE

- *looking at issues in a detached and impartial manner*

INSIDER INFO

College Board test writers deliberately avoid using critical reading passages that present CONTENTIOUS (controversial) topics such as abortion, gay rights, or health care. Instead, they typically select passages that present an OBJECTIVE view on neutral topics such as string theory in physics, prehistoric cave paintings, and the origins of traffic rules. The tone of these passages is best described as OBJECTIVE, because the authors present events and facts in a detached and impartial manner.

80. MEASURED

- *the quality of being calm and restrained; unhurried and deliberate*

AP U.S. HISTORY

When students hear the word *MEASURE*, they usually think of using rulers and yardsticks to determine the length of something; however, *MEASURE* can also describe a carefully thought out response that employs a calm and restrained tone. For example, on March 4, 1861, Americans nervously waited to hear how Abraham Lincoln would respond to the secession of seven southern states. His inaugural address adopted a carefully MEASURED tone that was both firm and CONCILIATORY (willing to lessen conflict). While insisting that the "Union of the United States is perpetual," Lincoln also pledged that "the government will not assail you. You can have no conflict without being yourselves the aggressors."

CHAPTER 9
THE TOP TWENTY PEOPLE
PART 1

SAT questions often ask you to identify specific types of people. Chapters 9 and 10 will introduce you to the Top Twenty People you might encounter on your SAT. For example, in this chapter you will meet HEDONISTS who seek pleasure, SAGES who dispense wisdom, and BENEFACTORS who support a cause.

81. HEDONIST
- *a person who is devoted to seeking sensual pleasure*

POP CULTURE
The first known HEDONISTS were ancient Greeks and Romans who devoted themselves to carefree lives of pleasure. They would no doubt agree with the philosophy of partying now advocated by LMFAO in their hit song "Party Rock Anthem." The LMFAO duo are modern HEDONISTS who proudly announce that "party rock is in the house tonight." Like true HEDONISTS, they invite everyone to "just have a good time."

82. REPROBATE
- *a person who is depraved, unprincipled, and wicked*

POP CULTURE
Who do you think are the most wicked male and female movie REPROBATES, or villains, of all time? My candidate for the number one male REPROBATE is Batman's archenemy the Joker. The Joker is a MISANTHROPE (hater of humankind) and master criminal who kills rival gangsters and innocent citizens without COMPUNCTION (regret). My candidate for the number one female REPROBATE is Lord Voldemort's fanatical follower Bellatrix Lestrange. Bellatrix is an IMPLACABLE (can't be appeased) enemy of Harry Potter who boasts about killing Sirius Black while taking great pleasure in acts of torture and cruelty.

83. INTERLOPER

- *a person who intrudes where he or she is not wanted; an uninvited guest*

DID YOU KNOW?

During the 17th century, the British East India Company enjoyed a LUCRATIVE (very profitable) trading monopoly with India. Envious independent English merchants called *INTERLOPERS* or *trespassers* repeatedly attempted to break into this monopoly. Today, the word *INTERLOPER* is still used to describe intruders or uninvited guests. For example, in the video "Last Friday Night," Katy Perry is initially an INTERLOPER at Rebecca Black's party.

84. ACOLYTE

- *a person who is a devoted fan or follower of someone famous*

POP CULTURE

Lady Gaga is currently one of the world's best known and most popular entertainers. Her music and fashion have attracted millions of ACOLYTES who buy her songs, attend her concerts, and imitate her fashions. Lady Gaga affectionately refers to her ACOLYTES as "Little Monsters."

85. ICONOCLAST

- *a person who attacks cherished ideas, traditions, and institutions*

AP ART HISTORY

Impressionist paintings are now among the world's most admired and valuable works of art. But this was not always the case. At first, outraged critics denounced the Impressionists as ICONOCLASTS who violated SACROSANCT (long-cherished) artistic traditions. For example, the Impressionists rejected the idealized figures, balanced compositions, and polished surfaces advocated by conservative members of the then all-powerful French Academy. Instead, the young Impressionist ICONOCLASTS used quick brush strokes to capture slices or impressions of contemporary life. As Western art's first ICONOCLASTS in five centuries, the Impressionists above all wanted UNFETTERED (unrestrained) freedom of expression.

86. MENTOR

- *a person who acts as a wise and trusted advisor*

POP CULTURE

Justin Bieber was a young and unknown Canadian singer when he first auditioned for the well-known singer Usher; however, Usher immediately recognized Justin's potential star quality and quickly became his musical MENTOR. Usher proved to be a particularly ASTUTE (shrewd) MENTOR. He taught Bieber how to command the stage, perform smooth dance moves, and adopt a confident "swagger." Under Usher's expert TUTELAGE (instruction), Bieber quickly developed from a promising up-and-comer to a full-fledged global pop superstar.

87. BENEFACTOR

- *a person who helps people or institutions*

DID YOU KNOW?

Phil Knight is the co-founder of Nike and one of the world's wealthiest people. He is also a generous BENEFACTOR who has donated over $300 million to his alma mater, the University of Oregon. As the university's most important BENEFACTOR, Knight enjoys a number of special privileges and honors. In addition to using "the best seats in the house" for any university sports event, Knight has an athletic building named for him, a library named for his wife, a law school named for his father, and a basketball arena named for his son.

88. INNOVATOR

- *a person who creates new inventions, ideas, or ways of doing things*

INSIDER INFO

Students usually associate the word *INNOVATOR* with famous inventors such as Thomas Edison, Alexander Graham Bell, and Steve Jobs. It is important to keep in mind that College Board test writers often construct sentence completion questions in which the INNOVATOR is an author who utilizes new writing techniques. For example, James Joyce was an INNOVATIVE novelist who pioneered and perfected the use of stream-of-consciousness writing.

89. PROPONENT

- *a person who fights for a cause, idea, or movement; a CHAMPION*

IN THE NEWS

Dr. Daphne Sheldrick has dedicated her life to being a PROPONENT for wildlife conservation in Kenya. Poachers kill elephants for their valuable ivory tusks. As a result, the elephant population in Kenya has plummeted from 100,000 in 1980 to just 25,000 today. As a dedicated PROPONENT of saving endangered African wildlife, Dr. Sheldrick runs an elephant orphanage and works tirelessly to raise public awareness of the threat to an irreplaceable global treasure. You can learn more about Dr. Sheldrick and her work by visiting her website: www.sheldrickwildlifetrust.org.

90. SAGE

• *a person who is renowned for his or her wisdom and SAGACITY*

AP WORLD HISTORY

The two wisest SAGES of ancient India and China lived at the same time but never heard of each other. The highest, most formidable mountain barrier in the world—the Himalayas—separated their two civilizations. Yet by an odd coincidence, these two SAGES both sought to find wisdom and to know the truth about life. For Buddha, wisdom lay in giving up all selfish desires so that one's soul might escape the pain of life and death. For Confucius, wisdom lay in respecting one's elders and rulers so that families and kingdoms could live in harmony.

CHAPTER 10
THE TOP TWENTY PEOPLE
PART 2

SAT questions often ask you to identify specific types of people. Chapters 9 and 10 introduce you to the Top Twenty People you might encounter on your SAT. For example, in this chapter you will meet DEMAGOGUES who inflame popular passions, PUNDITS who give opinions, and HERETICS who oppose established authorities.

91. PHILANTHROPIST

- *a person who gives money or gifts to charities; a wealthy person with a generous nature and concern for human welfare*

IN THE NEWS
Bill Gates is the richest person in America and one of the wealthiest individuals in the world. Although he began his career as the RUTHLESS (merciless) founder of Microsoft, Gates has transformed himself into one of the world's foremost PHILANTHROPISTS. The Bill and Melinda Gates Foundation has given away almost $28 billion over the last two decades. The foundation's donations have helped fund INNOVATIVE education programs, medical research, and a MYRIAD (a large number) of other worthwhile PHILANTHROPIC projects.

92. MISANTHROPE

- *a person who distrusts and is contemptuous of other people; MISANTHROPY is thus a general hatred of humankind*

POP CULTURE
What do the Joker in *The Dark Knight* and Lord Voldemort in the *Harry Potter* series have in common? Both are MISANTHROPES who have contempt for other people. Heath Ledger described the MISANTHROPIC Joker as a "psychopathic, mass-murdering schizophrenic clown with zero empathy." J. K. Rowling used similar language when she described the MISANTHROPIC Lord Voldemort as "a raging psychopath, devoid of the normal human responses to other people's suffering."

93. CONNOISSEUR

- *a person who, through study and interest, has a fine appreciation for something*

MEET VINAY

OK, I admit it—I am a CONNOISSEUR of aviation. My love affair with aviation began at age six when I got lost in the gigantic Amsterdam Airport. I wandered for hours, staring at row after row of gleaming airplanes. I was particularly ENTHRALLED (fascinated) by the majestic Boeing 747, the Queen of the Skies. Over the next twelve years I VORACIOUSLY (greedily) consumed all the information that I could find about aviation. Most people could not care less about airline schedules and network planning. But to me, the reason why Delta Air Lines flies a 777-200ER between Detroit and Seoul and schedules it to leave Detroit at 6:50 PM is the most fascinating thing in the world. I guess that's why I'm part of an extraordinarily rare breed—a true CONNOISSEUR of aviation.

94. NEOPHYTE

- *a person who is new at an occupation or task; a beginner; a NOVICE*

MEET VINAY

Planes and aviation have always fascinated me (See Word 93 above). Just over four years ago, I confidently began my career as an aviation blogger, journalist, and writer extraordinaire. But I was a NEOPHYTE. My first blog, entitled "Aviation Lover," was amateurish, inadequate, and filled with content and grammatical errors. It was little wonder that the established players in the blogosphere considered me a total NOVICE; however, four years of hard work and struggle have paid off for me. Today I am a well-respected aviation journalist who has been published and even quoted as a source in various industry publications. I now write for two of the top fifteen aviation blogs in the world. It is safe to say that I am no longer a NEOPHYTE, but rather a veteran.

95. DILETTANTE

- *an amateur who "dilly-dallies" or engages in an activity without serious intentions; a dabbler*

INSIDER INFO

Students frequently confuse *DILETTANTE* with *CONNOISSEUR* (see Word 93). Both DILETTANTES and CONNOISSEURS are amateurs. While a DILETTANTE shows SUPERFICIAL (shallow) interest in a topic or activity, however, a CONNOISSEUR displays a solid appreciation for the subject he or she is studying. Thus, Vinay is a

CONNOISSEUR of aviation and not a DILETTANTE!

96. DEMAGOGUE

- *a political leader who inflames popular emotions and passions*

AP U.S. HISTORY

During the early 1950s Senator Joseph McCarthy of Wisconsin was a DEMAGOGUE who exploited the Cold War climate of paranoia. On February 9, 1950, McCarthy told an audience in Wheeling, West Virginia, that America's foreign policy failures could be linked to Communist infiltration of the State Department. Although McCarthy failed to uncover a single Communist agent, his DEMAGOGIC campaign of INNUENDO (veiled accusations) and half-truths made him one of the most powerful and feared politicians in America.

97. PUNDIT

- *a knowledgeable commentator who offers informed opinions on a topic*

MEET MY STUDENTS: DAVID

David was born to be a political PUNDIT. His insights into current political events were so great that I always reserved two minutes at the end of each AP Government class for David to offer his opinions on a key concept or controversial issue. My students had so much respect for David that they affectionately nicknamed him "The Pundito." Needless to say, David scored a five on his AP Government exam and went on to have a distinguished academic record at the University of Virginia. He is currently a political analyst for the prestigious Cook Political Report and has even appeared as a PUNDIT on NBC News. I am very proud of David and fondly remember the days when our "Pundito" concluded our AP Government classes with his famous two-minute commentaries.

98. HERETIC

- *a person who opposes accepted and established beliefs*

AP U.S. HISTORY

Anne Hutchinson and Roger Williams are the best known HERETICS in the AP U.S. History curriculum. Both challenged the ORTHODOX (accepted and established) teachings and authority of the Puritan magistrates. Outraged by their HERETICAL views, the Massachusetts authorities banished Hutchinson and Williams to Rhode Island. PARADOXICALLY, religious intolerance in Massachusetts promoted religious tolerance in Rhode Island.

99. PROGENITOR

- *a person who was an originator or major*
  contributor to an artistic style or trend

INSIDER INFO

A PROGENITOR can be the originator or major contributor to any musical, artistic, or literary style. College Board test writers, however, seem to have a PREDILECTION (preference) for modern jazz drummers. For example, Tony Williams was a PROGENITOR because he "paved the way for later jazz-fusion musicians." Similarly, Max Roach was a PROGENITOR because he was "one of the first artists to exploit the melodic possibilities of the drum."

100. ZEALOT

- *a person who is full of enthusiasm and zeal for a cause*

IN MY LIFE

I have always been a ZEALOT for learning new vocabulary words. When I was your age I kept a list of vocabulary words that I called the "Word Herd." I am still a vocabulary ZEALOT. Now I am committed to AUGMENTING (increasing) your SAT LEXICON (special vocabulary) of Level 3, 4, and 5 words. My motto is and always will be: "Vocabulary! Vocabulary!! Vocabulary!!!"

CHAPTER 11
THE TOP TWENTY WORDS WITH PREFIXES
PART 1

A prefix is a word part found at the beginning of a word. Chapter 11 focuses on ten commonly tested words that begin with the following four prefixes: *de-*, meaning "down;" *ex-*, meaning "out;" *re-*, meaning "back;" and *mal-*, meaning "bad." Knowing these four prefixes can help you unlock the meaning of many SAT vocabulary words.

101. DELETERIOUS
- *harmful; dangerous; destructive*

IN YOUR LIFE
Smoking cigarettes is a DELETERIOUS habit that can cause lung cancer and a number of heart diseases. The DELETERIOUS effects of smoking are not confined to the smoker. Nonsmokers are also affected by inhaling the cigarette smoke of others.

102. DEMISE
- *the end of existence or activity; death*

POP CULTURE
The last few years have witnessed the DEMISE of a number of famous American companies. For example, the Internet helped cause the DEMISE of Blockbuster and Borders Books. At the same time, the demand for healthy foods contributed to the DEMISE of Hostess Brands, the makers of Twinkies and other popular but nutritionless snack foods.

103. DESPONDENT

- *feeling downcast and disheartened*

POP CULTURE

In her song "Back to December," Taylor Swift is feeling DESPONDENT because of the CALLOUS (insensitive) way she broke up with her boyfriend. On a fateful day in December he gave Taylor roses and she "left them there to die." Taylor remembers "all the beautiful times" they shared during the summer and now misses his "sweet smile" and how he held her in his arms. These memories make Taylor feel even sadder and more DESPONDENT. Taylor knows she can't turn back time, so her song is a plea for forgiveness.

104. EXONERATE

- *to free from accusation or blame; to EXCULPATE*

INSIDER INFO

SAT test writers often link *EXONERATE* with the word *COMPLICITY* to create tricky sentence completion questions. *COMPLICITY* means "to be linked to a crime." So if evidence establishes a defendant's COMPLICITY, then that person would not be EXONERATED from the charge of committing a crime. On the other hand, if the evidence fails to establish COMPLICITY, then the defendant would be EXONERATED and freed from blame.

105. EXORBITANT

- *unreasonably expensive; inordinately priced; literally out of orbit*

IN YOUR LIFE

Some of America's most prestigious private colleges now cost almost $60,000 a year for tuition, fees, room and board. As a result, many parents and students are now beginning to question what they say is the EXORBITANT cost of attending an elite college.

106. RECIPROCATE

- *to return in kind or degree; to give or take mutually*

POP CULTURE

In his hit song "Grenade," Bruno Mars is deeply in love with an unnamed woman. Bruno promises to do anything for his true love, including saving her life by jumping in front of a train or even catching a grenade. Unfortunately, the woman does not RECIPROCATE Bruno's feelings. She tosses his love in the trash and leaves him alone and heartbroken.

107. RESILIENT

- *able to bounce back from adversity*

IN THE NEWS

On May 31, 1985, Apple's board of directors stripped Steve Jobs of all authority at the company he cofounded. At first Jobs was devastated and didn't know what to do. But Jobs proved to be RESILIENT; he soon started both NeXT and Pixar. In 1997 the RESILIENT Jobs made his triumphant return to Apple.

108. RESURGENCE

- *surging back to prominence; rising again*

IN THE NEWS

Apple faced a seemingly bleak future when Steve Jobs returned to the company in 1997. At that time Apple was worth $3 billion and its stock sold for just $4 a share. Michael Dell and other tech leaders predicted that Apple would soon collapse. Jobs chose to ignore Dell's dire prediction. Instead, he launched a series of revolutionary products that sparked a RESURGENCE in Apple's popularity and profits. Today, with its stock worth over $400 a share, Apple is one of the most valuable companies in the world!

109. MALAISE

- *a feeling of mental, moral, or spiritual unease*

AP U.S. HISTORY

Americans seemed gripped by a powerful feeling of MALAISE during the summer of 1979. Earlier that year militant Muslim fundamentalists overthrew the pro-American Shah of Iran and promptly cut the flow of oil to the United States and its allies. As gasoline prices soared, Americans reluctantly came to realize that the era of cheap energy prices had ended forever. President Carter then perplexed an already uneasy public by chiding his fellow citizens for "falling into a moral and spiritual crisis." Instead of inspiring the country, Carter's "MALAISE" speech worsened the mood of social and economic uncertainty. The feeling of MALAISE finally lifted when President Reagan won election in 1980 and promised a "new morning in America."

110. MALICIOUS

- *having or showing a desire to cause harm*

IN MY LIFE

The seniors at a high school where I taught had a long tradition of doing clever pranks at the end of the school year. For example, one year the seniors filled the vice principal's office with helium balloons. The prank wasn't MALICIOUS, and the vice principal was a good sport; however, at a nearby high school the pranks got out of hand when a group of seniors let the air out of the tires of the district's entire fleet of buses. The MALICIOUS prank had a number of consequences. The school day had to be canceled and everyone had to attend a Saturday make-up day. School officials caught the seniors and banned them from attending the prom and graduation.

THE TOP TWENTY WORDS WITH PREFIXES
PART 2

A prefix is a word part found at the beginning of a word. Chapter 12 focuses on ten commonly tested words that begin with the prefix *un-*, meaning "not." Knowing this prefix can help you unlock the meaning of a number of frequently tested SAT vocabulary words.

111. UNCOUTH

• *displaying deplorable manners that are CRUDE, rude, and BOORISH*

POP CULTURE

Teenagers have a well-known PENCHANT (liking) for movies that feature the antics of UNCOUTH but lovable characters who delight in exhibiting deplorable manners. For example, in *Superbad*, Seth and Evan attend a party where they outdo themselves in their display of UNCOUTH behavior. In one particularly outrageous scene, a drunken Seth accidentally head-butts Jules, leaving her with a black eye.

112. UNFETTERED

• *free from restraint or restriction; free and open*

DID YOU KNOW?

Fetters are leg irons that are used to physically restrain the feet and thus prevent running or kicking. Interestingly, the term *fetter* shares a root with the word *foot*. Since fetters restrain movement, the word UNFETTERED means to be free from restrictions or limitations. On the SAT, UNFETTERED is usually used to indicate free and open inquiry or free and open artistic expression.

113. UNCORROBORATED

- *unsupported by other evidence; unsubstantiated*

IN THE NEWS

Scientists have long speculated that water once flowed on Mars' surface, but their speculations were UNCORROBORATED by actual evidence. Pictures from the Curiosity rover now provide evidence that CORROBORATES (supports) the conclusion that Mars was once home to moving bodies of water.

114. UNNERVED

- *filled with apprehension; deprived of courage and strength*

IN MY LIFE

Have you ever wanted something so badly that it was all you thought about? I was consumed with wanting to make our high school varsity basketball team. Knowing that the first practice was a crucial audition, I mentally rehearsed my game plan. Then I suddenly spotted a procession of seniors wearing varsity blue and gray uniforms. The arrival of confident, trash-talking seniors totally UNNERVED me. I completely missed my first shots as I struggled unsuccessfully to maintain my composure. Needless to say, I couldn't overcome my nerves and didn't make the team.

115. UNDAUNTED

- *not discouraged or disheartened; resolutely courageous; INTREPID*

AP EUROPEAN HISTORY

In 1434, no European had ever sailed beyond Cape Bojador, a treacherous cape located 1,000 miles south of Portugal. Superstitious Europeans believed that boiling seas filled with monsters awaited any mariner foolish enough to venture into these waters. While fainthearted sea captains preferred to avoid the dangerous seas near Cape Bojador, Portugal's Prince Henry the Navigator remained UNDAUNTED. In 1434, Prince Henry ordered Captain Gil Eannes to "strain every nerve" to pass Cape Bojador. Like Prince Henry, Eannes was UNDAUNTED by the mission's psychological and geographical challenges. His successful voyage marked the beginning of a golden age of Portuguese exploration and commercial expansion.

116. UNSAVORY

- *distasteful or disagreeable; morally offensive*

INSIDER INFO

UNSAVORY was originally used to describe foods that are not (*un*) SAVORY (tasty). UNSAVORY, however, is now often used to describe people or actions that are morally offensive and thus leave a bad taste in one's mouth. SAT test writers typically use UNSAVORY to describe questionable business tactics and corrupt politicians.

117. UNFAILING

- *the quality of being sure and certain; constant*

AP PSYCHOLOGY

Noam Chomsky is a renowned linguist who argues that young children possess an innate capacity to learn and produce speech. Chomsky notes that children in widely different cultures UNFAILINGLY progress through the same stages of language development. For example, infants UNFAILINGLY begin to babble sounds in their native language at around nine months of age. Somewhere near their first birthday, infants delight their parents by UNFAILINGLY saying "mama" and "dada."

118. UNAFFECTED

- *the quality of being emotionally unmoved by outside events*

IN THE NEWS

Scientists now believe that unless the world's nations radically curb emissions of greenhouse gases, the planet's temperature will rise by several degrees Fahrenheit before the end of the century. Although the planet may be warming, public interest in the problem is cooling. A significant number of political leaders remain UNAFFECTED by the dire warnings of melting polar ice caps and rising sea levels.

119. UNSCRUPULOUS

- *the quality of being unprincipled; lacking standards of what is right or honorable*

AP U.S. HISTORY

During the early 1900s, journalists known as *muckrakers* exposed the UNSCRUPULOUS activities of corrupt business and political leaders. For example, Ida Tarbell wrote a devastating expose of the UNSCRUPULOUS practices John D. Rockefeller used to eliminate competitors and build the Standard Oil Company into the "Mother of Trusts." Another muckraker, David Graham Philips, published an essay entitled "The Treason of the Senate," which charged that most U.S. Senators were puppets controlled by UNSCRUPULOUS corporate robber barons.

120. UNPRETENTIOUS

- *characterized by a modest and natural manner; not STILTED or unnatural*

IN MY LIFE

During my career as an SAT and AP teacher I have had the opportunity to teach the children and close relatives of Nobel Prize winners, corporate executives, and even national political leaders. Although a handful of the students were POMPOUS (self-important) and boastful, most were surprisingly hardworking and UNPRETENTIOUS.

CHAPTER 13
THE TOP TWENTY WORDS WITH A HISTORY
PART 1

Words often have fascinating histories. SAT test writers have a long-standing practice of using "historic words" in sentence completion questions. These questions are a clever way of testing both your vocabulary and your knowledge of history. Chapters 13 and 14 focus on twenty words that have deep historic roots.

121. MYRIAD

- *many; a large number*

DID YOU KNOW?

MYRIAD is actually an ancient Greek word meaning "ten thousand." The largest number the ancient Greeks could conceive of was MYRIAD MYRIAD, or 10,000 times 10,000! It is interesting to note that both centipedes and millipedes are arthropods that have a large, or MYRIAD, number of legs. That is why they belong to the subphylum *Myriapoda*!

122. NARCISSISTIC

- *characterized by excessive self-absorption, especially about one's personal appearance*

POP CULTURE

In Greek mythology, Narcissus was a strikingly handsome youth who saw an image of himself reflected in a pool of water. The more he looked, the deeper he fell in love with his own image. Narcissus would probably be pleased to know that NARCISSISM is alive and well in the modern world. For example, in his hit song "Sexy and I Know It," LMFAO's Redfoo proudly boasts, "When I walk in the spot, this is what I see. Everybody stops and they staring at me." According to the NARCISSISTIC Redfoo, girls look at his sexy body because he supposedly works out.

123. MORIBUND

- *approaching death; on the verge of becoming OBSOLETE*

DID YOU KNOW?

In Roman mythology, Mors was the cold and merciless god of death who cast spells causing eternal sleep. Mors' name continues to live in the SAT word *MORIBUND*. Any product or company that is MORIBUND has been visited by Mors and is on the verge of dying. For example, more and more people are choosing to watch streaming videos of movies and television shows on the Internet. As a result, the DVD is fast becoming a MORIBUND medium.

124. VOLUPTUOUS

- *full of delight or pleasure; having a shapely and pleasing appearance*

DID YOU KNOW?

In ancient Roman mythology, Cupid, the handsome son of Venus, used golden arrows to inspire romantic love in those they struck. Cupid accidentally struck himself with a golden arrow and promptly fell in love with the beautiful maiden Psyche. The two lovers finally overcame Venus' opposition and married. They had a daughter, Voluptas, who was of course very beautiful. Voluptas gave her name to the modern word *VOLUPTUOUS*, meaning "full of delight or pleasure." It is interesting to note that *VOLUPTUOUS* can also refer to a woman's shapely appearance.

125. PROTEAN

- *capable of assuming many different shapes and forms; extremely variable*

INSIDER INFO

Proteus was a sea-god who could change his shape at will. The modern adjective *PROTEAN* refers to this unique ability to change forms. *PROTEAN* often appears in Level 4 and 5 sentence completion questions, where it is used to describe a rapidly changing virus that ELUDES (evades) the body's immune system.

126. SOPHISTRY

- *the deliberate use of SUBTLY deceptive and misleading arguments*

INSIDER INFO

SOPHISTRY was originally used to describe the techniques taught by a group of respected RHETORIC teachers in ancient Greece. Today, *SOPHISTRY* is a negative term used to describe the clever use of misleading arguments. By juggling words, a skilled SOPHIST can make bad seem good, and good seem bad. Thus far, SAT test writers have confined *SOPHISTRY* and *SOPHISTIC* to Level 5 sentence completion questions. Be alert for lawyers and debaters who are notorious for being SUBTLY deceptive.

127. LACONIC

- *marked by few words; very brief and to the point; SUCCINCT*

AP WORLD HISTORY

The ancient Spartans were warriors who lived in a region of Greece called Laconia. Unlike the Athenian SOPHISTS, the Spartans valued deeds far more than words. The Spartans were famous for their concise, or LACONIC, diplomatic messages. When the powerful conqueror Philip of Macedon invaded Greece, he sent the Spartans a message asking if they wanted him to come as a friend or foe. The Spartans upheld their reputation for LACONIC replies when they returned the one-word answer, "Neither!"

128. TRIVIAL

- *of little worth or importance; trifling; insignificant;
  characterized by MINUTIAE*

DID YOU KNOW?

TRIVIAL derives from the Latin words *tri*, meaning "three," and *via*, meaning "road." In ancient Rome, TRIVIAL literally referred to a place where three roads met. Remember, the ancient Romans did not have cars or motorcycles. Most people traveled on foot. At three-way intersections people often paused to exchange small talk about their everyday lives. *TRIVIAL* thus came to mean "of little importance, insignificant."

129. QUIXOTIC

- *characterized by an IDEALISTIC but impractical quest*

IN MY LIFE

I always enjoy teaching my students about Miguel de Cervantes' great novel *Don Quixote*. Cervantes described the adventures of a would-be knight determined to undo the wrongs of the world. Although he failed to fulfill his romantic dreams, Don Quixote did bequeath us the SAT word *QUIXOTIC*, meaning "IDEALISTIC but impractical."

130. HUBRIS

- *OVERBEARING pride and arrogance*

AP EUROPEAN HISTORY

Mary Shelley's novel *Frankenstein* focuses on the tragic consequences of Dr. Victor Frankenstein's HUBRIS. In ancient Greek literature, HUBRIS is a flaw leading one to overestimate one's abilities and take actions that produce tragic consequences. Dr. Frankenstein thought that he was furthering the cause of science by creating a living being from dead flesh. The monster then wreaked terrible vengeance upon Frankenstein for the HUBRIS that made him believe he could USURP (encroach upon) nature.

THE TOP TWENTY WORDS WITH A HISTORY
PART 2

Words often have fascinating histories. SAT test writers have a long-standing practice of using "historic words" in sentence completion questions. These questions are a clever way of testing both your vocabulary and your knowledge of history. Chapter 14 focuses on a second set of ten words with deep historic roots.

131. CAVALIER

- *characterized by a haughty disregard for others; arrogant and OVERBEARING*

AP EUROPEAN HISTORY

During the mid-1660s in England, the term *CAVALIER* referred to a gallant gentleman who supported King Charles I in his struggle with Parliament. The term continues to have a positive association as the nickname of the University of Virginia and the Cleveland NBA basketball team, but don't be fooled by these positive associations. To their opponents, the CAVALIERS were haughty and arrogant aristocrats. SAT test writers now use *CAVALIER* as a negative adjective to describe people who display an arrogant disregard for others.

132. ANTEDILUVIAN

- *ridiculously old and out-of-date; ARCHAIC; ANTIQUATED*

DID YOU KNOW?

In Christian religious writings, *ANTEDILUVIAN* refers to events that occurred before (*ante*) the biblical flood (*diluvian*) described in the Book of Genesis. Today *ANTEDILUVIAN* is used to describe anything that is extremely old and thus out of date. For example, many high schools have computers that are ANTEDILUVIAN and need to be replaced.

133. INDOMITABLE

- *cannot be tamed or subdued; unconquerable*

IN YOUR LIFE

The Latin word *domitare* means "to tame" and gives us the word *domesticate*. A domesticated animal is one that can be tamed or subdued. An animal or person who is INDOMITABLE, however, cannot be tamed and is thus unconquerable. I have always taught my students that developing an INDOMITABLE will is one of the keys to achieving a high SAT score. As you take the test, remain focused and INDOMITABLE. Above all, never give up!

134. CATHARSIS

- *an experience that cleanses the spirit and leaves a person feeling emotionally refreshed*

AP WORLD HISTORY

CATHARSIS stems from a Greek verb meaning "to purify or purge." As conceived by Aristotle, tragic drama produces a cleansing effect or emotional release in the audience. Today, *CATHARSIS* can be used to describe any emotional release. SAT test writers have used physical exercise and writing a novel as examples of CATHARTIC experiences, since they both release emotional tension and refresh the spirit.

135. DRACONIAN

- *describes laws, rules, and punishments that are very harsh and severe*

POP CULTURE

Draco was an ancient Greek ruler whose code of laws called for very severe or DRACONIAN penalties for even the smallest offense. Draco would no doubt approve of the harsh DRACONIAN laws imposed by President Snow to control the citizens of Panem. In *Catching Fire*, for example, Gale is almost whipped to death for illegally hunting outside the District 12 fence.

136. NEFARIOUS

- *describes people and actions that are extremely wicked and evil; VILE*

POP CULTURE

Wicked people have unfortunately been a part of society since the dawn of history. In ancient Rome, the Latin word *nefarius* referred to a criminal. The word *NEFARIOUS* is now used to describe a person who is extremely evil. The Wicked Witch of the West (*The Wizard of Oz*), Bellatrix Lestrange (the *Harry Potter* series), and Talia al Ghul (*The Dark Knight Rises*) form a TRIUMVIRATE (group of three) of particularly NEFARIOUS female villains.

137. PROLIFIC

• *very productive; fruitful*

DID YOU KNOW?

In ancient Rome the proletariat formed a social class of citizens who owned little or no property. The proletariat did, however, produce an abundant supply of *proles*, or children. The modern word *PROLIFIC* is derived from the Latin word *prole*. PROLIFIC still retains its original meaning of "being fruitful and productive." SAT test writers typically use *PROLIFIC* to describe authors who write numerous books and essays.

138. MERCURIAL

• *unpredictable and given to constantly shifting moods*

DID YOU KNOW?

In ancient mythology, Mercury was the messenger of the gods, who flew with the aid of his winged sandals. Mercury was active, swift, and above all changeable. Today, *MERCURIAL* is used to describe a person who is born under the planet Mercury and is thus unpredictable and given to rapidly shifting moods. For example, a MERCURIAL person would be AFFABLE (friendly) one moment and ALOOF (distant, detached) the next.

139. MAUDLIN

• *excessively sentimental; emotional and tearful*

DID YOU KNOW?

MAUDLIN originally referred to Mary Magdalene, a New Testament figure whom artists typically depicted weeping or having red, swollen eyes. In English, *Magdalene* was pronounced "maudlin." The word soon came to mean "excessively emotional and sentimental." For example, *Titanic*, *The Notebook*, and *Bambi* are movies that feature heartbreaking scenes that brought MAUDLIN audiences to tears.

140. ERUDITE

• *learned and SCHOLARLY*

IN MY LIFE

ERUDITE is a frequently used SAT word that has a surprising origin. It comes from the Latin word *erudire*, meaning "to free from rudeness (*rudis*)." *ERUDITE* thus describes a person who is learned and SCHOLARLY and therefore no longer rude. When I was in high school I compiled a list of vocabulary words that I called the "Word Herd" to help me prepare for the SAT. The more words I learned, the more ERUDITE I became. *The Essential 500 Words* is thus an updated "Word Herd," designed to help you become an ERUDITE SCHOLAR who will ace the critical reading sections of the SAT!

CHAPTER 15
THE TOP TWENTY SYNONYM PAIRS
PART 1

A synonym pair is a set of two words that share the same definition. Learning synonym pairs is an efficient way to AUGMENT your vocabulary rapidly. Chapter 15 is the first of a two-part series of chapters devoted to defining and illustrating the top twenty synonym pairs.

141. CAPRICIOUS &
142. FICKLE

- *both words mean "very changeable and impulsive"*

POP CULTURE
In the video "Baby," Justin Bieber falls for a VIVACIOUS (full of life) girl played by Jasmine Villegas. Justin eagerly looks forward to a romance in which he and Jasmine "will never ever-ever be apart." But Justin is shocked when he learns that Jasmine says they are "just friends." Blindsided by the news, a visibly distressed Justin asks, "What are you sayin'?" Sorry to break it to you, Justin, but Jasmine is CAPRICIOUS and thus given to shifting moods. As you might guess, the break-up proves to be very brief. By the end of the video, Justin and the FICKLE Jasmine are back together again.

143. ENMITY &
144. ANIMUS

- *both words mean "a feeling of intense dislike and ANIMOSITY; ANTIPATHY"*

POP CULTURE
In the movie *Harry Potter and the Sorcerer's Stone*, Draco Malfoy arrogantly advises Harry, "You'll soon find that some wizarding families are much better than others, Potter. You don't want to go making friends with the wrong sort. I can help you there." Offended by Draco's DISDAINFUL attitude, Harry rejects his advice, thus creating an ENMITY that lasts through the rest of their years at Hogwarts.

145. ADAMANT &
146. INTRANSIGENT

- *both words describe behavior that is unyielding and inflexible; OBSTINATE, RECALCITRANT, OBDURATE, and INTRACTABLE are other frequently used synonyms*

POP CULTURE

In her song "We Are Never Ever Getting Back Together," Taylor Swift admits that she once believed that she and her boyfriend "were forever." However, all that has changed now. Taylor ADAMANTLY insists that their relationship is totally over. Although the guy says that he still loves her, Taylor remains INTRANSIGENT as she EMPHATICALLY proclaims, "We are never ever ever getting back together."

147. PAINSTAKING &
148. METICULOUS

- *both words mean "very careful and precise; EXACTING"*

IN THE NEWS

Steve Jobs was the legendary co-founder of Apple. Jobs was a PERFECTIONIST who was renowned for his PAINSTAKING attention to detail and his relentlessly high standards. For example, architects and designers spent a year building a model Apple Store in a secret warehouse near the company's headquarters. Jobs' search for the perfect layout was so METICULOUS that he rejected the model and ordered his designers to start over. Jobs' PAINSTAKING work paid off. Today there are more than 400 Apple Stores worldwide.

149. LOQUACIOUS &
150. GARRULOUS

- *both words mean "very talkative"*

IN MY LIFE

As an SAT "guru" I am frequently invited to visit classes and talk about the importance of building a strong vocabulary. On one memorable occasion a third-grade class proudly informed me that they knew the meaning of the "big" SAT word *GARRULOUS*. When I asked how they knew this difficult Level 5 SAT word, the children all made a honking sound to imitate the GARRULOUS geese in *Charlotte's Web*. Too bad *Charlotte's Web* did not also include LOQUACIOUS ladybugs!

151. TENDENTIOUS &
152. PARTISAN

- *both words describe strong and biased views on controversial issues*

INSIDER INFO

Each SAT contains a dual passage comparing and contrasting the views of two authors on a topic. The topics rarely feature TENDENTIOUS views on a controversial topic. However, the October 2011 SAT did include a dual passage in which two PARTISAN authors debated the merits of investing in nuclear power or coal power. Unlike most bland SAT critical reading passages, both authors EMPHATICALLY expressed their BIASES in a TENDENTIOUS manner.

153. CASTIGATE &
154. EXCORIATE

- *both words mean "to express very strong and harsh SCATHING disapproval"*

POP CULTURE

Rebecca Black is a fifteen-year-old California pop singer. She became an instant celebrity when her 2011 single "Friday" attracted over 160 million YouTube views in just three months. Music critics CASTIGATED the song by calling it "a mind-meltingly horrific song" and "the worst song ever." So what did the song and video do to deserve such severe criticism? Critics began by EXCORIATING such inane lyrics as, "Yesterday was Thursday, Thursday. Today is Friday, Friday …Tomorrow is Saturday. And Sunday comes afterwards." But that is not all. At one point in the video Rebecca is in a QUANDARY (dilemma) over whether she should take the front seat or the back seat in a car driven by an underage driver. On top of all this, her lip-synching is off and her voice is auto-tuned. No wonder over three million harshly critical viewers CASTIGATED her by hitting "dislike" on their computer screens.

155. DEXTEROUS &
156. ADROIT

- *both words mean "skillful"*

DID YOU KNOW?

The Latin word *dexter* means "right hand." Since the ancient Romans believed that right-handed people had more manual skill than left-handed people, the word DEXTEROUS came to mean "very skillful." Similarly, ADROIT is a French word meaning "to the right." Like the Romans, the French believed that right-handed people were the most skillful. These long-standing linguistic BIASES can still be seen in the SAT words DEXTEROUS and ADROIT. Both words are used to describe people who are skilled with their hands.

157. HISTRIONIC &
158. OVERWROUGHT

• *both words describe an exaggerated and theatrical display of emotion; MAWKISH*

POP CULTURE

The reality TV series *Keeping Up with the Kardashians* thrives on showing viewers the HISTRIONIC reactions of members of the Kardashian family to the problems and rumors surrounding their lives. The level of OVERWROUGHT emotions reached a new high (or low) immediately following the much-hyped marriage between Kim Kardashian and Kris Humphries. Within weeks celebrity magazines reported that (gasp!) their marriage was falling apart. The rumors proved to be true when Kim divorced Kris just 72 days after saying "I do."

159. ESOTERIC &
160. RECONDITE

• *both words describe knowledge that is obscure and hard for non-specialists to understand; ARCANE*

MEET VINAY

As a CONNOISSEUR (knowledgeable amateur) of aviation, I am able to spout tons of ESOTERIC aviation knowledge at the drop of a hat. For example, I can quickly tell you that a Boeing 787-8 burns seventeen percent less fuel than an Airbus A330-200 on a 5,000-mile flight, because it is made of carbon fiber-reinforced plastic as opposed to the aluminum-based used by the A330. Unfortunately, unlike little-known details about movies, celebrities, and rappers, my RECONDITE aviation knowledge isn't of much use at parties. I was really pleased, however, when RECONDITE recently turned up as the answer to a Level 5 sentence.

CHAPTER 16
THE TOP TWENTY SYNONYM PAIRS
PART 2

A synonym pair is a set of two words that share the same definition. Learning synonym pairs is an efficient way to AUGMENT your vocabulary rapidly. Chapter 16 is the second of a two-part series of chapters devoted to defining and illustrating the top twenty synonym pairs.

161. BRUSQUE &
162. CURT

- *both words describe behavior that is rude, blunt, and PEREMPTORY in manner*

AP U.S. HISTORY

On December 1, 1955, a then-unknown African American seamstress named Rosa Parks boarded a Montgomery city bus to ride home from work. Tired from a long day, Rosa took a seat in a row reserved for "colored people." When the bus unexpectedly filled up, the white driver BRUSQUELY demanded that Rosa give up her seat to a white passenger. Although she was exhausted, Rosa was even more tired of enduring the daily humiliations imposed by Jim Crow segregation laws. When Rosa did not respond, the driver CURTLY asked, "Are you going to stand up?" Rosa refused, saying just one fateful word, "No." Her historic act of defiance mobilized Montgomery's African American community and led to the successful Montgomery Bus Boycott.

163. UNORTHODOX &
164. UNCONVENTIONAL

- *both words refer to ways of doing something that break with established practices or customary procedures*

INSIDER INFO

UNCONVENTIONAL and *UNORTHODOX* are often used by the media to refer to the outlandish behavior of rock stars and other celebrities. In contrast, SAT test writers often use these adjectives to describe treatments that are not a part of mainstream medical practices. For example, many patients prefer herbal therapy to chemotherapy to treat some forms of cancer. Test writers typically point out that while UNORTHODOX and UNCONVENTIONAL treatments may have merit, they are usually viewed with SKEPTICISM (doubt) by the medical establishment.

165. INEPT &
166. MALADROIT

- *both words describe behavior that lacks grace and is thus clumsy and ineffective*

IN MY LIFE

I have a confession to make. I have always wanted to be a skilled dancer. In my favorite fantasy I ADROITLY (skillfully) moonwalk across the classroom while simultaneously teaching Level 5 vocabulary words. Unfortunately, I am a very INEPT dancer. My most MALADROIT performance occurred at a school talent show when I completely bungled a line dance from the Gladys Knight song "Midnight Train to Georgia." The audience (which included my wife) roared with laughter as I fell out of synch with the other dancers. Some people even thought my INEPT performance was a deliberate attempt to be funny. It wasn't!

167. PLATITUDINOUS &
168. HACKNEYED

- *both words describe TRITE, often-repeated statements presented as if they were significant and original*

POP CULTURE

It is characteristic of popular culture to take a word or phrase and use it with such regularity that it becomes PLATITUDINOUS and HACKNEYED. For example, "amazing," "awesome," and "life is a journey" have all become TRITE (clichéd) from overuse. If you have become tired of hearing "amazing" used to describe everything from a new prom dress to a new smartphone, don't worry. The fad for "amazing" will soon pass, and a new word will become PLATITUDINOUS and HACKNEYED.

169. FLAMBOYANT &
170. THEATRICAL

- *both words describe fashions that are exaggerated, showy, and intended to attract attention; OSTENTATIOUS*

POP CULTURE

In the movie The Hunger Games, the residents of the Capitol are portrayed as particularly vain and FLAMBOYANT people who love to adorn themselves with THEATRICAL fashions. The women of the Capitol covet ultra-white skin, long false lashes and bright eye shadow. For example, Venia is a member of Katniss's prep team who is well known for her aqua colored hair and gold facial tattoos. The Capitol's men are equally FLAMBOYANT and THEATRICAL. For example, Flavius loves to dye his hair orange and wear purple lipstick.

171. IMPERTURBABLE &
172. UNFLAPPABLE

- *both words describe people who are calm and composed, especially under great duress*

MEET MY STUDENTS: RISHI

On March 26, 2011, East Coast students opened their SAT test booklets and read the following essay question: "Do people benefit from forms of entertainment that show so-called reality, or are such forms of entertainment harmful?" The question shocked and flustered students unfamiliar with reality TV programs. While many confused students panicked, Rishi remained IMPERTURBABLE. Rishi later told me that at first he wasn't sure what to do. Although under great duress, he calmly wrote down the names of the only three reality shows he could think of—*American Idol*, *The Biggest Loser*, and *Dancing With the Stars*. Even though he had never seen *The Biggest Loser*, Rishi understood the show's basic premise and quickly made up an imaginary contestant who benefited from the show by losing over 100 pounds. By remaining UNFLAPPABLE, Rishi successfully completed his essay and later received a 12!

173. WRY &
174. DROLL

- *both words refer to a dry sense of humor, often with a touch of sarcasm*

INSIDER INFO

WRY and *DROLL* have the distinction of being the two most frequently used correct answers on critical reading questions. Many students have told me that they are misled by the answer choices "a WRY sense of humor," or a "DROLL sense of humor." After all, students rarely find anything remotely funny in an SAT critical reading passage. It is important to understand that *WRY* and *DROLL* do not refer to the type of slapstick humor in a scene from one of the *Hangover* movies. Both WRY and DROLL humor are "dry" because they appeal to your intellect. SAT passages that illustrate WRY and DROLL humor always have a touch of sarcasm. For example, when a modern archaeologist was asked to compare ancient and modern garbage, he WRYLY replied, "Modern waste is fresher."

175. PENCHANT &
176. PREDILECTION

- *both words describe a strong liking or preference for something*

MEET MY STUDENTS: SANJANA

Sanjana has a PENCHANT for ice cream. She loves to go with her friends to nearby Princeton where she can buy mango or cookies 'n' cream at the Bent Spoon. In addition, Sanjana has a special PREDILECTION for a flavor known as Rocky Road that includes nuts and marshmallows mixed with chocolate ice cream. Yum—that does sound like a very SAVORY (tasty) treat!

177. HAUGHTY &
178. IMPERIOUS

- *both words describe an attitude that conveys arrogance,*
  superiority, and pride; SUPERCILIOUS

AP EUROPEAN HISTORY

Louis XIV was an absolute monarch who ruled France from 1643 to 1715. Unlike the English king, Louis XIV did not share his power with a parliament. The HAUGHTY self-proclaimed "Sun King" believed that he and France were one and the same. Louis IMPERIOUSLY boasted, "*L'etat, c'est moi*," meaning, "I am the state."

179. **THWART &**
180. **STYMIE**

- *both refer to obstacles that HAMPER, HINDER,*
  or hold back progress and movement

POP CULTURE

The plot of action adventure movies often involves the story of how a superhero THWARTS the plan of a NEFARIOUS (evil) villain. For example, in Marvel's *The Avengers*, Iron Man, The Incredible Hulk, Thor, Captain America, Hawkeye, and Black Widow join forces to STYMIE Loki's plan to conquer Earth. In *The Dark Knight Rises*, Batman and Catwoman defeat Bane and Talia al Ghoul and STYMIE thier plan to destroy Gotham City.

CHAPTER 17
THE TOP TEN ANTONYM PAIRS

An antonym pair is a set of two words that have contrasting definitions. Learning antonym pairs is an efficient way to AUGMENT your vocabulary rapidly and prepare for contrast sentence completion questions. Chapter 17 is devoted to defining and illustrating the top ten antonym pairs.

181. MAGNANIMOUS VERSUS
182. VINDICTIVE

- *MAGNANIMOUS is used to describe people who are noble, tolerant and generous in spirit. In contrast, VINDICTIVE is used to describe people who are vengeful and unforgiving.*

AP EUROPEAN HISTORY

When World War I finally ended, President Wilson MAGNANIMOUSLY called for a just and lasting peace based upon the ideals expressed in his Fourteen Points. But the Allies, led by France and Great Britain, were in no mood to be MAGNANIMOUS victors. They demanded that Germany pay for the immense suffering inflicted by the war. The Versailles Treaty reflected the Allies' VINDICTIVE attitude toward Germany. The treaty forced Germany to accept full responsibility for starting World War I and to pay reparations later set at $33 billion. These VINDICTIVE terms humiliated Germany and played a key role in Adolf Hitler's subsequent rise to power.

183. NAÏVE VERSUS
184. SAVVY

- *NAÏVE describes a person who is innocent, GULLIBLE, and guileless. In contrast, SAVVY describes a person who is perceptive and SHREWD.*

POP CULTURE

In the movie *The Wizard of Oz*, Dorothy is a young Kansas farm girl who is suddenly swept by a powerful tornado to the beautiful but mysterious land of Oz. Dorothy's main concern is returning home. She NAÏVELY believes that all she needs to do is travel to the Emerald City, where the all-powerful Wizard of Oz will magically return her to Kansas. As Dorothy travels along the Yellow Brick Road she meets the Scarecrow, Tin Man, and Cowardly Lion. During their journey to the Emerald City, Dorothy gradually becomes a SAVVY judge of the true strengths of her new friends. By the end of the movie, Dorothy is no longer a NAÏVE and helpless little girl. Aided by Glinda, the SAVVY Good Witch of the North, Dorothy taps the heels of her ruby slippers together and returns home to Kansas.

185. PLACATE VERSUS
186. INFLAME

- *PLACATE describes actions intended to calm angry feelings, often by making concessions. In contrast, INFLAME describes actions that arouse passionate feelings.*

AP U.S. HISTORY

Fannie Lou Hamer was a Black civil rights activist in Mississippi during the early 1960s. In 1964 an all-white and anti-civil rights delegation represented Mississippi at the Democratic National Convention. As Vice-Chair of the rival Mississippi Freedom Democratic Party (MFDP), Hamer challenged the credentials of the regular delegation on the grounds that it did not represent all citizens of the state. Democratic Party leaders attempted to PLACATE the MFDP by offering the delegation two non-voting seats. This concession, however, further INFLAMED Hamer and her supporters. Hamer defiantly rejected the compromise by declaring, "We didn't come all the way up here to compromise...Nobody's free until everybody's free."

187. RUTHLESS VERSUS
188. COMPASSIONATE

- *RUTHLESS describes behavior that lacks mercy or pity. In contrast, COMPASSIONATE describes behavior that shows sympathy for another's suffering.*

AP WORLD HISTORY

Ashoka ruled the Mauryan Empire in India from about 270 B.C.E. to 231 B.C.E. At first Ashoka was a RUTHLESS ruler who rejoiced when his army conquered Kalinga in a battle that claimed over 100,000 lives. As he toured the battlefield, however, Ashoka saw the mangled bodies of the dead and heard the agonized pleas of the living. "What have I done?" Ashoka cried out. "If this is victory, what's a defeat?" Filled with REMORSE, Ashoka rejected violence, adopted Buddhism, and devoted the rest of his reign to becoming a COMPASSIONATE ruler. Ashoka even employed "officials of righteousness" to look out for the welfare of all the people in his empire.

189. CAJOLE VERSUS
190. COERCE

- *CAJOLE means "to persuade or coax by using flattery and compliments." In contrast, COERCE means "to compel by using force and power."*

POP CULTURE

In Marvel's movie *The Avengers*, Nick Fury, the Director of S.H.I.E.L.D., sends Natasha Romanoff (the Black Widow) to India to find and CAJOLE Dr. Bruce Banner (the Hulk) into joining the Avenger Initiative to THWART (block) the villainous Loki. In contrast, Loki relies upon force as he attempts to conquer Earth and COERCE all humans into accepting him as their king.

191. BREVITY VERSUS
192. PROLONGED

- *BREVITY describes situations or forms of communication that are short or FLEETING. In contrast, PROLONGED describes situations or forms of communication that are stretched out and long.*

POP CULTURE

In their music video "We Owned the Night," Lady Antebellum remembers a perfect night spent with a girl who was "the purest beauty." Although their relationship only lasted for a night, its BREVITY did not detract from its intensity. For a brief romantic moment the couple "owned the night" and "made the world stand still." Lady Antebellum acknowledges that the relationship could not be PROLONGED and that "we'd never speak again." Still, despite the evening's BREVITY, the couple created a cherished memory that would last forever.

193. **ELITIST** VERSUS
194. **EGALITARIAN**

- *ELITIST beliefs stress giving privileges only to a select group. In contrast, EGALITARIAN beliefs stress the political equality of all people.*

AP EUROPEAN HISTORY

The French Revolution began as a revolt against the ELITIST privileges of the Old Regime. For example, although the nobles made up less than two percent of the French population, they owned twenty percent of the land, paid no taxes, and held the highest offices in the church, army, and government. EGALITARIAN leaders attempted to REDRESS (remedy) these inequities by proclaiming a new society based upon the ideals of "Liberty, Equality, Fraternity" as they abolished the Old Regime's special privileges. PARADOXICALLY, many of the revolutionary leaders who espoused EGALITARIAN slogans also engaged in ELITIST practices that repressed freedom in the name of public safety.

195. **REVERENT** VERSUS
196. **IRREVERENT**

- *REVERENT describes behavior and attitudes characterized by great respect. In contrast, IRREVERENT describes behavior and attitudes characterized by an often SATIRICAL lack of respect.*

POP CULTURE

Most college marching bands perform CONVENTIONAL shows that display REVERENCE for their school's traditions. In contrast, the Leland Stanford Junior University Marching Band (LSJUMB) of Stanford University is renowned for its IRREVERENT performances. The band plays at sporting events, student activities, and "anywhere there is fun and merriment." The LSJUMB members don't play traditional marching band music or wear CONVENTIONAL uniforms. Instead their shows are famous for making IRREVERENT fun of other universities. For example, the LSJUMB was banned from visiting Notre Dame after a halftime show at Stanford in which the drum major dressed as a nun and conducted the band using a wooden cross as a baton.

197. THEORETICAL VERSUS
198. EMPIRICAL

- *THEORETICAL knowledge is based upon speculation rather than experiment or observation. In contrast, EMPIRICAL knowledge is based upon experiment or observation rather than speculation.*

IN THE NEWS

Which air-breathing animal is the sea's deepest diver? For years, marine biologists were forced to rely upon THEORETICAL guesswork. But now new time-depth radio tags are enabling scientists to gather EMPIRICAL evidence about the diving ability of bottlenose whales. For example, northern bottlenose whales swimming in a submarine canyon off Novia Scotia dove 4,767 feet in dives that lasted an incredible seventy minutes.

199. INNOCUOUS VERSUS
200. INSIDIOUS

- *INNOCUOUS describes behavior or actions that are harmless and inoffensive. In contrast, INSIDIOUS describes behaviors or actions that spread in a hidden and usually harmful manner.*

IN YOUR LIFE

Have you ever posted an embarrassing photo of yourself on Facebook or tweeted an off-color joke to a friend? Like most Internet users, you probably believed that no one outside of your circle of friends would ever see your INNOCUOUS posts. But seemingly INNOCUOUS pictures and jokes can live forever on the Internet and come back to haunt you when you apply for a job. Companies can now assemble all of your so-called INNOCUOUS Internet chatter and pictures into a dossier for a prospective employer. So what seems INNOCUOUS today could have INSIDIOUS consequences when you are older.

CHAPTER 18

THE TOP 100 LEVEL 5 WORDS
PART 1

The SAT rates each question on a five-point scale of difficulty. Level 5 questions are the most challenging questions on the test. At least eighty percent of all test-takers miss a Level 5 question. What makes these questions so difficult? In most cases, the questions call for a knowledge of little-known and often misunderstood vocabulary words. This chapter is the first in a series of ten chapters that will define and illustrate 100 Level 5 vocabulary words. It is important to remember that the Level 5 questions are actually very easy if you know the words!

201. APLOMB

- *poise under pressure; coolness under strain*

IN MY LIFE

During my first year of teaching, my pants ripped when I bent over to pick up a paper. The students burst into laughter as my face turned bright red. But I kept my cool by laughing with the class at my embarrassing misfortune. Everyone agreed that I had handled the situation with APLOMB.

202. ECLECTIC

- *composed of elements drawn from various sources and styles; diverse; heterogeneous; MULTIFARIOUS*

INSIDER INFO

ECLECTIC is one of the SAT's most frequently used correct sentence completion answers. Be especially alert for a sentence completion question that includes a variety of different genres or stylistic elements. For example, Peruvian folklore is ECLECTIC because it includes songs, legends, and parables drawn from the nation's Incan and Spanish heritage. Recent tests have used *MULTIFARIOUS* as a synonym for *ECLECTIC*. Don't let the length of this word fool you. The prefix *multi*, meaning "many," tells you that *MULTIFARIOUS* means "very diverse."

203. BOMBASTIC

• *marked by PRETENTIOUS writing or speech that is STILTED or unnatural.*

DID YOU KNOW?

BOMBAST was originally a 16th-century name given to cotton padding or stuffing. BOMBASTIC gradually evolved into an adjective used to describe writing or speech that is overly padded, in the sense of being wordy and PRETENTIOUS. Here is an example of BOMBASTIC writing taken from an SAT essay written by one of my students: "The day began with a PLETHORA of OMINOUS clouds, which, compounded by a seemingly infinite bus ride, only AUGMENTED the pressure I felt." Try to avoid stuffing too many "big SAT words" into one sentence! SAT readers will not reward BOMBASTIC writing that is overly padded, wordy, and PRETENTIOUS.

204. CREDULOUS

• *disposed to believe reports and stories based upon little evidence; disposed to be overly GULLIBLE*

AP U.S. HISTORY

On Sunday evening, October 30, 1938, about six million Americans turned their radio dials to CBS. Shocked listeners soon heard a frantic announcer describing a terrifying creature with a *V*-shaped mouth, "saliva dripping from its rimless lips that seem to quiver and pulsate." The shaken announcer then grimly informed listeners that the fearsome creatures were "the VANGUARD of an invading army from the planet Mars." Soon CREDULOUS people all across America panicked as weeping families clung to one another for comfort and terrified people ran blindly into streets and fields. A subsequent Princeton University study found that the fictional broadcast deceived about one-third of the listeners. Today, we are INCREDULOUS that so many people were so CREDULOUS!

205. NUANCE

• *a very small difference in color, meaning, or feeling; a delicate shade of difference; a SUBTLE hint of feeling*

POP CULTURE

When the *Harry Potter* saga begins, Severus Snape is a malicious potions teacher with undisguised ANIMOSITY (dislike) towards Harry Potter. As the story unfolds, however, Snape's character becomes more complex and NUANCED. For example, what are Snape's true relationships with Lord Voldemort, Professor Dumbledore, and Harry Potter? J. K. Rowling deliberately creates a NUANCED character whose conflicting loyalties and motives are not revealed until the end of the final book.

206. DICHOTOMY

- *characterized by a division into two parts*

IN THE NEWS

Steve Jobs was known and feared as a person who had little tolerance for mediocre people. The Apple CEO used a strict DICHOTOMY to ARBITRARILY (based upon personal judgement) categorize everyone he met into two camps. You were either "enlightened" and thus deserving of respect or a "bozo" and thus deserving to be dismissed.

207. VITUPERATIVE

- *marked by harshly abusive criticism; SCATHING*

POP CULTURE

Reality TV celebrity Kim Kardashian stunned her fans by filing for a divorce just 72 days after her televised wedding to Kris Humphries. Kim didn't anticipate the public's swift and highly critical reaction to her decision. One VITUPERATIVE critic bluntly called Kim "a fame-addicted, money-hungry monster." Another offered this VITUPERATIVE observation: "She will only wear what she's being paid to wear. She has incorporated getting paid into every aspect of her life."

208. INNUENDO

- *an indirect and usually negative reference; an insinuation*

POP CULTURE

In an interview with a celebrity magazine, Mariah Carey discussed her new twins, exercise program, and marriage to Nick Cannon. Mariah couldn't resist making a sly INNUENDO directed at Kim Kardashian when she told the reporter: "Sometimes Nick and I make each other mad. But we always talk through our problems. That's why we aren't divorced after less than three months." Note that, rather than making a direct reference to Kim Kardashian's sudden divorce, Mariah relied instead on the much SUBTLER weapon of an INNUENDO.

209. EFFUSIVE

- *gushing with unrestrained enthusiasm*

MEET MY STUDENTS: REVATHY

Revathy had several reasons to be ECSTATIC (really happy) and EFFUSIVE. She and a friend had won front row VIP seats to attend a Central Park concert by The Wanted. Revathy lavished EFFUSIVE praise on the band, saying that they were even better than One Direction. In addition, *Good Morning America* broadcast clips of the concert that included several pictures of Revathy. But Revathy's story does not end there. During the concert, Revathy threw a special black and green "Irish Swag" t-shirt on the stage for Siva. The next day Siva used Twitter to post a picture of himself holding the t-shirt. He even added this EFFUSIVE tweet: "Cool t-shirt a fan got for me;)!"

210. VENAL

- *marked by corrupt dealings; open to bribery*

IN THE NEWS

Samuel Eshaghoff was a bright but VENAL student at Emory University who saw a way to make some extra money. According to investigators, six Great Neck North high school students paid Eshaghoff between $1,500 and $2,500 to take the SAT in their place. The VENAL Eshaghoff took their money and delivered higher test scores. His unethical and VENAL action, however, also delivered criminal charges and a probe into cheating at other Long Island high schools.

CHAPTER 19
THE TOP 100 LEVEL 5 WORDS
PART 2

Chapter 19 is the second of our ten-part series of chapters devoted to defining and illustrating the top 100 Level 5 words. Always remember that the hard questions are easy if you know the words!

211. CHICANERY

- *deception by artful trickery; subterfuge*

INSIDER INFO
CHICANERY is one of the most frequently used correct answers for Level 5 sentence completion questions. It is important to remember that *CHICANERY* is a negative word that is used to describe actions that are dishonest and tricky. The Trojan Horse in the *Iliad* is a famous example of a cunning plan based on CHICANERY. College Board test writers often use *CHICANERY* as an answer in double-blank questions in which *WRONGHEADED* is the first answer.

212. ANACHRONISM

- *an error in chronology that occurs when a person, event, or object is chronologically out of place*

POP CULTURE
Hollywood movies often contain ANACHRONISMS that embarrass their directors but amuse eagle-eyed fans. For example, in the hit movie *Titanic*, Jack tells Rose that "when I was a kid me and my father were ice-fishing out on Lake Wissota." In reality, Lake Wissota is a man-made reservoir that wasn't created until five years after the *Titanic* sank. Even *The Godfather* was not immune to the problem of ANACHRONISMS. In one scene set in the 1950s, two long-haired bearded hippies from the early 1970s can be seen in the lobby of a Las Vegas hotel.

213. IDIOSYNCRASY

- *a behavior that is distinctive and peculiar to an individual; an ECCENTRICITY*

MEET MY STUDENTS: KAJEN

Although *idio* seems like it means "stupid," it is really Latin for "one's own." IDIOSYNCRASIES are thus one's own, usually odd, behavior. For example, when I asked Kajen to name a personal IDIOSYNCRASY, he admitted to taking showers that last up to two hours. Needless to say, I was INCREDULOUS (in a state of disbelief). However, it turns out that several of my students have IDIOSYNCRASIES that involve taking a shower. For example, Pranay confessed that he has actually fallen asleep in the shower!

214. OBSTREPEROUS

- *characterized by loud, unruly behavior and noisy, stubborn defiance*

IN MY LIFE

OBSTREPEROUS young children are the BANE (ruin) of air travel. Several years ago I used my hard-earned frequent flier miles to upgrade to a business class seat. I was so excited! But my excitement proved to be short-lived. A mother and her three OBSTREPEROUS young children sat behind and across from me. They cried, screamed, and repeatedly kicked the back of my seat. I finally gave up and moved to what turned out to be a quiet coach seat.

215. COPIOUS

- *large in quantity; plentiful; abundant; VOLUMINOUS*

POP CULTURE

In the movie *Harry Potter and the Half-Blood Prince*, Harry obtains a copy of a potions book that was once owned by a mysterious "Half-Blood Prince." The Half-Blood Prince wrote COPIOUS notes in the margins that enabled Harry to excel in class. At the end of the movie, Snape reveals that he is the Half-Blood Prince and thus the author of the COPIOUS notes.

216. WATERSHED

- *a historic turning point that marks a momentous change of course*

POP CULTURE

On January 9, 2007, Steve Jobs unveiled the iPhone to a cheering audience at the MacWorld convention in San Francisco. Jobs dramatically proclaimed, "Every once in a while a revolutionary product comes along that changes everything … Today Apple is going to reinvent the phone." Jobs was right. The iPhone was indeed a revolutionary new product that marked a WATERSHED in the history of personal communications by ushering in a new era of smart and easy-to-use mobile phones.

217. UBIQUITOUS

- *characterized by being everywhere at the same time; PERVASIVE*

POP CULTURE

Cell phones are now UBIQUITOUS. You can see teenagers using them in malls and passengers using them in airport terminals. Recently, as my wife and I were walking across a nearby college campus, we were struck by the UBIQUITY of cell phones. Almost every student we saw was either talking on a cell phone, reading a text message, or sending a text message.

218. LICENTIOUS

- *characterized by a lack of moral discipline, especially in sexual conduct; DISSOLUTE*

POP CULTURE

In 2010, Charlie Sheen was the highest paid actor on television. He earned an astounding $1.8 million per episode of *Two and a Half Men*. However, Sheen's LICENTIOUS conduct in his personal life soon made headlines around the world. Sheen's LICENTIOUS behavior included alcohol and drug use, allegations of domestic violence, and DISSOLUTE (lacking moral restraint) parties with porn stars. Public outrage at Sheen's LICENTIOUS behavior finally forced CBS and Warner Bros. to fire him from his role in *Two and a Half Men*.

219. RECTITUDE

- *the quality of great moral integrity and honesty, PROBITY*

POP CULTURE

In the novel *To Kill a Mockingbird*, Atticus Finch is a lawyer in a small town in Mississippi, where he is known for his personal RECTITUDE. Unlike the rest of the white majority, Atticus believes that race should have nothing to do with a person's guilt or innocence. Atticus therefore decides to accept the responsibility for defending Tom Robinson, a 25-year-old black man accused of assaulting and raping a white woman. Despite Atticus' best efforts, a BIASED (partisan, prejudiced) all-white jury finds Tom guilty. Although he suffers a legal defeat, Atticus wins a moral victory by demonstrating great personal and professional RECTITUDE.

220. SPATE

- *a large number or amount of something*

POP CULTURE

SPATE is used to describe a large number of something. For example, Hollywood studios release a SPATE of action-adventure movies each summer. The summer of 2012 featured a SPATE of action-adventure movies including *The Avengers*, *Men in Black 3*, *Snow White and the Huntsman*, *The Amazing Spider-Man*, *The Dark Night Rises*, and *The Bourne Legacy*.

THE TOP 100 LEVEL 5 WORDS
PART 3

Chapter 20 is the third of our ten-part series of chapters devoted to defining and illustrating the top 100 Level 5 words. Always remember that the hard questions are easy if you know the words!

221. SOPORIFIC

- *causing or tending to cause feelings of drowsiness or sleepiness*

MEET MY STUDENTS: NIKITA

My students often have amusing stories to illustrate the word *SOPORIFIC*. For example, Nikita told our class about her SOPORIFIC history teacher. The teacher loves to tell long-winded stories about what their high school was like in the early 1970s. His seemingly endless stories were so SOPORIFIC that Nikita could barely keep her eyes open. Fearing that she would fall asleep in class Nikita asked to go to the bathroom. Once there she promptly fell asleep and missed the rest of the class! Don't expect to see SAT sentence completion questions that feature a SOPORIFIC teacher. It is important to remember that lectures, medicines, and even foods can be SOPORIFIC.

222. PRODIGIOUS

- *extraordinarily large in size, amount, or extent*

IN THE NEWS

The devastating tsunami that hit Japan in March 2011 created a PRODIGIOUS amount of debris. Boats, cars, appliances, tires, and even homes were all washed out to sea. A PRODIGIOUS debris field is now drifting across the Pacific Ocean. The leading edge of the debris is now reaching the west coast of the United States, where it is beginning to create a PRODIGIOUS mess!

223. INCONGRUOUS

• *lacking harmony; inconsistent or incompatible with something else*

IN MY LIFE

I have a favorite New York Yankees baseball hat and a favorite Boston Red Sox jacket. I like to wear the combination on brisk Fall days. This INCONGRUOUS combination often confuses people. How can I be a Yankees fan and a Red Sox fan? The two teams are in fact bitter rivals. I usually explain that I bought the two items on business trips and don't care that the combination—"Boston Yankees"—is INCONGRUOUS. The hat and jacket are comfortable, and that is all that matters to me.

224. MYOPIC

• *shortsighted; lacking foresight*

IN MY LIFE

I once had a very bright student who wanted to drop her AP U.S. History class because she didn't like her teacher. I cautioned Natalie not to be so MYOPIC. I pointed out that the Ivy League colleges she was applying to would expect to see AP U.S. History on her high school transcript. But Natalie was ADAMANT (stubborn and unyielding) and switched to a regular U.S. History class. Her MYOPIC decision proved to be costly. Although she had outstanding SAT scores, excellent grades, and an impressive record of community service, Ivy League colleges turned down Natalie's application. The moral of this story is clear: don't be MYOPIC. Keep your eyes on your long-term goals!

225. APOPLECTIC

• *filled with rage; IRATE*

AP U.S. HISTORY

On February 16, 1898, Americans awoke to the shocking news that a mysterious explosion sank the U.S.S. *Maine* in Havana Harbor. Theodore Roosevelt, then the Assistant Secretary of the Navy, was APOPLECTIC. "The *Maine*," he angrily wrote, "was sunk by an act of dirty treachery on the part of the Spaniards." TR became even more APOPLECTIC as he contemptuously watched President McKinley's diplomatic efforts to avoid a conflict with Spain. The BELLICOSE (warlike) Roosevelt exploded in anger and exclaimed, "McKinley has no more backbone than has a chocolate éclair."

226. EDIFY

• *to instruct and enlighten*

AP WORLD HISTORY

The ancient Chinese SAGE (wise person) Confucius used proverbs to EDIFY his disciples. For example, one proverb that he used to teach his unique vision of an ordered society was, "Our greatest glory is not in never falling, but in getting up every time we do." Although it is 2,500 years old, modern teachers could still use this proverb to EDIFY today's students about PERSEVERANCE.

227. ACERBIC

- *characterized by a bitter, cutting tone, CAUSTIC*

POP CULTURE

Simon Cowell is a talent judge on the television show *The X Factor*. He is best known for using his ACERBIC wit to berate contestants he deems INEPT and annoying. For example, Simon unleashed his ACERBIC wit by telling one off-key contestant, "If you sang like this two thousand years ago, people would have stoned you to death."

228. BALEFUL

- *PORTENDING evil and harm; SINISTER and forbidding*

POP CULTURE

In the movie *The Lion King*, Scar is a fearsome and treacherous lion who kills his own brother Mufasa to seize the throne as King of the Jungle. With his coal-black mane, SINISTER smile, and terrifying roar, it is little wonder that Scar's BALEFUL appearance fills the other animals in the jungle with TREPIDATION (fear).

229. EPITOMIZE

- *to embody the essential characteristics of a trait; to typify*

POP CULTURE

Movie stars often EPITOMIZE key cultural traits. For example, John Wayne EPITOMIZED the rugged individual, Marilyn Monroe EPITOMIZED the blond bombshell, and the Indian superstar Amitabh Bachchan EPITOMIZED the "angry young man" of Hindi cinema.

230. EPHEMERAL

- *very brief; short-lived; FLEETING*

DID YOU KNOW?

EPHEMERAL is both a beautiful and a sad word. It is derived from the Greek word *hemera*, meaning "a day." *EPHEMERAL* reminds us that we should "seize the day" and treasure the beautiful moments of our lives. For example, rainbows are both beautiful and EPHEMERAL. While the unique combination of rain and sunshine creates a wondrous effect, you can only enjoy a rainbow for a few moments before it dissipates.

CHAPTER 21
THE TOP 100 LEVEL 5 WORDS
PART 4

Chapter 21 is the fourth of our ten-part series of chapters devoted to defining and illustrating the top 100 Level 5 words. Always remember that the hard questions are easy if you know the words!

231. IGNOMINIOUS

- *a condition of great public shame, dishonor, and humiliation*

IN THE NEWS

Like many tyrants, Colonel Qaddafi's final moments were IGNOMINIOUS. On October 20, 2011, jubilant rebels discovered the Libyan dictator hiding IGNOMINIOUSLY in an abandoned drainage pipe. They then shot Qaddafi and displayed his battered body in a cold meat locker.

232. DISINGENUOUS

- *characterized by giving a false appearance of honesty; deceptive and therefore not straightforward, candid, or FRANK*

POP CULTURE

Major online dating sites receive almost 600 million visits a month. The online daters have a strong tendency to write DISINGENUOUS profiles about themselves. About 81 percent of all online daters deliberately misrepresent their height, weight, or age. For example, women DISINGENUOUSLY describe themselves as being 8.5 pounds thinner than they really are. Researchers explain that online daters are DISINGENUOUS because of a desire to create idealized profiles that will make them more attractive to others.

233. INDELIBLE

- *impossible to remove, erase, or wash away; memorable*

AP U.S. HISTORY

On July 20, 1969, millions of people all over the world watched on their television sets as Neil Armstrong, an American astronaut, climbed slowly down the ladder of his lunar landing vehicle and stepped onto the surface of the moon. Pictures of Armstrong's historic lunar footprint have created an INDELIBLE image of human triumph and achievement. Since the moon does not have an atmosphere, there is no wind. As a result, Armstrong's footprint will remain INDELIBLE and can only be erased by a random meteor. I hope my vocabulary examples, like Armstrong's footprint, are leaving an equally INDELIBLE impression on your minds!

234. EQUANIMITY

- *emotional calmness and composure in times of stress*

AP U.S. HISTORY

On the morning of September 11, 2001, President George W. Bush visited a second grade class in Sarasota, Florida. As the excited students proudly read a story entitled *The Pet Goat*, the President's Chief of Staff Andrew Card unexpectedly entered the classroom. Card walked over to the President and whispered in his ear, "America is under attack." Despite the alarming news, Bush maintained his EQUANIMITY. He remained with the students for another seven minutes and attentively listened to them complete their lesson. While some later criticized Bush for not immediately leaving the room, most Americans praised the president for his display of EQUANIMITY. One of the second graders later perceptively noted, "If he wanted the country to stay calm, he needed to show that he was calm."

235. MELLIFLUOUS

- *a sound that is full and sweet and thus pleasing to hear*

DID YOU KNOW?

The modern Level 5 word *MELLIFLUOUS* actually has ancient roots. It is derived from the Latin word *mel*, meaning "honey." Since the root *fluus* means "to flow," *MELLIFLUOUS* literally means "honey-flowing." *MELLIFLUOUS* almost always refers to singers who have voices that are full and sweet. For example, Justin Bieber has a MELLIFLUOUS voice in his Christmas ballad "Under the Mistletoe."

236. ETHEREAL

- *very delicate; airy and light; exquisitely refined*

POP CULTURE

Taylor Swift's video "Love Story" contains a scene in which Taylor and her "Prince Charming" dance in a romantic candlelit castle ballroom. The beautiful aristocratic ladies all wear ETHEREAL gowns made of fine silk. Of course, Taylor's ETHEREAL grace captures the heart of her true love.

237. BASTION

- *a stronghold or fortification; a group or place that defends a way of life*

IN THE NEWS

The South has always prided itself on being a BASTION of good manners. GENTEEL (polite and refined) southern gentlemen are famous for opening doors for their girlfriends and saying "Yes, sir" or "No, ma'am" to adults. But many sociologists believe that digital communications and recent immigration trends are combining to erode southern manners. They predict that the South's status as America's last BASTION of CIVILITY (politeness) may be changing forever.

238. AMALGAM

- *a blend of different elements; a mixture; a SYNTHESIS*

AP U.S. HISTORY

In his famous *Letters from an American Farmer* (1782), the French-born essayist J. Hector St. Jean de Crevecoeur perceptively wrote that America featured a unique AMALGAM of immigrants, "which you will find in no other country." Over two centuries later, America continues to be an AMALGAM, or "melting pot," that includes millions of immigrants from all over the world.

239. ENTRENCHED

- *solidly established, dug in; strongly ingrained*

AP U.S. HISTORY

As the 1950s began, the long-established system of Jim Crow racial segregation remained deeply ENTRENCHED in the American South. For example, at the start of the 1953–1954 school year, 2.5 million African American children attended all-black schools in seventeen Southern states and the District of Columbia. However, on May 17, 1954, the United States Supreme Court issued a landmark decision in *Brown v. Board of Education*, striking down the ENTRENCHED doctrine of "separate but equal."

240. CUPIDITY

- *extreme greed for material wealth; characterized by AVARICE*

IN THE NEWS

In the hit movie *Wall Street*, Gordon Gekko is an UNSCRUPULOUS (unprincipled) investment banker who proudly proclaims, "Greed is good. Greed works." Today, many Americans wonder if Gekko was right. Many critics argue, for example, that the reckless CUPIDITY of Wall Street bankers caused the recent Great Recession.

CHAPTER 22
THE TOP 100 LEVEL 5 WORDS
PART 5

Chapter 22 is the fifth of our ten-part series of chapters devoted to defining and illustrating the top 100 Level 5 words. Always remember that the hard questions are easy if you know the words!

241. INEFFABLE
- *something that is hard to express and difficult to put into words*

POP CULTURE
In the movie *Titanic*, Rose secretly meets Jack near the bow of the ship. Jack asks Rose to hold his hand, close her eyes, and step up to the railing. When she opens her eyes Jack holds her arms as she extends them out into the ocean breeze and gasps, "I'm flying!" Jack and Rose then share an INEFFABLE moment as they kiss for the first time and unknowingly witness the Titanic's final sunset.

242. CHARISMATIC
- *full of personal charm and magnetism*

POP CULTURE
CHARISMA is similar to the contemporary word *swagger*. A person with CHARISMA exudes a natural charm that enables him or her to move with confidence and own any room. For example, former presidents John F. Kennedy and Ronald Reagan were both very CHARISMATIC. In his song "6 Foot 7 Foot," Lil Wayne summed up the modern meaning of *CHARISMA* when he described it as "vodka with spritzer."

243. LUGUBRIOUS

- *expressing the grief and sorrow associated with an irreparable loss; mournful and gloomy*

POP CULTURE

The final fifteen minutes of the movie *A Walk to Remember* features one of the most POIGNANT (touching) and LUGUBRIOUS scenes in film history. The movie, based upon a Nicholas Sparks novel, tells the love story of Landon and Jamie, played by Shane West and Mandy Moore. At the beginning of the movie, Landon is a SURLY (ill-tempered and rude) teenager who is the ANTITHESIS (opposite) of the bookish and religious Jamie. But an accident brings them together, and they soon fall in love. However, just as Landon realizes that he wants to do something with his life, Jamie reveals that she has terminal leukemia and will die before she turns eighteen. In the movie's final LUGUBRIOUS scenes, Jamie and Landon marry just before her tragic death.

244. ELUCIDATE

- *to make clear by explanation; clarify*

AP BIOLOGY

On April 25, 1953, James Watson and Francis Crick published a groundbreaking ELUCIDATION of the double-helix structure of DNA, the molecule essential for passing on our genes and "the secrets of life." Unknown to the public, their ELUCIDATION actually depended upon the pioneering work of another biologist, Rosalind Franklin. Her X-ray image, "Photo 51," proved to be a vital clue in Watson and Crick's decoding of the double helix. While Watson and Crick went on to win a Nobel Prize in 1962 for their ELUCIDATION of DNA's structure, Franklin never received adequate recognition for her discovery. She died in 1958 at age 37 from ovarian cancer.

245. CONUNDRUM

- *a puzzling question or problem that is difficult to resolve*

AP PSYCHOLOGY

Lawrence Kohlberg was an American psychologist who created a series of hypothetical ethical CONUNDRUMS in order to study moral reasoning. In one of his CONUNDRUMS, a woman faced a PROLONGED (extended) period of suffering from a rare form of cancer that could only be cured by a drug just discovered by a local pharmacist, who charged ten times what the medicine cost to produce. The sick woman's husband could only raise about $1,000, or half the price. Explaining that his wife was suffering and could die, the husband begged the druggist to reduce the price. But the pharmacist refused, saying, "I discovered the drug, and I deserve to make a profit." The DISTRAUGHT husband now faced an excruciating CONUNDRUM. Should he steal the medicine, because his wife's right to life superseded the druggist's right to private property? Or should he obey the law and allow his wife to suffer and die?

246. PERNICIOUS

- *causing harm in a hidden and injurious way*

IN MY LIFE

Jody was my first official girlfriend. I was a NAÏVE (innocent) ninth grader who trusted everyone, including Jody's best friend Paula. Little did I realize that Paula was actually a PERNICIOUS person who secretly spread lies about me to Jody. For example, PERNICIOUS Paula told Jody that I was flirting with other girls at a party. To find out what happened, see Word 247 below.

247. INCREDULOUS

- *not willing to believe; unbelieving*

IN MY LIFE

PERNICIOUS (quietly harmful) Paula's campaign of lies worked (see Word 246 above). I'll never forget what happened next. On April Fools' Day, Paula came to me and said, "Jody doesn't want to go out with you anymore." I was stunned and INCREDULOUS. At first I refused to believe Paula. But it was true. My first girlfriend broke up with me on April Fools' Day. I learned the hard way that "the first cut is the deepest."

248. PANTHEON

- *a select group of illustrious people who have done the same thing*

DID YOU KNOW?

PANTHEON is a Level 5 SAT word that would have been known by all citizens of ancient Rome. The Roman PANTHEON was a famous temple dedicated by Emperor Hadrian to all (*pan*) of the gods (*theoi*). The modern word *PANTHEON* still retains the ancient temple's sense of exclusivity. Today, a *PANTHEON* refers to a select group of notable people who do the same thing. For example, Henry Ford, Walt Disney, and Steve Jobs form a PANTHEON of great American inventors and entrepreneurs.

249. CHAGRIN

- *strong feelings of embarrassment and mortification caused by a failure or keen disappointment*

INSIDER INFO

Sentence completion questions using *CHAGRIN* often provide an example of an embarrassing blunder that mortifies a person. For example, a tailor would be CHAGRINED if he first misplaced an order to alter a prom dress and then, when he found the gown, accidentally spilled coffee on it.

250. INIMICAL

• *injurious or harmful in effect*

IN YOUR LIFE

INIMICAL comes from the Latin word *inimicus*, meaning "enemy." Doctors and public health officials would all agree that smoking is an enemy that is INIMICAL to your health. Smoking can cause lung cancer and a number of heart diseases. The INIMICAL effects of smoking are not confined to the smoker. Nonsmokers are also affected by inhaling the cigarette smoke of others. So let me be EMPHATIC (forceful and clear) and REITERATE (repeat) this earnest ADMONITION (warning): Don't smoke—it's INIMICAL to you and to your friends!

CHAPTER 23
THE TOP 100 LEVEL 5 WORDS
PART 6

Chapter 23 is the sixth of our ten-part series of chapters devoted to defining and illustrating the top 100 Level 5 words. Always remember that the hard questions are easy if you know the words!

251. REFRACTORY

- *obstinately resistant to authority or control; unmanageable and unruly*

IN MY LIFE

My greatest teaching challenge occurred during my first year when my soaring ideals collided with the reality of teaching 39 REFRACTORY first-period "Basics." The Basics were assigned to me because they were all unruly students who had failed U.S. History the previous year. When I asked my department chair for advice, he replied, "They're Basics. They resist authority and are almost impossible to control. Be flexible and try anything. Good luck." To find out what happened next, see Word 252.

252. DISCONCERTED

- *describes a condition of being unsettled and thrown into a state of confusion*

IN MY LIFE

On the first day of class I calmly and confidently handed the Basics a thick U.S. History textbook and assigned Chapter 1 for homework. The Basics were INCREDULOUS (in a state of disbelief). They promptly lived up to their reputation for being REFRACTORY by loudly protesting, "We're the Basics. We don't do homework!" Needless to say, their loud and EMPHATIC protest left me totally DISCONCERTED. Unsettled by a class of 39 rebellious Basics, I didn't know what to say or do. To find out what happened next, see Word 253.

253. CONCILIATORY

- *describes an approach that is flexible and YIELDING;*
  willing to make CONCESSIONS to restore harmony

IN MY LIFE

The Basics' CATEGORICAL (absolute) opposition to doing any homework left me totally DISCONCERTED (unsettled). Faced with 39 REFRACTORY Basics, I chose a PRAGMATIC (practical) and CONCILIATORY approach. I sternly reminded the Basics that they had to pass U.S. History to graduate. But I also told them that I wanted them to enjoy history and relate it to their lives. My CONCILIATORY approach worked. Instead of beginning with a chapter on European explorers, we began with a unit on contemporary problems in American society.

254. PRECIPITATE

- *to cause to happen especially suddenly or prematurely*

AP U.S. HISTORY

On June 25, 1950, the North Korean army suddenly attacked South Korea. The attack stunned the United States and PRECIPITATED the Korean War. President Truman saw the invasion as a test of containment and an opportunity to prove that Democrats were not "soft" on Communism.

255. CONFLUENCE

- *a merger or coming together of several factors; flowing together*

AP PSYCHOLOGY

Schizophrenia affects approximately one percent of the U.S. population. Its symptoms include delusional beliefs, hallucinations, and fragmented thinking. Psychologists agree that schizophrenia does not have a single cause. Instead, it is PRECIPITATED (caused) by a CONFLUENCE of several factors, including stress, overactive dopamine neurons, and genetic inheritance.

256. PHLEGMATIC

- *sluggish, lethargic and thus not easily aroused into action*

INSIDER INFO

What words do you associate with Basset hounds? Most people would probably list *friendly*, *loyal*, *social*, and *sleepy* as prime characteristics. Of course, College Board test writers are not most people. Their list of traits would feature *PHLEGMATIC*, since Basset hounds are "not easily aroused into action." You can remember *PHLEGMATIC* by associating it with phlegm, the thick, slow-moving liquid secreted by the mucous membrane during a cold or respiratory infection.

257. SEMINAL

- *highly influential in an original way*

AP U.S. HISTORY

What do Edgar Allen Poe's detective story "The Murders in the Rue Morgue" and Jack Kerouac's novel *On the Road* have in common? Both were SEMINAL works in American literature. Poe's short story marked the beginning of modern detective fiction. Kerouac's novel marked the defining expression of the Beat Generation's philosophy of rebelling against mindless conformity by living spontaneously.

258. CONTENTIOUS

- *always ready to argue or provoke a dispute; quarrelsome*

MEET MY STUDENTS: KARLEE

CONTENTIOUS is a very tricky word. In one of my SAT classes many students saw the root word *content* and mistakenly believed that *CONTENTIOUS* means "full of contentment." When I pointed out that in a debate a contention is a point of argument, many students still seemed confused. At this point, Karlee offered a clever way to remember the meaning of *CONTENTIOUS*. She reminded everyone of a *Hannah Montana* episode ("Ooh, Ooh, Itchy Woman") that featured a class overnight camping trip. Mr. Picker assigned Hannah and Lilly to share a tent with their archrivals Amber and Ashley. Predictably, the four girls proceeded to have a CONTENTIOUS argument over who put up the tent. Karlee's tip worked, and all of my students now remember that *CONTENTIOUS* means "argumentative."

259. RUMINATE

- *to think deeply about a subject; to REFLECT; to contemplate*

POP CULTURE

In his song "Somebody That I Used to Know," Gotye RUMINATES about the times when he and his former girlfriend were together. Gotye cannot erase the memory of when they were a couple. His feelings for her remain "an ache" he cannot forget. Filled with a sadness that won't go away, Gotye reluctantly concludes, "Now you're just somebody that I used to know."

260. HARBINGER

- *a precursor or forerunner; an indicator that someone or something is approaching*

INSIDER INFO

In recent years environmentalists, the public, and College Board test writers have become increasingly concerned with the problems posed by global warming. Recent tests have focused upon the HARBINGERS or indicators of global warming. For example, melting icebergs, rising sea levels, and declining populations of polar bears and penguins are all HARBINGERS of rising temperatures.

CHAPTER 24
THE TOP 100 LEVEL 5 WORDS
PART 7

Chapter 24 is the seventh of our ten-part series of chapters devoted to defining and illustrating the top 100 Level 5 words. Always remember that the hard questions are easy if you know the words!

261. TRUNCATE

- *to cut short; to abbreviate*

INSIDER INFO

The five-paragraph, three-example essay is a very popular SAT format. If done properly, it usually generates a double-digit score. The format does have problems, however. Many students devote too much space to their first and second examples and are then forced to TRUNCATE both their third example and conclusion. The imbalance can result in a lower score. Practice will help you write three evenly balanced examples and avoid the problem of being forced to TRUNCATE an example.

262. INDEFATIGABLE

- *tireless; filled with an inexhaustible supply of energy*

INSIDER INFO

Many of my students choose to write personal essays describing their athletic teams. The essays often feature a performance in a big game. *INDEFATIGABLE* can be a very useful descriptive word in this type of essay. For example, one of my students wrote, "As we charged onto the field we looked like a team that was ready to win. We were INDOMITABLE (resolute and determined) and INDEFATIGABLE." These two sentences demonstrated a varied, accurate and apt vocabulary. My student received a 12 on her essay.

263. CIRCUMVENT

- *to cleverly go around or bypass a rule, to evade and thus avoid*

AP U.S. HISTORY

The Fifteenth Amendment (1870) prohibited states from denying black males the right to vote because of "race, color, or previous condition of servitude." During Reconstruction, however, the Southern states quickly found ways to CIRCUMVENT the amendment. Property qualifications, poll taxes, literacy tests, and the infamous grandfather clause, for example, all denied black males the vote without making skin color a determining factor. By the early 1900s, African Americans had effectively lost their political rights in the South.

264. ACQUIESCE

- *to accept passively; to give your assent to a plan or action without protest*

AP EUROPEAN HISTORY

The Treaty of Versailles demilitarized the Rhineland, a strategic strip of German land along the French border. In 1936 Adolf Hitler broke the treaty by sending German troops into the Rhineland. Although Hitler expected the French to retaliate, they instead ACQUIESCED to this blatant violation of the Versailles Treaty. Hitler later admitted, "The forty-eight hours after the march into the Rhineland were the most nerve-wracking in my life. If the French had then marched into the Rhineland, we would have had to withdraw." Emboldened by the French AQUIESCENCE, Hitler planned additional aggressive actions.

265. URBANE

- *characterized by elegant manners, DISCRIMINATING taste, and a BROAD education*

POP CULTURE

Have you seen "The Most Interesting Man in the World" commercial? The URBANE "Interesting Man" has elegant manners, discriminating taste, and is of course always surrounded by beautiful, admiring women. He is obviously a sophisticated person who is rich in stories and life experiences. However, his famous line "Stay thirsty, my friends" is very AMBIGUOUS (unclear). Does it mean to stay thirsty so you can acquire more knowledge and thus be even more URBANE? Or does it mean to stay thirsty so you can buy more Dos Equis beer? (I wonder what score the URBANE "Interesting Man" received on his SAT!).

266. SALUTARY

• *beneficial and thus tending to promote physical well-being*

IN YOUR LIFE

Taking the SAT, preparing for AP courses, applying to colleges, and participating in extracurricular activities can all be very stressful. Learning how to relax can have a SALUTARY effect on your mood and help restore balance into your hectic lifestyle. Popular relaxation techniques include meditating, breathing deeply, listening to soft music, watching a movie, and of course, reading this vocabulary book!

267. VOLATILE

• *subject to sudden and violent changes in temperament; unstable*

IN MY LIFE

Everyone in the high school where I taught knew that Greg had a VOLATILE personality. But we all underestimated just how VOLATILE his temper really was. Greg was dating a very pretty girl named Karen. Perhaps sensing that Greg was unstable, Karen decided to end their relationship right after lunch. As he returned to class, Greg's VOLATILE temper got the best of him as he violently punched a glass window. The blow caused severe lacerations and left a trail of blood in the hall. I'll never forget the horrified look on our students' faces as they saw Greg's bloody hand. Amazingly, Karen and Greg soon RECONCILED (reunited). Karen ignored Greg's VOLATILE temper and said the smashed window proved that he had strong feelings for her.

268. DILATORY

• *inclined to waste time and be habitually late; PRONE to tardiness*

MEET VINAY

If there were an award for the most DILATORY student in the history of Montgomery High School, it would be on my mantelpiece. During my junior year, I was tardy a record 29 times, including six days when I showed up with less than four hours left in the school day. My DILATORY habits even extend to academics. I vividly remember putting off writing a fifteen-page AP Bio paper on animal physiology until hours before it was due. My DILATORY ways did not extend to the SAT and AP tests, however. Not wanting to incur the wrath of my teachers, parents, and Mr. Krieger, I showed up for the tests on time.

269. ARTIFICE

• *a deceptive maneuver; a crafty RUSE; a clever stratagem*

INSIDER INFO

ARTIFICE was the answer to a difficult sentence completion question on a recent PSAT. College Board test writers paired *ARTIFICE* with *RUSES* by saying that a person "ran out of RUSES when his ARTIFICES were exposed." George Washington's famous decision to cross the Delaware River and surprise the Hessians on Christmas Eve 1776 is perhaps the most famous ARTIFICE in American military history. The Trojan Horse that allowed the Greeks to conquer Troy in the historical epic the *Iliad* is the most famous ARTIFICE in literary history.

270. FORBEARANCE

• *to show great patience or tolerance*

INSIDER INFO

One way to remember *FORBEARANCE* is to link the word *bear* with the popular expression, "Bear with me for a moment." When a coach, teacher, or parent asks you to bear with them, they are asking for your patience or FORBEARANCE.

THE TOP 100 LEVEL 5 WORDS
PART 8

Chapter 25 is the eighth of our ten-part series of chapters devoted to defining and illustrating the top 100 Level 5 words. Always remember that the hard questions are easy if you know the words!

271. ENERVATE

- *to feel mentally and physically weakened; to lack strength and* energy

INSIDER INFO

Many students believe that *ENERVATE* means "energized." Although the two words do sound alike, they are actually antonyms. *ENERVATE* means "to lack energy or vigor." For example, many students understandably feel ENERVATED after a long day at school followed by band or athletic practice. But don't worry. You'll revive after reading the entertaining and DIDACTIC (instructive) examples in *The Essential 500 Words*.

272. SQUALID

- *run-down and foul; very dirty and wretched*

AP U.S. HISTORY

In his book *How the Other Half Lives*, Jacob Riis documented the SQUALID conditions endured by late-19th-century immigrants living in New York City's Lower East Side. At that time, a single square mile in the Lower East Side contained 334,000 people, making it the most densely populated place in the world. Riis's photographs exposed the dirty, disease-ridden slums where families considered themselves lucky to live in a SQUALID one-room apartment lacking plumbing and proper ventilation.

273. JUXTAPOSITION

- *two or more contrasting people or things placed next to each other; a side-by-side comparison*

INSIDER INFO

The word *JUXTAPOSITION* drew a lot of attention on a recent SAT. A sentence completion described a modern sculptor who created a "sculpture wall" by JUXTAPOSING a number of contrasting objects. Many students incorrectly answered *SEMBLANCE*. *SEMBLANCE* refers to an outward appearance that is deliberately misleading. In contrast, *JUXTAPOSITION* refers to a side-by-side comparison.

274. UNEQUIVOCAL

- *admitting no doubt or misunderstanding; having only one meaning and interpretation*

POP CULTURE

In her song Stronger (What Doesn't Kill You), Kelly Clarkson's ex has left her alone. He thinks Kelly is "broken down" and will "come running back." But he was "dead wrong!" Kelly is a fighter who UNEQUIVOCALLY insists that "what doesn't kill you makes you stronger." Don't expect SAT authors to express opinions that are quite as emphatic as those expressed in Kelly's song. For example, in one recent passage Peter Schwartz expresses his UNEQUIVOCAL opposition to coal and other fossil fuels by writing that they are "driving climate change" and are "a luxury that a planet with six billion energy-hungry souls can't afford." Note that both Kelly Clarkson and Peter Schwartz can be characterized as UNEQUIVOCAL because of the strength of their convictions.

275. SCOURGE

- *something that causes misery, affliction, or destruction; a BANE*

IN YOUR LIFE

Have you ever read an Internet post written by a "troll"? If so, then you know that trolls are anonymous provokers who flood the Internet with inflammatory insults, threats, and profanity. Although trolls have existed since the beginning of the Internet, in recent years they have become a SCOURGE. Trolls often overwhelm website discussion boards with INVECTIVE-filled (verbally abusive) posts that are often profane and threatening.

276. IMPUNITY

- *freedom from punishment or pain*

IN THE NEWS

The Internet protects trolls (see Word 275) by allowing them to remain anonymous. In addition, the First Amendment protects the right of trolls to be as rude or offensive as they like. As a result of these protections, trolls can ASSAIL (attack) their victims with IMPUNITY. Fortunately, more and more websites are beginning to EXCISE (remove) objectionable posts from their comment boards.

277. IMPLACABLE

- *characterized by a relentless hatred that cannot be appeased; merciless and unforgiving*

POP CULTURE

What do the Evil Queen in the Snow White films and Raoul Silva in the James Bond film *Skyfall* have in common? Both share an IMPLACABLE hatred for their rivals. The Evil Queen is a villainous ruler who has an IMPLACABLE hatred for her beautiful step-daughter Snow White. Raoul Silva is a ruthless cyberterrorist who has an IMPLACABLE hatred for M, the head of MI6, the British Secret Intelligence Service.

278. IMPUGN

- *to attack or ASSAIL with words; to verbally challenge something as false or wrong*

INSIDER INFO

The key to unlocking the meaning of *IMPUGN* is to know that the Latin root *pugnare* means "to fight." *IMPUGN* is used to describe situations in which someone uses words to attack another person verbally. For example, politicians often IMPUGN the credibility of their rivals, and lawyers often IMPUGN the testimony of witnesses.

279. POLEMIC

- *a controversial argument often published as an essay or pamphlet attacking a specific opinion or doctrine*

AP EUROPEAN HISTORY

In November 1894 a French court sentenced a Jewish artillery officer, Captain Alfred Dreyfus, to life imprisonment on Devil's Island in French Guiana. Although high-ranking members of the French General Staff were aware of Dreyfus' innocence, they FABRICATED (invented) a web of lies to convict Dreyfus. Emile Zola, a popular French novelist, published an open letter entitled *"J'Accuse,"* attacking the irregularities in the Dreyfus trial. Zola concluded his POLEMIC by declaring, "The truth is on the march and nothing will stop it." Zola's famous POLEMIC forced the French courts to reopen the case and ultimately EXONERATE (free from guilt) Captain Dreyfus.

280. PERFIDIOUS

- *characterized by treacherous and deceitful behavior; traitorous*

POP CULTURE

In the movie *The Dark Knight Rises*, Miranda Tate pretends to be a wealthy socialite dedicated to using Wayne Enterprises' nuclear fusion technology to generate a clean source of energy. Tate soon becomes Bruce Wayne's trusted confidant and the new CEO of Wayne Enterprises. But in reality, Tate is a PERFIDIOUS villain who is actually Talia al Ghoul, the daughter of Batman's NEMESIS (a source of harm or ruin) Ra's al Ghoul. The PERFIDIOUS Talia's real goal is to crush Batman and fulfill her father's mission of destroying Gotham City.

CHAPTER 26
THE TOP 100 LEVEL 5 WORDS
PART 9

Chapter 26 is the ninth of our ten-part series of chapters devoted to defining and illustrating the top 100 Level 5 words. Always remember that the hard questions are easy if you know the words!

281. CURSORY
- *performed in a hasty and SUPERFICIAL manner without attention to details*

INSIDER INFO
Recent tests have included challenging questions that feature uses of the word *CURSORY*. For example, in one critical reading passage, the narrator is a young Korean girl who discovers a random page from a book. She then shows the page to her girlfriend Sunny. Far more interested in batting a shuttlecock, Sunny glances at the page and then tentatively identifies the print as *hangul*, a native Korean alphabet. Sunny's SUPERFICIAL glance is best described as CURSORY.

282. GALVANIZE
- *to energize and stir into action, to arouse*

AP U.S. HISTORY
On December 1, 1955, a white Montgomery City Lines bus driver BRUSQUELY (CURTLY, rudely) ordered Rosa Parks to give up her seat to a white passenger. Although she was tired from a long day at work, Rosa was even more tired of enduring the injustices of racial segregation. Rosa therefore refused the bus driver's order by saying just one fateful word—"No!" Rosa's historic refusal to give up her seat GALVANIZED Montgomery's black community and led to the successful Montgomery Bus Boycott. The boycott played a key role in GALVANIZING the Civil Rights Movement.

283. EXTEMPORIZE

- *to perform without preparation; IMPROVISE*

AP U.S. HISTORY

Political leaders now give speeches that are carefully written and delivered with the aid of a teleprompter. Students are therefore very surprised to learn that Dr. King EXTEMPORIZED most of his famous "I Have a Dream" speech. Dr. King's great speech left an INDELIBLE (can't be removed) impression on his listeners by successfully articulating the hopes and dreams of black and white Americans for a just society based upon racial equality.

284. TACITURN

- *RESERVED and not talkative; LACONIC*

POP CULTURE

In the *Men in Black* film series, Agent K (played by Tommy Lee Jones) is the MIB's top agent. Unlike his partner, the LOQUACIOUS (talkative) Agent J (played by Will Smith), Agent K is a TACITURN man who takes the MIB creed that "silence is your native tongue" very seriously. Agent K rarely jokes or smiles and typically responds to J's rambling thoughts with his trademark TACITURN expression, "All right, kid, here's the deal."

285. UNAMBIGUOUS

- *clear and precise; exhibiting no uncertainty; CATEGORICAL*

IN THE NEWS

Steve Jobs' innovative ideas changed the way technology is used in our society. For example, the iPod reinvented the way we listen to music and the iPhone reinvented the way we communicate with each other. These dramatic advances did not come easily. Jobs was an aggressive and demanding leader who insisted on maintaining high standards of excellence. "We have an environment where excellence is really appreciated," Jobs UNAMBIGUOUSLY asserted. That's my job – to make sure everything is great."

286. CONSTERNATION

- *a sudden and alarming amazement that results in confusion and dismay*

MEET MY STUDENTS: PRIYAL

Going through airport security is one of the BANES (sources of misery) of modern travel. When Priyal was just fourteen years old, Amsterdam airport security officials unexpectedly pulled her aside and began a full search of her bags and person. Needless to say, Priyal and her family were shocked and filled with CONSTERNATION. The security officers sternly insisted that they were just doing their jobs. As the time-consuming search dragged on and on, Priyal and her apprehensive family felt an even greater sense of CONSTERNATION. Why was Priyal being searched, and what would happen if they missed their flight? After several alarming minutes the search finally ended, and Priyal and her family ran to the gate and barely made it to the plane on time.

287. PORTEND

- *to serve as an omen or warning; to foreshadow danger*

POP CULTURE

The movie *The Avengers* ends with the victory of the Avengers over Loki and the Chitauri invaders. However, after the first set of credits, viewers see a glimpse of the villain who sent Loki to Earth. He is Thanos, a sinister demi-god whose name is derived from Thanatos, the Greek god of death. Thanos is one of the most dangerous villains in the universe. His appearance PORTENDS future danger for Earth and for the Avengers. Fans believe that Thanos and the Avengers will be on a collision course in *The Avengers 2*.

288. INSCRUTABLE

- *very hard to figure out; incomprehensible*

INSIDER INFO

SAT double-blank sentence completion questions often use unexpected examples and surprising cause and effect relationships. For example, on one recent question, fans of a new video game were CONFOUNDED (puzzled) by INSCRUTABLE new features. While I can imagine archaeologists being CONFOUNDED by INSCRUTABLE Mayan carvings, I find it unrealistic that modern gamers would be CONFOUNDED by INSCRUTABLE videogame features. But then, College Board test writers are often INSCRUTABLE.

289. CRYSTALLIZE

- *to take a definite form or shape*

IN YOUR LIFE

Your junior and senior years in high school can be a very stressful time. The SATs, college admission forms, and AP tests are all formidable hurdles that must be overcome. Although your plans have not CRYSTALLIZED, well-meaning parents, relatives, and teachers will all question you about a future that still seems NEBULOUS (not fully formed). But don't worry. You will achieve high test scores, college admission letters will arrive, and your plans will suddenly CRYSTALLIZE.

290. PUERILE

- *childish and immature; CALLOW*

MEET MY STUDENTS: TIFFANY

Tiffany is an experienced cheerleader currently teaching a group of eight-year-olds how to cheer. While the young girls are enthusiastic, they are also very PUERILE. The girls demand constant attention, complain about everything, and sometimes ignore Tiffany's instructions. Of course, Tiffany understands that the girls are young and that it is hard to control their PUERILE antics. We're confident that Tiffany will prevail and that the girls will ultimately perform precisely choreographed cheers.

THE TOP 100 LEVEL 5 WORDS
PART 10

Chapter 27 is the tenth of our ten-part series of chapters devoted to defining and illustrating the top 100 Level 5 words. Always remember that the hard questions are easy if you know the words!

291. PROFLIGATE

- *characterized by SQUANDERING (wasting) time and money*

POP CULTURE

When Justin Bieber's girlfriend Selena Gomez dropped a hint that she really wanted to see the movie *Titanic*, the Biebs decided to create a date she would never forget. JB surprised Selena by taking her to the Staples Center, the 20,000-seat home of the Los Angles Lakers. After a private dinner of steak and pasta at the Lexus Club, the evening became even more romantic when *Titanic* began playing on a huge screen in the empty arena. When my students heard about this amazing but extravagant date, most criticized JB for being a PROFLIGATE spender. After all, he could have rented *Titanic* for a lot less than the $100,000 it costs to rent the Staples Center for one night. But was Bieber really being PROFLIGATE? It turns out that Biebs was actually very FRUGAL (thrifty), because management allowed him to use the arena for free as a thank you for his string of three previous sold-out concerts.

292. FOREBODING

• *a strong inner feeling or premonition of future misfortune*

AP U.S. HISTORY

On December 7, 1941, the Japanese launched a surprise air attack on Pearl Harbor that sank or damaged eighteen American warships while losing just 29 planes. While his EXULTANT (triumphant) officers celebrated their victory, the Japanese commander Admiral Yamamoto spent the day sunk in apparent depression. Yamamoto had a FOREBODING that the war with America would end in disaster. "I fear all we have done," he warned, "is to awaken a sleeping giant and fill him with a terrible resolve." Yamamoto's feeling of FOREBODING proved to be correct. Resolved to crush Japan, an angry and now united America entered World War II.

293. IRASCIBLE

• *easily angered; PRONE to outbursts of temper*

INSIDER INFO

What do the words *IRATE* and *IRASCIBLE* have in common? Both words contain the Latin root *ira*, meaning "anger or rage." So if you are IRATE you are very angry, and if you are IRASCIBLE you are easily angered. *IRASCIBLE* is a negative trait that is often paired in double-blank sentence completion questions with other negative traits such as *BRUSQUE* (abrupt, CURT), *HEADSTRONG* (impulsive) and *CANTANKEROUS* (irritable, cranky).

294. INDULGENT

• *characterized by excessive generosity; overly lenient and tolerant*

POP CULTURE

According to celebrity magazines, Tom Cruise is determined to be an INDULGENT dad when he is with his young daughter Suri. For example, the newly single dad flew Suri on his private jet to Orlando, where she enjoyed a lavish four-day visit to Disney World. Her loving and INDULGENT father showered Suri with toys, treats, and an adorable *Little Mermaid* costume. Tom treated Suri like a princess as he arranged for her to chat with costumed characters and even spend a night in Disney's exclusive Cinderella Castle Suite.

295. PEDANTIC

• *characterized by being OSTENTATIOUS (showy) in displaying one's knowledge; bookish*

POP CULTURE

The character of Sheldon Lee Cooper on the TV program *The Big Bang Theory* is renowned for his PEDANTIC demonstrations of obscure information. Whether RUMINATING about Bose-Einstein condensates or describing the precise location of retroflectors on the moon's surface, Sheldon never misses an opportunity to show off what he knows.

296. OFFICIOUS

- *describes someone who acts more official than they actually are; annoyingly meddlesome*

POP CULTURE

OFFICIOUS is a tricky word that students often think refers to an office or an official. Instead, *OFFICIOUS* describes busybodies who act more official than they actually are. For example, in the *Harry Potter* series Percy Weasley is portrayed as having an unhealthy obsession with following rules. When the Ministry of Magic denies that Lord Voldemort has returned, the OFFICIOUS Percy insists that Harry and the members of the Order of the Phoenix accept the official but ERRONEOUS (wrong) viewpoint.

297. BOHEMIAN

- *describes a person who is known for UNCONVENTIONAL behavior; a nonconformist*

MEET MY STUDENTS:DHARA

I find that most of my students have never heard the word *BOHEMIAN*. My explanation that the 1950s beatniks and the late-1960s hippies both led BOHEMIAN lifestyles did not seem to RESONATE (evoke a shared feeling) with my 21st-century students. Fortunately, my student Dhara helped me by pointing out that the word *BOHEMIAN* reminded her of the Boho Chic style of clothing. Dhara's tip worked, and all of my students now remember that *BOHEMIAN* describes UNCONVENTIONAL behavior.

298. PROSCRIBE

- *to forbid or prohibit an activity*

IN MY LIFE

I recently attended my niece's wedding reception. I arrived early and went to the country club's now-empty bar to order a snack and a soft drink. The bartender stunned me by politely but firmly saying, "I'm sorry, but I can't serve you. Club rules PROSCRIBE serving gentlemen who are not wearing a jacket." I was impressed by the bartender's correct use of *PROSCRIBE* but furious at the club's INANE (absurd, silly) rule. The waiter made matters worse when he offered to let me wear a secondhand bright green sports jacket that was several sizes too large. Rather than look like a clown, I refused the offer and walked out.

299. FACETIOUS

- *cleverly amusing in tone; not meant to be taken seriously*

POP CULTURE

Richard Castle is one of the most FACETIOUS characters on television. His quick wit provides timely comedic relief on a program that focuses on solving gruesome murders. Castle's FACETIOUS sense of humor can be clearly seen in this exchange with his partner, Detective Beckett:

Beckett: "Crime scene. Dead body. Little respect here."

Castle: "I don't think he can hear me."

300. PUNCTILIOUS

- *strictly attentive to minute details of conduct; very precise and METICULOUS*

INSIDER INFO

Most of my students are BEFUDDLED (confused) by the word *PUNCTILIOUS*. They claim never to have seen it before and have no idea what it means. I then invite my students to take a close look at *PUNCTILIOUS*. It is really a combination of the word *PUNCTUAL*, meaning "prompt," and the suffix *-ous*, meaning "full of." So *PUNCTILIOUS* means "full of promptness," in the sense of paying careful attention to details. A PUNCTILIOUS person would not challenge traditions or take a CURSORY (hasty) glance at an important document.

CHAPTER 28
THE TOP 100 LEVEL 4 WORDS
PART 1

The SAT rates each question on a five-point scale of difficulty. Level 4 questions are the second most challenging questions on the test. At least 65 percent of all test-takers miss a Level 4 question. What makes these questions so difficult? In most cases, the questions call for a knowledge of little-known and often misunderstood vocabulary words. This chapter is the first in a series of ten chapters that will define and illustrate 100 Level 4 vocabulary words. It is important to remember that the Level 4 questions are actually very easy if you know the words!

301. AUSPICIOUS
- *favorable and promising; accompanied by good omens and therefore PROPITIOUS*

WORLD CULTURES
In Chinese culture certain numbers are believed to be either AUSPICIOUS or INAUSPICIOUS. For example, *two* is often considered an AUSPICIOUS number because "good things come in pairs." In contrast, *four* is often considered an INAUSPICIOUS number because its pronunciation is very similar to the word for death. As a result, many buildings in East Asia do not have a fourth floor. This is very similar to the Western practice of eliminating the thirteenth floor, since thirteen is believed to be an INAUSPICIOUS number.

302. EVOCATIVE

- *characterized by using the power of imagination to call forth a memory*

INSIDER INFO

On the SAT, *EVOCATIVE* describes an experience that has generated a number of answers for challenging sentence completion and critical reading questions. The questions typically deal with an EVOCATIVE portrayal of a person or an author's EVOCATIVE tone describing a place. For example, in one recent passage, an archaeologist's tone is EVOCATIVE because he imagines hearing "the echoes of the ancient city" and the voices of its residents "over pots of steaming coffee."

303. ENIGMA

- *a riddle shrouded in mystery and thus something*
  that is puzzling and INSCRUTABLE

POP CULTURE

In his song "6 Foot 7 Foot," Lil Wayne points out that being misunderstood is not necessarily bad when he asks, "What's a world without ENIGMA?" Lil Wayne is right. Life would be MUNDANE (commonplace) without ENIGMAS to discuss and solve. It is important to note that the adjective *ENIGMATIC* means "mysterious." For example, Da Vinci's *Mona Lisa* is world-famous for her ENIGMATIC smile.

304. SUPERFICIAL

- *shallow; lacking intellectual or emotional depth*

POP CULTURE

In the movie *Clueless*, Cher is an attractive, popular, and hip teenager at a fashion-obsessed Beverly Hills high school. However, these traits do not impress Josh, her socially conscious ex-stepbrother. Josh teases Cher for being selfish, vain, and most of all SUPERFICIAL. According to Josh, Cher's only direction in life is "toward the mall." Cher denies that she is SUPERFICIAL, pointing out that she is a serious person who donates her used clothes to charity. Cher may be "clueless," but at least she can define SUPERFICIAL!

305. PRECOCIOUS

- *characterized by the exceptionally early development or maturity of a talent*

IN MY LIFE

My niece Sierra is very PRECOCIOUS. Naturally, when I visit with Sierra I enjoy teaching her SAT vocabulary words. When she was just five years old, I told Sierra that she was PRECOCIOUS because she had a big vocabulary. Sierra then gleefully told everyone in the room that she was PRECOCIOUS!

306. STIGMATIZE

- *to brand or mark as inferior*

AP U.S. HISTORY

On May 17, 1954, the United States Supreme Court reversed the long-standing "separate but equal" doctrine of *Plessy v. Ferguson* by issuing a landmark decision in *Brown v. Board of Education of Topeka*. Speaking for a unanimous Court, Chief Justice Earl Warren agreed with NAACP lawyer Thurgood Marshall that separate schools were inherently unequal because they unjustly STIGMATIZED black children.

307. INFINITESIMAL

- *incalculably small; MINUSCULE*

AP BIOLOGY

Pfiesteria piscicida are microscopic one-celled microorganisms. The organism is INFINITESIMAL in size. Amazingly, thousands of them could fit on the exclamation point dot at the end of this sentence!

308. VITRIOLIC

- *characterized by a harsh and nasty tone; SCATHING*

AP U.S. HISTORY

In her groundbreaking book *Silent Spring*, Rachel Carson warned that the continued INDISCRIMINATE (not selective) use of DDT and other chemical pesticides posed a dire threat to wildlife and human health. The chemical industry promptly attacked both Carson and her book. VITRIOLIC critics denounced Carson as a "hysterical woman," "a fanatic," and "a Communist." Nevertheless, Carson demonstrated great courage and conviction by refusing to COMPROMISE her principles. Today, Rachel Carson is widely ACCLAIMED (praised) for her role in helping to ban DDT and GALVANIZE (energize) the global environmental movement.

309. PROLIFERATE

- *to grow rapidly; multiply quickly; to BURGEON*

IN THE NEWS

The song "Gangnam Style" has focused global attention on the lifestyle of the people who live in the Gangnam district of Seoul, South Korea. The "Gangnam style" includes a fascination with cosmetic plastic surgery. Visitors to Gangnam have noted the astonishing PROLIFERATION of plastic surgery clinics. There are now over 430 such clinics in the district, making it the plastic surgery center of South Korea. The PROLIFERATION of clinics has triggered a boom in cosmetic procedures. South Korea now has the highest per capita rate of cosmetic surgery in the world.

310. RESPLENDENT

- *characterized by great beauty, splendor, and dazzling jewel-like colors; not DRAB*

WORLD CULTURES

Traditional Indian weddings are often very elaborate affairs that can last for days. Brides and grooms are usually treated like royalty. Many brides wear sarees that are renowned for their RESPLENDENT jewel-like colors, gorgeous lace, and intricate embroidery.

THE TOP 100 LEVEL 4 WORDS
PART 2

Chapter 29 is the second of our ten-part series of chapters devoted to defining and illustrating the top 100 Level 4 words. Always remember that the hard questions are easy if you know the words!

311. EXHORT

- *to spur on; to encourage*

IN MY LIFE

In *Harry Potter and the Order of the Phoenix*, Harry EXHORTED his classmates at Hogwarts to join "Dumbledore's Army" to learn how to fight the evil Lord Voldemort. On my InsiderTestPrep.com website, I EXHORT students to study my list of essential vocabulary words to fight evil questions on the SAT.

312. AMELIORATE

- *to improve; make better*

IN THE NEWS

America has a long list of notable reformers who have worked to AMELIORATE social problems. For example, in the early 20th century Jane Addams worked to AMELIORATE the condition of poor immigrants in Chicago. Today Brad Pitt's Make It Right Foundation is working to AMELIORATE a housing shortage in New Orleans' IMPOVERISHED (very poor) Ninth Ward.

313. COMPUNCTION

* *a feeling of deep regret caused by a sense of guilt;
  great REMORSE and CONTRITION*

POP CULTURE

In the movie *Snow White and the Huntsman*, the Evil Queen admits that she once felt COMPUNCTION for being the cause of bloody battles that claimed many innocent lives. "It once pained me," she confesses, "to know that I am the cause of such despair." But the Evil Queen's feelings have hardened, and she no longer feels any sense of COMPUNCTION for causing such great suffering. Instead, she defiantly proclaims, "their cries give me strength."

314. MENDACITY

* *the trait of being deliberately untruthful; DUPLICITOUS*

AP EUROPEAN HISTORY

Is lying ever justified? In his book *The Prince*, Machiavelli argued that for the good of the state, a prince should resort to MENDACITY to trick his enemies. His ideal ruler was the crafty Spanish king, Ferdinand of Aragon. When the king of France complained that Ferdinand had deceived him twice, the MENDACIOUS Ferdinand boasted, "He lies, the drunkard. I have deceived him more than ten times."

315. FORTUITOUS

* *an accidental but lucky chance; filled with good fortune*

IN THE NEWS

Tom Morris always bought three $1 Powerball tickets each week. On Saturday, August 13, 2011, Tom entered a SuperAmerica store to purchase his usual three tickets. He reached into his pocket and discovered that he only had a $5 bill. Tom briefly paused and then decided to buy five tickets and let the machine pick random numbers. Tom's spontaneous decision proved to be FORTUITOUS. The fourth set of numbers was the winner in a Powerball jackpot worth $228.9 million! The 61-year-old sales engineer celebrated his FORTUITOUS good luck by retiring from his job and promising his ECSTATIC (very happy) family, "We're going to have fun!"

316. DEBACLE

- *a complete disaster; a FIASCO*

AP U.S. HISTORY

On April 24, 1980, President Jimmy Carter ordered a daring mission to rescue 52 Americans held captive at the U.S. Embassy in Tehran, Iran. Code-named Operation Eagle Claw, the mission quickly turned into a DEBACLE when a sand cloud forced one helicopter to crash land and another to return to the aircraft carrier U.S.S. *Nimitz*. Carter then approved the ground commander's request to abort the mission. The DEBACLE became even worse when a helicopter crashed into a transport aircraft and caused the deaths of eight American servicemen. The humiliating DEBACLE damaged American prestige and played a key role in Carter's overwhelming defeat in the 1980 presidential election.

317. INADVERTENT

- *unintentional and accidental; unwitting*

MEET MY STUDENTS: MUKHI

Mukhi's full name is very long and very difficult to pronounce. Here it is—Saimukeshvarma Bhupatiraju. Needless to say, many people have trouble pronouncing this name. In fact, on the first day of school, teachers often address Mukhi as "the kid with the very long name." In the eighth grade, Mukhi earned an award for his high academic average. At the awards assembly the announcer INADVERTENTLY mispronounced Mukhi's name so badly that he did not know that he was being called to the stage. Thinking that Mukhi was absent, the announcer went on to the next person. Mukhi and his friends now remember the INADVERTENT slight as a humorous middle school incident. Mukhi wants everyone to know that he did receive his certificate a few days later.

318. PERFUNCTORY

- *characterized by casual INDIFFERENCE; performing in a routine manner*

IN MY LIFE

It is commonly assumed that students who achieve high SAT scores are smarter than students who achieve low scores. My experience suggests otherwise. Students who achieve high scores ASSIDUOUSLY (diligently) study vocabulary words, practice critical reading, and take several timed tests. In contrast, students who receive low scores typically make only a PERFUNCTORY effort. They postpone practice, make excuses, and conveniently forget to take practice tests.

319. AUSTERITY

• *great self-denial, especially when refraining from spending*

INSIDER INFO

Students who keep up with the news will recognize the word AUSTERITY. The economic crisis in Europe has forced governments in Greece, Italy, and Spain to enact AUSTERITY programs designed to cut government spending. Similarly, budget cuts have forced state and local governments in the United States to undertake AUSTERITY measures. Recent SAT sentence completions have also focused attention on the word AUSTERITY. Double-blank sentence completion questions often pair *AUSTERITY* with the word *CURTAIL*, meaning "to cut back, limit, or TRUNCATE (cut short)." For example, a town council would undertake AUSTERITY measures by CURTAILING the number of new public projects.

320. INDIGENOUS

• *a plant, animal, or person that is native or ENDEMIC to an area*

DID YOU KNOW?

The American Beauty rose is renowned for its exceptional beauty and fragrance. It is a particular favorite with home gardeners and is one of the mainstays of the cut-flower industry. Despite its name, the American Beauty rose is not INDIGENOUS to the United States. It is actually native to France and was first introduced in the United States in 1875 by the botanist George Valentine Nash. It is interesting to note that Nash had nothing to do with the use of roses on Valentine's Day.

THE TOP 100 LEVEL 4 WORDS
PART 3

Chapter 30 is the third of our ten-part series of chapters devoted to defining and illustrating the top 100 Level 4 words. Always remember that the hard questions are easy if you know the words!

321. LITANY

- *a long and familiar list often recited by rote*

IN MY LIFE
My wife Susan once got a speeding ticket for driving 35 miles per hour in a 25-mph zone. She thought the ticket was unfair and prepared a good excuse. The traffic magistrate greeted a room filled with speeding offenders by warning everyone not to bother insulting his intelligence. He then recited a LITANY of tired excuses that included a broken speedometer (her excuse), rushing to a funeral, and worst of all claiming, "I had to go to the bathroom." After hearing the magistrate recite this LITANY of excuses, Susan decided to pay the $75 fine.

322. ESTRANGE

- *to alienate; drive apart*

INSIDER INFO
We often hear *ESTRANGE* used to describe the break-up of a celebrity marriage. This seems appropriate since *ESTRANGE* contains the word *strange*, suggesting that a couple has literally become strangers. Don't expect to see an SAT sentence completion question featuring a celebrity couple that has become ESTRANGED. While *ESTRANGE* is widely used to describe a personal relationship, it can also be used to describe a person's relationship to the environment. For example, massive and impersonal apartment complexes can ESTRANGE people from their surroundings.

323. GREGARIOUS

• *marked by a liking for companionship; sociable; AFFABLE*

AP BIOLOGY

Killer whales are very GREGARIOUS animals that live with their mothers in very stable family groups called *pods*. Since a female killer whale can live to be ninety years old, as many as four generations of whales can travel together. Their GREGARIOUS nature enables killer whales to develop sophisticated hunting techniques and vocal behaviors that marine biologists believe can be transmitted across generations.

324. IMPASSE

• *a deadlock or stalemate*

AP U.S. HISTORY

The election of 1860 marked a fateful moment in American history. Southern "fire-eaters" threatened to secede from the Union if the "sectional" Abraham Lincoln won the election. At the same time, northern abolitionists vowed to prevent the expansion of slavery into the western territories. The United States thus confronted a dangerous IMPASSE. Lincoln's election led to the secession of seven southern states. Senator Crittendon and other leaders worked tirelessly to craft a COMPROMISE that would break the IMPASSE and save the Union. But their efforts failed, and a civil war between the North and the South became inevitable.

325. ARDUOUS

• *describes a difficult task that requires a great deal of strenuous work*

MEET MY STUDENTS: ADITI

Aditi is committed to participating in Relay for Life activities designed to raise money for cancer research. For example, last year Aditi and her team wrote emails, sold cancer bracelets, and participated in a twelve-hour walk. Although these volunteer activities required long and ARDUOUS work, Aditi is proud that she raised $1,800 and that her team raised over $4,600. Way to go Aditi—we are all very proud of you!

326. ESCHEW

• *to avoid something deliberately*

WORLD CULTURES

Approximately 250,000 Amish live in North America. The Amish are known for ADHERING (strictly following) to a traditional lifestyle that ESCHEWS many modern conveniences. For example, Amish families ESCHEW using electricity, making telephone calls, and driving automobiles. In addition, the Amish ESCHEW modern clothing fashions, preferring to ADHERE (closely follow) to a strict dress code that rejects personal vanity.

327. PRECLUDE

- *to make impossible, especially beforehand; to prevent or to FORESTALL something from happening*

AP ART HISTORY

Vincent Van Gogh was not PRECLUDED from becoming famous by a lack of talent. One of history's most original artists, Van Gogh painted a variety of dazzling landscapes, vibrant still lifes, and revealing portraits that pioneered the Post-Impressionist style. Unrecognized and unappreciated in his own life, Van Gogh fought a desperate and ultimately losing struggle against poverty, hunger, alcoholism, and insanity. He fatally shot himself when he was 37, thus PRECLUDING the recognition and fame he deserved.

328. POSTHUMOUS

- *occurring or coming into existence after a person's death*

AP ART HISTORY

Vincent Van Gogh sold only one painting during his lifetime; however, his works enjoyed enormous POSTHUMOUS fame in the years following his death in 1890. Critics and the general public now recognize Van Gogh as one of history's greatest artists.

329. IMPETUS

- *the moving force behind something; a stimulus that moves something along*

AP EUROPEAN HISTORY

The spice trade provided the primary IMPETUS for the first Portuguese and Spanish voyages of exploration. Peppers that could be purchased in Calicut for three Venetian ducats could be sold in Europe for eighty ducats, a 2,700-percent markup. Profit thus provided the most compelling IMPETUS for the voyages of Vasco da Gama and Christopher Columbus.

330. PRISTINE

- *immaculately clean; unspoiled; free from contamination*

IN THE NEWS

In the early 1990s, Russian scientists discovered a PRISTINE lake two miles beneath the surface of Antarctica. Named Lake Vostok, the isolated body of water may be home to many unusual life forms. Researchers must now determine how to investigate the lake without contaminating its PRISTINE ecosystem.

THE TOP 100 LEVEL 4 WORDS
PART 4

Chapter 31 is the fourth of our ten-part series of chapters devoted to defining and illustrating the top 100 Level 4 words. Always remember that the hard questions are easy if you know the words!

331. ERRONEOUS

- *incorrect; mistaken; wrong; filled with errors*

POP CULTURE

In the movie *The Social Network*, Lawrence Summers, the President of Harvard University, confidently predicted that Facebook would have limited public appeal and even less commercial value. Summers' prediction proved to be ERRONEOUS. Facebook now has over 850 million active users, and its founder Mark Zuckerberg is one of the wealthiest people in the world.

332. ADMONISH

- *to counsel against, to warn EARNESTLY*

POP CULTURE

In 1995 J. K. Rowling, then an obscure single mom, began her search to find a publisher for a children's fantasy book she had just completed. One publishing executive ADMONISHED Rowling by warning her that young readers would not be able to identify with her characters and that there was little chance of making money by writing a children's book. Needless to say, his ADMONITION proved to be ERRONEOUS. Rowling's series of books about a boy wizard named Harry Potter have now sold over 450 million copies in 67 languages.

333. DEMARCATE

- *to clearly set or mark the boundaries of a group or geographic area*

AP U.S. HISTORY

Columbus's discoveries prompted the Spanish to ask Pope Alexander VI to DEMARCATE the boundaries between lands claimed by Spain and Portugal. The Pope obliged by issuing the Papal Line of DEMARCATION. As its name implies, the proclamation DEMARCATED or marked the boundaries of so-called "heathen lands" that would be controlled by Spain and by Portugal. Although the Line of DEMARCATION gave the lion's share of New World land to Spain, Portugal received title to lands that ultimately became Brazil.

334. FOSTER

- *to promote and encourage*

IN MY LIFE

The administration and staff at Jordan-Matthews High School tried very hard to FOSTER a climate of racial harmony. But FOSTERING racial tolerance proved to be difficult. The community had to overcome a historic legacy in which the ancestors of some of our white students had owned the ancestors of some of our black students. Football played a key role in breaking down barriers and FOSTERING a greater sense of togetherness. As the Jordan-Matthews Jets won victory after victory, the school and community came together to support their team.

335. FLORID

- *excessively ornamental, as in a very flowery style*
  of writing; neither plain nor STARK

DID YOU KNOW?

The Italian city of Florence, the American state of Florida, and the SAT word *FLORID* all derive from the Old French word *flor*, meaning "flower." Florence is thus a flowery city, Florida is a flowery state, and *FLORID* is a flowery word. FLORID writers are known for using flowery descriptions. For example, Edward Bulwer-Lytton began his novel *Paul Clifford* with the following classic example of FLORID writing: "It was a dark and stormy night; the rain fell in torrents…rattling the housetop; and fiercely agitating the scanty flame of the lamps that struggled against the darkness."

336. CHURLISH

- *characterized by SURLY and rude behavior; sullen and devoid of CIVILITY*

IN THE NEWS

Serena Williams was once best known for her skill as a tennis player and flair as a fashion model. She is now increasingly known for her CHURLISH behavior during tennis matches. For example, in the 2011 U.S. Open, Williams called the official "a loser," "a hater," and "unattractive, on the inside." Williams continued to demonstrate CHURLISH behavior when she refused the customary post-match handshake with the umpire.

337. CIRCUMSCRIBE

- *to limit, restrict, or confine*

POP CULTURE

In her song "Fly," Nicki Minaj realizes that fame has a price. She protests that managers, producers, and even fans "try to box me in." Nicki doesn't want others to CIRCUMSCRIBE her life. She vows to soar and thrive. Don't expect College Board test writers to use lyrics from a Nicki Minaj song to test your knowledge of the word *CIRCUMSCRIBE*. Past SAT examples included social customs that CIRCUMSCRIBED the lives of Renaissance women and STRINGENT (very strict) rules that CIRCUMSCRIBED the range of paint colors available to a group of homeowners.

338. PROVISIONAL

- *temporary; not permanent*

INSIDER INFO

For most American teenagers the word *PROVISIONAL* calls to mind a PROVISIONAL driver's license. Don't expect to see this example on your SAT. Instead, test writers typically focus on PROVISIONAL theories of the universe that are not definitive and PROVISIONAL governments that are not permanent.

339. PASTORAL

- *an idealized portrayal of country life; RUSTIC; BUCOLIC*

AP ART HISTORY

John Constable is often described as England's greatest landscape artist. His PASTORAL paintings feature lush green meadows, picturesque villages, and lazy streams flowing under old stone bridges. To this day, his PASTORAL masterpieces draw large admiring crowds at London's National Gallery. The scenes he immortalized are preserved along a Painter's Trail in a portion of Suffolk now known as "Constable Country."

340. CONVIVIAL

- *characterized by being full of life and good company; JOVIAL and festive*

POP CULTURE

In the music video "Last Friday Night (TGIF)," Rebecca Black is the CONVIVIAL hostess of a "best ever" party that is "absolutely incredible." Rebecca generously welcomes her nerdy neighbor Kathy Beth Terry (Katy Perry) and quickly transforms her into a CONVIVIAL party girl. The festive guests enjoy a CONVIVIAL scene that includes Kenny G playing a sax solo on the roof and Hanson as the house band.

CHAPTER 32
THE TOP 100 LEVEL 4 WORDS
PART 5

Chapter 32 is the fifth of our ten-part series of chapters devoted to defining and illustrating the top 100 Level 4 words. Always remember that the hard questions are easy if you know the words!

341. BURGEON

- *to grow and multiply rapidly; to FLOURISH*

AP U.S. HISTORY

In the mid-19th century, as many as sixty to 100 million bison roamed the Great Plains. Less than three decades later the transcontinental railroads had enabled hunters to nearly exterminate these once-great herds. By 1912, a tiny herd of fewer than 100 bison remained in Yellowstone National Park; however, the determined work of dedicated conservationists has brought the bison back from the brink of extinction. The bison population is now BURGEONING, with an estimated 350,000 living on ranches and parks throughout the United States.

342. CONFOUND

- *to perplex and confuse; to leave baffled, BEWILDERED, and NONPLUSSED*

AP ART HISTORY

In 1950, Jackson Pollock stunned and CONFOUNDED the art world with an Abstract Expressionist painting entitled *Autumn Rhythm*. The painting did not contain images of Fall or any other recognizable objects. Instead, Pollock literally hurled paint onto a canvas and claimed that the resulting maze of lines and drips represented the process of painting. Needless to say, critics attacked Pollock's work and called him "Jack the Dripper." Even today, most museum visitors are still CONFOUNDED by Pollock's paintings and by his Abstract Expressionist message.

343. BEMOAN

- *to moan and groan; to express great regret; to LAMENT*

IN MY LIFE

I met Mr. Withers in the faculty lounge. He was a veteran teacher who sat in "his" rocking chair everyday at lunch. Mr. Withers loved to BEMOAN recent trends in education. According to him, our students lacked discipline, study skills, and manners. He also BEMOANED the quality of new teachers like me. According to Mr. Withers, we were too lenient and of course failed to manage our classrooms properly.

344. QUIESCENT

- *marked by inactivity and quiet; a state of tranquility*

AP U.S. HISTORY

American college students have alternated between QUIESCENT periods of inactivity and restless periods of protest. For example, the Vietnam War and the Civil Rights Movement transformed the QUIESCENT 1950s into the turbulent 1960s.

345. REAFFIRM

- *to make a renewed commitment to something; to confirm*

IN THE NEWS

Malala Yousufzai is a teenage Pakistani human rights activist who has become a global symbol of defiance against Taliban oppression. In 2009, the Taliban issued a PEREMPTORY (arbitrary) order banning all girls from attending schools in the town in northwestern Pakistan where Malala lived. Malala refused to SUCCUMB (submit) to the Taliban and instead began a blog exposing the horrors they imposed on the girls in her hometown. The Taliban retaliated in October 2012 by attempting to assassinate Malala as she rode home on her school bus. Malala survived the attack and is now recognized as a courageous CHAMPION (supporter) of women's rights. UNDAUNTED (not discouraged) by continuing Taliban threats, Malala had REAFFIRMED her commitment to human rights vowing, "I shall raise my voice."

346. ACRIMONIOUS

- *marked by feelings of ill will and hostility; great resentment; RANCOROUS in tone*

AP U.S. HISTORY

The ACRIMONIOUS blood feud between the Hatfields and McCoys has fascinated Americans for over a century. The two rival families lived on opposite sides of the Big Sandy River in the mountains between Kentucky and West Virginia. The ACRIMONY began in 1878 when Randolph McCoy accused Floyd Hatfield of stealing one of his prized pigs. The incident sparked a lethal feud between the two families that lasted for decades. Over time the two clans finally RECONCILED and even appeared together in 1979 on the *Family Feud* game show. In 2012 a record television audience watched the History Channel's epic mini-series on the Hatfields and McCoys.

347. RANCID

• *having a rotten taste or smell; sour*

DID YOU KNOW?

Honey has special chemical properties that prevent it from spoiling or becoming RANCID. Archaeologists have found unspoiled honey stored in the tombs of ancient Egyptian pharaohs. Incredibly, the honey was still edible!

348. LARGESSE

• *generous giving; LIBERAL bestowing of gifts*

INSIDER INFO

LARGESSE is normally associated with generous acts of PHILANTHROPY and selfless giving. However, acts of LARGESSE can have ulterior motives. For example, the pharmaceutical industry in the United States is noted for its LARGESSE. The industry entertains lavishly and sponsors numerous medical conventions. But it also promotes its political interests by spending more on lobbyists than any other industrial group.

349. EPIPHANY

• *an unexpected moment of sudden inspiration*

IN MY LIFE

Back in the early 1990s, as I was driving home from an SAT class, I thought about how hard it is to teach students difficult SAT vocabulary words. I turned the radio channel to an oldies station just as the DJ began playing Bon Jovi's hit song "Livin' on a Prayer." I suddenly had an EPIPHANY. What if I used the stories in popular songs and movies to illustrate challenging SAT vocabulary words! For example, "Livin' on a Prayer" tells the story of a working class couple who are down on their luck. But Gina is RESOLUTE (determined) and refuses to SUCCUMB (give up). She EXHORTS (encourages) Tommy "to hold on to what we've got." This EPIPHANY marked the beginning of a revolutionary way to teach SAT vocabulary. The pop culture examples in this book all are inspired by my EPIPHANY as I listened to "Livin' on a Prayer."

350. VINDICATE

• *to justify or prove something's worth*

IN MY LIFE

I was very excited about my decision (see Word 349) to use popular songs and scenes from movies to provide memorable examples of difficult SAT vocabulary words; SKEPTICS (doubters), however, questioned my new approach. They insisted that rote memorization and REPETITION were the best ways to learn SAT vocabulary words. I refused to let the critics dampen my enthusiasm. Within a short time my students reported dramatic increases in their critical reading scores. Being VINDICATED (proven right) felt good, and helping my students felt even better.

CHAPTER 33
THE TOP 100 LEVEL 4 WORDS
PART 6

Chapter 33 is the sixth of our ten-part series of chapters devoted to defining and illustrating the top 100 Level 4 words. Always remember that the hard questions are easy if you know the words!

351. AMBIGUOUS

- *open to more than one interpretation; unclear*

POP CULTURE

The movie *The Amazing Spider-Man* ends with an intentionally AMBIGUOUS mid-credits scene. Dr. Curt Conners (The Lizard) is incarcerated in a high-security cell for his diabolical plot to transform everyone in New York City into a reptile. A shadowy figure suddenly appears and asks Dr. Connors, "Did you tell the boy about his father?" Dr. Connors answers, "No," and the man in the shadows replies, "Well, that's very good, so we'll let him be for now." The boy is of course Peter Parker (Spider-Man); however, everything else is AMBIGUOUS. Who is the mysterious figure, and how did he get into the cell? Although there is much speculation, the scene is AMBIGUOUS, and the answers to these questions are all unknown. We'll have to wait for *The Amazing Spider-Man 2* to find out the truth.

352. ENTHRALL

- *fascinating and spellbinding; CAPTIVATING*

AP U.S. HISTORY

Frederick Douglass was a former slave who became America's foremost black abolitionist during the antebellum period. A gifted orator, Douglass ENTHRALLED audiences with his commanding personal presence and authentic stories about the horrors of slavery. For example, he told a spellbound audience in Massachusetts, "I appear before the immense assembly this evening as a thief and a robber. I stole this head, these limbs, this body from my master, and ran off with them."

353. VIVACIOUS

- *full of life and spirit; animated*

MEET MY STUDENTS: NICOLE

I am fortunate to have many VIVACIOUS students who enliven my classes with their spirit and energy. But few students can surpass Nicole's wit and VIVACITY. I can always count on Nicole for a funny story about the antics of celebrities such and Kim Kardashian, Snooki, and of course Kristen Stewart. In addition, Nicole has an uncanny ability to spontaneously use clever facial expressions and hand gestures to illustrate difficult vocabulary words.

354. IMPULSIVE

- *acting with a lack of forethought or deliberation; rash*

POP CULTURE

In her song "Call Me Maybe," Carly Rae Jepsen sees a hot guy and has a sudden innocent crush. Although Carly knows "this is crazy," she IMPULSIVELY gives the guy her number and says, "So call me, maybe?" If her IMPULSIVE action works out, it will be the perfect way to start a summer romance—or not!

355. AUDACIOUS

- *fearlessly and often recklessly bold and daring*

POP CULTURE

In the movie *The Hunger Games*, Katniss is forced to display her fighting skills during a private session with Seneca Crane and the other Gamesmakers. Normally a skilled archer, Katniss's first shot misses the target. Although Katniss's next shot is a bullseye, the bored Gamesmakers focus their attention on a roast pig placed on their banquet table. Furious that she has been ignored and upstaged by a dead pig, Katniss AUDACIOUSLY targets an apple in the roast pig's mouth. Her arrow pierces the apple as the stunned Gamesmakers stare at her in disbelief. Impressed by her AUDACITY, the Gamesmakers award Katniss an eleven out of twelve for her skill and boldness.

356. BELLWETHER

- *a person, group, or statistic that serves as a leading indicator of future events*

AP ECONOMICS

Economists and Wall Street stock analysts use BELLWETHER statistics to help them predict changes in the economy. For example, economists use the consumer confidence index to predict future economic growth. Other fields also have BELLWETHERS. Paris and Milan are BELLWETHER cities for the high fashion industry. Copies of the clothes supermodels wear in these fashion centers will soon end up on store shelves in your nearby shopping mall.

357. FASTIDIOUS

- *marked by careful attention to details; METICULOUS*

MEET MY STUDENTS: SRUTI

What does your clothing closet look like? Are your clothes neatly arranged or are they placed in no particular order? I asked Sruti this question and she replied that her entire wardrobe is arranged by type and by color. Wow - Sruti is very FASTIDIOUS! However, not all of my students are so METICULOUS. Keyur admits that he puts his clothes in a big pile and then randomly picks out what to wear. He was not AFFRONTED (offended) when Sruti called him SLOVENLY.

358. METEORIC

- *similar to a meteor in speed, brilliance, or BREVITY; characterized by a sudden, very rapid rise or fall*

POP CULTURE

Nicki Minaj's platinum single "Starships" is a good METAPHOR (comparison) for her METEORIC career rise. Just three years ago, Minaj was making dresses for herself in the basement of her home in Queens, New York. Now the rapper is a global superstar who headlines sold-out concerts and represents international companies such as Pepsi. Although Minaj is on top now, she should remember that in the music industry a METEORIC rise to fame is often followed by an equally METEORIC fall into obscurity.

359. CULL

- *to select from a large quantity or collection*

MEET MY STUDENTS: ALIN

Alin is the entertainment editor of *The Clarion*, the East Brunswick High School student newspaper. Alin admits that her job is not easy. Students often submit a number of reviews for popular movies, albums, and concerts. Alin must then CULL the best stories for publication. Because of space limitations, *The Clarion* must sometimes publish a TRUNCATED (abbreviated) version of the original article.

360. REVULSION

- *a strong feeling of REPUGNANCE or disgust*

AP U.S. HISTORY

In his muckraking novel *The Jungle* (1906), Upton Sinclair wrote the following graphic description of the filthy conditions in a Chicago meatpacking factory: "There would be meat stored in great piles in rooms; and the water from leaky roofs would drip over it; and thousands of rats would race about it." Sinclair's vivid and disturbing description produced a wave of public REVULSION. Congress responded to the public outcry by promptly passing the Meat Inspection Act and the Pure Food and Drug Act.

CHAPTER 34
THE TOP 100 LEVEL 4 WORDS
PART 7

Chapter 34 is the seventh of our ten-part series of chapters devoted to defining and illustrating the top 100 Level 4 words. Always remember that the hard questions are easy if you know the words!

361. INSIPID

- *lacking flavor or interest; flat and BLAND*

POP CULTURE

In the movie *Ratatouille*, Anton Ego is a sharp-tongued French food critic who is known as "the Grim Eater." Ego strikes fear into the hearts of proud French chefs by branding their dishes as INSIPID and unoriginal. It is important to remember that *INSIPID* can also be used to describe works of art and literature that lack flair or vitality.

362. SNIDE

- *expressing DISDAIN (contempt) in an insulting or contemptuous manner*

POP CULTURE

In the movie *Ratatouille*, Anton Ego (see Word 361 above) is a sharp-tongued French food critic who is known for his SNIDE remarks. For example, he gleefully tells the young and obviously nervous Linguini, "You're slow for someone in the fast lane." Note that on the SAT, an attitude of DISDAIN (contempt) is the key driving force behind a SNIDE remark.

363. SUCCUMB

- *to submit to an overpowering force or YIELD to an overwhelming desire; to give up or give in*

POP CULTURE

High school students are often urged to make good decisions and to avoid SUCCUMBING to the temptations of drugs, alcohol, and tobacco. If today's students would watch *Star Wars Episode III: Revenge of the Sith*, they would learn a valuable lesson about the danger of SUCCUMBING to temptation. As the movie begins, Anakin Skywalker is a justice-loving Jedi Knight who fights on behalf of the citizens of the Republic. But as the film progresses, Anakin's growing fears and insecurities combine with the MACHINATIONS (SINISTER schemes) of the evil Emperor Palpatine to tempt the young Jedi to go over to the Dark Side of the Force. Although his friend Obi-Wan Kenobi and his wife Padme try to prevent his downfall, Anakin finally SUCCUMBS to the Dark Side and becomes the Sith Lord, Darth Vader.

364. EXECRABLE

- *unequivocally detestable, abominable, and repulsive*

INSIDER INFO

Do you think that EXECRABLE sounds like a "good" word or a "bad" word?
When I asked my students this question, 100 percent confidently responded that EXECRABLE is a "bad" word. My students were right! Perhaps EXECRABLE sounds like a "bad" word because it is very similar to the word excrement. SAT test writers often use EXECRABLE to describe the extremely negative responses that critics and preview audiences have to abominable books and movies that contain detestable and repulsive content.

365. SHREWD

- *marked by mental alertness and clever calculation; ASTUTE*

POP CULTURE

What do Simon Cowell and Warren Buffett have in common? Both are SHREWD judges of talent. Cowell is best known as a judge of musical talent. He SHREWDLY formed One Direction to fill the need for a boy band. Buffett is best known as a judge of business talent. His SHREWD investments have made him the second richest person in the United States with a net worth of over $45 billion. Buffett is also known for his SHREWD common-sense advice. For example, he SHREWDLY warned investors that, "You can't make a good deal with a bad person."

366. ASSIDUOUS

- *characterized by being very diligent, industrious, and hardworking*

MEET MY STUDENTS: JOHN

John's musical career began in New Zealand when he was just ten years old. Hoping to learn how to play the drums, John visited a local music conservatory. The drum classes were full, however, and the only open classes were for the flute and clarinet. John rejected the flute as a "girly instrument" and chose the clarinet. His decision proved to be FORTUITOUS (fortunate). John worked ASSIDUOUSLY to develop his clarinet skills. His dedication paid off. Today, John is a distinguished musician who was selected to be part of America's All National Honor Ensemble.

367. AUTOCRATIC

- *having absolute power; dictatorial and DESPOTIC*

POP CULTURE

In the *Hunger Games* trilogy, Coriolanus Snow is the AUTOCRATIC ruler of the Capitol and all of Panem. Though seemingly laid-back, Snow's outward manner BELIES (misrepresents) the fact that he is in reality a cruel and manipulative ruler, determined to govern Panem with an iron hand.

368. POIGNANT

- *moving and heart-rending; deeply touching*

IN THE NEWS

Marina Keegan graduated from Yale on May 25, 2012. The future filled the 22-year-old aspiring writer with enthusiasm. In an essay written for the *Yale Daily News*, Marina confidently reminded her classmates, "What we have to remember is that we can still do anything. We can change our minds. We can start over… The notion that it's too late to do anything is comical. It's hilarious. We're graduating college. We're so young." Just a few days later Marina died in a car crash when her boyfriend lost control of his car. Marina's sudden and POIGNANT death stunned her family, friends, and classmates. Her devastated parents take SOLACE (comfort) from the knowledge that Marina's final, POIGNANT words are inspiring young people to live their lives to the fullest and to aspire always to make a difference.

369. TACTLESS

- *displaying a lack of consideration; thoughtless and INDISCREET*

MEET MY STUDENTS: RITIKA

Ritika and her family have a beloved pet dog named Leo. One day her sister shocked and upset her entire family by asking, "What will we do when Leo drops dead?" Although her sister's question raised an important point, it was very TACTLESS. Ritika scolded her sister and pointed out that it would have been far more TACTFUL (diplomatic) to ask, "What will we do when Leo is no longer with us?"

370. DEPRECATE

- *to show strong disapproval*

INSIDER INFO

The prefix *de-*, meaning "down," signals that *DEPRECATE* is a negative word that is used to express disapproval. For example, many Americans express their low approval of Congress by DEPRECATING politicians who seem unable to resolve pressing national issues. When people DEPRECATE themselves it is called SELF-DEPRECATION. For example, on the TV show *The X-Factor*, one very obese contestant SELF-DEPRECATINGLY asked the audience to "give a fat boy a chance." His inspirational performance thrilled the cheering audience.

CHAPTER 35
THE TOP 100 LEVEL 4 WORDS
PART 8

Chapter 35 is the eighth of our ten-part series of chapters devoted to defining and illustrating the top 100 Level 4 words. Always remember that the hard questions are easy if you know the words!

371. ANTHROPOMORPHIC
- *characterized by attributing human characteristics to animals or inanimate things*

POP CULTURE
What do Mickey Mouse, Donald Duck, and Goofy have in common? All three are world-famous ANTHROPOMORPHIC Disney characters. Mickey Mouse is a fun-loving, brave, and caring character who is the official host at Disney theme parks around the world. In contrast, Donald Duck is Micky's IRASCIBLE (easily angered), impatient, and often jealous rival. And finally, Goofy is an ANTHROPOMORPHIC dog who is lovable, loyal, and silly.

372. DISTRAUGHT
- *very upset; deeply agitated with emotional conflict or pain*

POP CULTURE
In the movie *The Life of Pi*, Pi is a sixteen-year-old boy who is stranded in the Pacific Ocean on a lifeboat with a 450-pound Royal Bengal tiger named Richard Parker. Pi and Richard Parker WARILY (cautiously) coexist as they overcome the threats posed by dehydration, predatory marine life, treacherous sea currents, and exposure to the elements. After 227 agonizing days at sea, the lifeboat finally washes ashore along the coast of Mexico. Richard Parker promptly and unceremoniously runs into the nearby jungle, disappearing forever. Richard Parker's failure even to look back once leaves Pi feeling DISTRAUGHT. Shaken by this "bungled goodbye," the DISTRAUGHT Pi weeps uncontrollably, saying that the pain "is like an axe that chops at my heart."

373. ALOOF

- *RESERVED and detached; distant*

INSIDER INFO

ALOOF is a high-frequency vocabulary word that is used in both sentence completion and passage questions. In double-blank sentence completions, ALOOF people are often contrasted with people who are outgoing and AFFABLE (friendly). *ALOOF* is typically used in passage questions to describe a character who is detached and RESERVED. For example, in one recent passage a landlady was ALOOF because she "always kept in the background."

374. EMULATE

- *characterized by imitation; striving to equal or match*

MEET MY STUDENTS: ROSHNI

Many of my students have younger brothers and sisters. One of my students wrote this example to illustrate how her younger brother EMULATED everything she did: "He ordered the same ice cream flavors as me, listened to the same music as me and played the same video games as me. He followed me around everywhere and even wanted to go to the mall with me. EXASPERATED (annoyed) by this constant EMULATION, I complained to my dad. He patiently explained that my little brother was just looking up to me. His pattern of EMULATING my behavior was really a form of flattery."

375. COMPLICITY

- *association or involvement in a wrongful act*

POP CULTURE

In the *Harry Potter* saga, Peter Pettigrew betrayed James and Lily Potter's secret hiding place to Lord Voldemort. The Dark Lord then killed the couple but was THWARTED (blocked) in his attempt to kill Harry. Although he was COMPLICIT in this crime, Pettigrew successfully framed Sirius Black for the treacherous murders as well as the slaying of twelve innocent Muggles. The Ministry of Magic eventually EXONERATED (freed from blame) Black.

376. DISCREDIT

- *to cast doubt on the reputation of a person or the*
  efficacy of an idea; to be held in low esteem

IN THE NEWS

Tiger Woods was once known as a devoted husband and the world's greatest golfer. His smiling image graced billboard and televison advertisements across the world. Woods was DISCREDITED, however, following revelations that he repeatedly cheated on his wife. It is important to remember that ideas can also be DISCREDITED. For example, communism is now widely DISCREDITED as a failed economic philosophy.

377. OVERBEARING

- *having or showing an arrogant superiority to and DISDAIN for those one views as inferior or unworthy*

POP CULTURE

In the movie *Avatar*, Colonel Miles Quaritch is the OVERBEARING Chief of Security of Hell's Gate on Pandora. Quaritch has little respect for the Na'vi and other INDIGENOUS (native) life forms on Pandora. His OVERBEARING approach to diplomacy is clearly revealed when he informs new recruits that his strategy is, "Peace and prosperity to us all, through superior firepower."

378. REBUKE

- *to criticize sharply; to REPRIMAND*

AP EUROPEAN HISTORY

The Italian scientist Galileo Galilei is now REVERED (honored) for his key role in the rise of the Scientific Revolution. When he was alive, however, DOGMATIC (close-minded) church officials severely REBUKED Galileo for championing a heliocentric model of the solar system, in which the Earth orbits the sun. In a famous trial, Church authorities forced Galileo to RENOUNCE (take back) his views and spend the final years of his life under house arrest. The REBUKE of Galileo delayed, but did not reverse, the march of scientific progress.

379. VIRTUOSITY

- *great technical skill*

MEET MY STUDENTS: EMILY

Emily loves to draw. In fact, she began drawing her first pictures when she was just two or three years old. Emily admires the VIRTUOSITY of Old Masters who could depict delicate flowers, life-like animals, and even realistic tear drops rolling down a person's cheek. Even so, Emily admits that she finds the Old Masters a bit boring. So who is Emily's favorite artist? See Word 380 to find out!

380. VISCERAL

- *describes an instinctive and emotional approach to life and problem solving*

MEET MY STUDENTS: EMILY

Although Emily admires the VIRTUOSITY (great technical skill) of the Old Masters (Word 379), she is fascinated with the life and works of Vincent van Gogh. Unlike the CEREBRAL (intellectual) approach of the Old Masters, van Gogh's paintings emphasize a VISCERAL approach to his world. For example, Emily loves *The Starry Night* because van Gogh's stars seem to explode with life and energy.

CHAPTER 36
THE TOP 100 LEVEL 4 WORDS
PART 9

Chapter 36 is the ninth of our ten-part series of chapters devoted to defining and illustrating the top 100 Level 4 words. Always remember that the hard questions are easy if you know the words!

381. HAVOC
- *widespread disorder or destruction; mayhem*

POP CULTURE
In the movie *The Dark Knight Rises*, Bane more than lives up to his malevolent name by wreaking HAVOC on Gotham. After temporarily defeating Batman, Bane destroys Gotham's transportation links with the outside world. He then forcibly disbands the city's legal government, thus enabling his gang of mercenaries to loot the defenseless city. This HAVOC continues until Batman finally returns to Gotham to recapture the city and end Bane's reign of terror.

382. IMPERIL
- *to pose a threat to; to endanger*

AP BIOLOGY
More than half of the world's 633 types of primates are IMPERILED by RAMPANT (unrestrained) habitat destruction and illegal poaching. For example, 25 species of monkeys, lemurs, and gorillas are all on the brink of extinction and need global action to protect them.

383. CONFLATE

- *to combine; bring together; to MELD or blend together*

POP CULTURE

The assassination of President Kennedy remains one of the greatest unsolved mysteries in American history. The Oliver Stone movie *JFK* promotes the controversial theory that Lee Harvey Oswald did not act alone. The movie CONFLATES documentary footage and dramatizes re-enactments so skillfully that viewers sometimes do not know which scenes are real and which are not.

384. PAUCITY

- *a shortage or scarcity; a DEARTH of something*

MEET MY STUDENTS: DHARA

Dhara loves shoes. Her wardrobe currently includes fifteen pairs of shoes. Dhara complains that this is not enough, however, and that her wardrobe suffers from a PAUCITY of footwear. For example, she needs a pair of pumps, ballet shoes, combat boots, Sperries, Nike sneakers, and of course high heel platforms. While her friends all agree with Dhara, her parents think she has a PLETHORA (an abundance) of shoes.

385. SUPERFLUOUS

- *unnecessary and unneeded; nonessential*

INSIDER INFO

SUPERFLUOUS has recently become a frequent answer to challenging sentence completion and passage questions. It is important to remember that *SUPERFLUOUS* means "unnecessary and therefore nonessential." For example, a recent critical reading passage discussed how 8th-century B.C.E. Greek bards actually resisted the introduction of a written alphabet. It turns out that pre-alphabetic bards memorized and then chanted stories and legends. They therefore opposed the new alphabet because they had "little overt need for the new technology of reading and writing." The phrase "little overt need" tells us that ancient Greek bards thought that the alphabet was unnecessary and therefore SUPERFLUOUS.

386. UNTENABLE

- *incapable of being defended or justified; indefensible*

AP U.S. HISTORY

The Seneca Falls Convention in 1848 marked the beginning of a long and at times frustrating battle for women's suffrage. Opponents THWARTED (blocked) the women's suffrage movement by claiming that women were a "weaker sex" who should avoid public affairs and confine themselves to their domestic roles as wives and mothers. These arguments, however, finally proved to be UNTENABLE as a new generation of suffragists successfully argued that women's suffrage was consistent with America's commitment to equality. In 1920 the states ratified the Nineteenth Amendment, granting women the right to vote.

387. PRONE

- *having a tendency to do something*

MEET MY STUDENTS: KAVIN

Kavin is one of my go-to students when we need help solving a difficult Level 5 math problem. He is also a candidate master in chess who is currently ranked as one of America's top twenty players in his age group. Kavin is both a knowledgeable student of the game and a perceptive observer of his opponents. He reports that many players are PRONE to making rapid moves without carefully evaluating the consequences of their new positions. Kavin then ADROITLY (skillfully) exploits his opponent's vulnerable position.

388. RANCOR

- *having a feeling of deep or bitter anger and ill-will*

POP CULTURE

In the *Hunger Games* trilogy, the DESPOTIC (tyrannical) President Snow uses a combination of armed Peacekeepers, DRACONIAN (very severe) rules, and of course the Hunger Games to control Panem's oppressed citizens. Snow's harsh rule creates great RANCOR among the DESTITUTE (very poor) and powerless citizens of the twelve districts. Katniss ultimately turns this RANCOR into an outright rebellion against President Snow.

389. COVET

- *to desire and prize*

MEET MY STUDENTS: ALIN

Alin knew that she faced very low odds of winning one of Z-100's COVETED tickets to meet Justin Bieber. She would have to be the 100th person to call the popular New York City radio station immediately after they played a set of nine songs. Still, Alin felt that she had to try. So she placed her call and anxiously waited for an answer. To her shock and amazement the Z-100 DJ announced that Alin had won not one but two of the COVETED tickets. Needless to say, Alin was so EUPHORIC (very happy) that she jumped up and down screaming at the top of her lungs. She had an amazing time, and Justin Bieber is still her favorite recording artist.

390. **RESTITUTION**

• *the act of compensating a person or group for a loss, damage, or injury*

AP U.S. HISTORY

In the days and weeks following the attack on Pearl Harbor, frightened Americans displaced their rage against Japan onto the 110,000 people of Japanese birth and descent living on the West Coast. Although no specific charges were ever filed against these Japanese Americans, they were interned or confined in detention camps located on desolate lands owned by the federal government. In 1987, Congress approved a formal national apology and a tax-free RESTITUTION payment of $20,000 to more than 66,000 surviving Japanese Americans who were held in detention centers.

THE TOP 100 LEVEL 4 WORDS
PART 10

Chapter 37 is the tenth of our ten-part series of chapters devoted to defining and illustrating the top 100 Level 4 words. Always remember that the hard questions are easy if you know the words!

391. STRINGENT

- *very strict; demanding close attention to details and procedures*

AP U.S. HISTORY

The Compromise of 1850 seemed to defuse the crisis between the North and the South. However, the hoped-for sectional peace proved to be FLEETING. The Compromise included the STRINGENT new Fugitive Slave Act, which imposed heavy fines and even jail sentences for those who helped runaway slaves escape. These STRINGENT regulations intensified antislavery sentiment because they required Northerners to enforce slavery.

392. BANE

- *anything that is a source of harm and ruin*

POP CULTURE

In *The Dark Knight Rises*, Bane is a villain who more than lives up to his name by being a BANE to Bruce Wayne and Gotham City. Bane's ruinous actions include bankrupting Wayne Industries, destroying Gotham's bridges, and threatening to devastate the isolated city with a nuclear bomb.

393. BOON

- *a timely benefit; a blessing*

POP CULTURE

At the beginning of *The Dark Knight Rises*, Bruce Wayne is a BROODING (preoccupied with depressing memories) man who has given up his role as Batman and now has nothing to live for. Bane then adds to Wayne's woes by viciously breaking his back and then locking him inside a foreign prison from which escape is virtually impossible. Ironically, these disasters actually prove to be a BOON. Bruce Wayne recovers from his injury, escapes from prison, and THWARTS (stops) Bane's plan to destroy Gotham. The BOON that is Bane even forces Bruce Wayne to move on from his career as Batman and begin a new life with Selina Kyle (Catwoman).

394. OPAQUE

- *not transparent or clear, and thus dense and difficult to understand; impenetrably dense*

INSIDER INFO

OPAQUE is typically used to describe objects such as curtains that are not transparent and do not allow light to pass through them. However, *OPAQUE* can also be used to describe writing that is unclear and therefore difficult to understand. College Board test writers typically contrast *OPAQUE* with the antonym *LUCID*, meaning "clear." For example, newspaper editors would reject or rewrite a manuscript with OPAQUE writing, while they would accept a manuscript with LUCID writing.

395. LEVITY

- *lightness in manner or speech, especially an attempt to inject humor into an otherwise serious situation*

MEET MY STUDENTS: NICOLE, ROSHNI, & MEGHA

SAT classes typically require serious work. Fortunately, I have a number of students who can be counted on to add a touch of LEVITY to our classes. For example, Nicole delights in telling us PERTINENT (relevant) gossip about Kristen Stewart's ongoing relationship with Robert Pattinson. Roshni added some LEVITY to our vocabulary lesson when she pointed out that one way to remember AVARICE (greed) is to associate it with being greedy for rice. And not to be outdone, Megha pointed out that CAVALIER (arrogant) people are arrogant and HAUGHTY because they can afford to eat caviar.

396. REMUNERATION

- *the payment received for performing a job; compensation*

POP CULTURE

The REMUNERATION workers receive varies greatly from job to job. For example, the federal minimum wage in 2012 was $7.50 per hour. In contrast, Judge Judy earned an astounding $45 million a year for her small-claims court television show. Wow—now that is what I call REMUNERATION!

397. EGREGIOUS

- *conspicuously and outrageously bad*

DID YOU KNOW?

The prefix *e-* means "out," and the root *greg* means "group." So *EGREGIOUS* literally means "out of the group." Originally *EGREGIOUS* meant "standing out from the group" in the sense of being really good. Today, however, *EGREGIOUS* means "standing out from the group" in the sense of being really bad. For example, military history is filled with EGREGIOUS errors in judgment that cost thousands of lives and changed the fate of nations. Napoleon made an EGREGIOUS error in invading Russia, and Japan made an EGREGIOUS error in attacking Pearl Harbor.

398. LAUD

- *to praise, commend, EXTOL, ACCLAIM, and HAIL*

MEET MY STUDENTS: PALLAVI

The members of my East Brunswick SAT class helped Pallavi celebrate her Sweet Sixteen birthday party. The girls all enthusiastically LAUDED Pallavi for a fantastic evening. The party began with a chartered bus ride that took over twenty of Pallavi's friends to a special restaurant near Times Square in New York City. The girls enjoyed a SUMPTUOUS (splendid) buffet dinner at The View, a revolving roof-top restaurant. Everyone LAUDED the tasty desserts, EXTOLLED the spectacular PANORAMIC (sweeping) view of New York City, and of course ACCLAIMED Pallavi's amazing dress.

399. DRAB

- *gloomy and depressing; dreary and cheerless*

POP CULTURE

In the movie *The Hunger Games*, District 12 is portrayed as Panem's most IMPOVERISHED (very poor) district. The people work in dangerous coal mines and live in DRAB homes that are covered by a layer of coal dust. Katniss describes her DRAB district as a place "where you can starve to death in safety."

400. DETER

- *to discourage or prevent someone from taking an action*

AP U.S. HISTORY

During the peak of the Cold War, the United States and the Soviet Union had enough nuclear weapons to destroy each other and most life on Earth. This "balance of terror" DETERRED leaders of the two superpowers from starting a catastrophic world war. Although the Cold War is over, the United States still maintains a powerful military to DETER hostile countries such as Iran and North Korea.

CHAPTER 38
THE TOP FIFTY
LEVEL 3 WORDS
PART 1

The SAT rates each question on a five-point scale of difficulty. Level 3 questions are the third most challenging questions on the test. At least fifty percent of all test-takers miss a Level 3 question. What makes these questions so difficult? In most cases, the questions call for a knowledge of vocabulary words that seem familiar. There is a difference, however, between having heard a word and knowing its precise definition. This chapter is the first in a series of five chapters that will define and illustrate fifty commonly used Level 3 vocabulary words. It is important to remember that the Level 3 questions are actually very easy if you know the words!

401. ADULATION
• *great public admiration and over-the-top praise*
IN THE NEWS
Lance Armstrong enjoyed widespread public ADULATION for much of his career. As a road-racing cyclist he won the prestigious Tour de France a record-shattering seven consecutive times between 1999 and 2005. In addition, he overcame cancer and founded the Lance Armstrong Foundation for cancer support. Public ADULATION translated into LUCRATIVE (very profitable) endorsements from a number of companies. To find out what happened, see Word 402 below.

402. DISILLUSION

- *to disenchant and free from false beliefs or illusions*

IN THE NEWS

Armstrong's world collapsed in June 2012, when the U.S. Anti-Doping Agency (USADA) issued a detailed report charging him with having used illicit performance-enhancing drugs. The USADA banned Armstrong from all athletic competitions, branding him a "serial cheat who led the most sophisticated, professionalized, and successful doping program the sport of cycling has ever seen." The overwhelming evidence in the USADA report stunned and DISILLUSIONED Armstrong's fans and advertisers. The once-admired athlete is now REVILED (despised) as a cheat and a liar.

403. ELUSIVE

- *hard to pin down; skillful at ELUDING capture; EVASIVE*

POP CULTURE

In the *Harry Potter* saga, the Golden Snitch is a very ELUSIVE object that can sprout wings and ELUDE (evade) even the most skillful Quidditch players. Each team has a designated Seeker, whose sole task is to capture the ELUSIVE snitch.

404. FUTILE

- *ineffectual; producing no result; vain*

DID YOU KNOW?

FUTILE actually comes from the Latin word *futilis*, meaning "leaky." So pouring water into a leaky bucket would of course be FUTILE. Don't expect College Board test writers to ask you the derivation of *FUTILE*. Instead, remember that a FUTILE project is doomed to failure.

405. CHAOTIC

- *disorganized and confused; lacking visible order or organization*

AP U.S. HISTORY

As the New York Stock Exchange opened on Thursday, October 29, 1929, the brokers hoped for a profitable day of rising prices. Instead they faced a CHAOTIC day of record selling and losses. By 1 PM the stock ticker had fallen 92 minutes behind the transactions on the floor. Frightened brokers could not get a true picture of what was happening. The CHAOTIC shouting of 1,000 brokers and their assistants created what one observer called a "weird roar." Now known as Black Thursday, the CHAOTIC market crash marked the beginning of the Great Depression.

406. OBSOLETE

- *no longer produced or used; ANTIQUATED; out-of-date; ARCHAIC*

IN YOUR LIFE

The electronic revolution is having a dramatic effect on how today's high school students learn and prepare for class. Once upon a time, high school students used slide rules to solve difficult math problems and multi-volume encyclopedias to find obscure information. Both slide rules and encyclopedias are now OBSOLETE. High school students now use sophisticated calculators to solve math problems and Wikipedia to look up information.

407. DISPARITY

- *the condition of being unequal; a noticeable difference in age, income, or treatment*

INSIDER INFO

Look closely at the word *DISPARITY*. The Latin root *par* means "equal." That's why when golfers are par for a course they are literally equal to the course. So *PARITY* means "equality." In contrast, the word *DISPARITY* signals an inequality. The DISPARITY can be in age, rank, income, or treatment. For example, legal experts criticize regional DISPARITIES in the sentencing of people convicted of comparable crimes.

408. ANTECEDENT

- *an event or occurrence that precedes something similar in time; a forerunner*

DID YOU KNOW?

Pizza is one of the most popular foods in the United States. Approximately three billion pizzas are sold in the United States each year, or about 46 slices per person. Yet few Americans realize that the ANTECEDENTS for pizza can be traced back to flatbreads prepared by ancient Roman bakers.

409. SOMBER

- *characterized by being dark, gloomy, and depressed*

AP U.S. HISTORY

On November 21, 1963, most Americans optimistically looked forward to a future of peace and prosperity led by their popular young president, John F. Kennedy. But history can be unpredictable. No one foresaw the terrible tragedy that occurred the next day in Dallas, Texas. As the news of President Kennedy's assassination flashed across the country, stunned Americans watched a SOMBER Vice President Lyndon B. Johnson take the oath of office inside the presidential plane as a grief-stricken Jacqueline Kennedy stood by his side.

410. AUGMENT

• *to make something greater; to increase*

IN YOUR LIFE

It is THEORETICALLY possible to AUGMENT almost anything. For example, surgeons can AUGMENT the size of a woman's breasts, and workers can take a second job to AUGMENT the size of their incomes. I often tell SAT students that one of my primary goals is to help them AUGMENT their LEXICON (dictionary) of SAT vocabulary words. Needless to say, this book is designed to help AUGMENT your SAT vocabulary so that you can achieve a higher critical reading score.

CHAPTER 39
THE TOP FIFTY LEVEL 3 WORDS
PART 2

Chapter 39 is the second of our five-part series of chapters devoted to defining and illustrating the top fifty Level 3 words. Always remember that the hard questions are easy if you know the words!

411. STODGY

- *dull, uninspiring, and unimaginative*

IN MY LIFE

STODGY teachers dampen the enthusiasm of inquisitive students. For example, one of my high school teachers dictated notes to us almost every day. Our test questions required us to regurgitate our notes on a given topic.

412. ABSTEMIOUS

- *characterized by moderation in eating and drinking*

AP WORLD HISTORY

Before gaining enlightenment, Buddha ate only a single grain of rice each day. His stomach became so empty that when he poked a finger into it he could touch his backbone. Buddha later RENOUNCED extreme deprivation. Instead, he urged his companions to follow an ABSTEMIOUS lifestyle based upon moderation in eating and drinking.

413. DIGRESS

- *to stray from a topic in writing, speaking, or thinking; to go off on a TANGENT.*

IN YOUR LIFE

Have you ever heard a speaker DIGRESS or wander off his or her topic? Most audiences have little patience for a speaker who wastes time by DIGRESSING. The same principle applies to your SAT essay. College Board essay readers have little patience for student writers who DIGRESS from the assigned essay topic. So stay focused and don't go off on a TANGENT.

414. MISNOMER

- *an incorrect or inappropriate name*

DID YOU KNOW?

Dry cleaning, Chinese checkers, and *funny bone* are all MISNOMERS. Dry cleaning actually uses chemicals, Chinese checkers originated in Germany, and the funny bone is actually a nerve.

415. LUCRATIVE

- *refers to an enterprise or investment that is profitable*

AP EUROPEAN HISTORY

The LUCRATIVE spice trade provided a compelling economic motive for the Portuguese and Spanish goal of reaching India. For example, da Gama and other Portuguese captains purchased 100 pounds of pepper in Calicut for just 3 Venetian ducats. They could then sell the pepper in for 80 ducats in Venice for a 2,700 percent profit! Cinnamon, cloves, and nutmeg all commanded a similar LUCRATIVE markup.

416. SOLICITOUS

- *characterized by being overly attractive and caring; excessively concerned; INDULGENT*

POP CULTURE

It is all too easy for a boyfriend or girlfriend to be overly SOLICITOUS towards the person they care about. It is even possible to spoil a person by being too SOLICITOUS. For example, in his song *Grenade*, Bruno Mars admits that he would do anything for his girl. However, she is a taker who never gives back.

417. INTREPID

- *fearless and daring; bold; DAUNTLESS*

IN THE NEWS

Felix Baumgartner is an INTREPID and world-famous skydiver who is known as the "King of the Daredevils." Fearless Felix more than lived up to his reputation for undertaking extremely dangerous stunts when he jumped from a helium balloon floating at the edge of space, 24 miles above the Earth. As millions watched a streaming video on YouTube, the INTREPID Felix hurtled through the atmosphere at an estimated speed of up to 834 miles per hour. He thus became the first person to break the sound barrier without vehicular power.

418. AFFABLE

- *friendly and pleasant; gracious; GENIAL*

IN MY LIFE

Everyone in my high school liked Ann. She was captain of our cheerleading squad and our school's homecoming queen. Although Ann was very popular, she wasn't conceited or arrogant. Ann always greeted everyone with an AFFABLE smile and never complained. Sadly, cancer recently took Ann's life. At her funeral, her husband Harry noted that Ann never said a bad word about anyone. He challenged the mourners to remember Ann's AFFABLE hello and to try to go through each day without saying or thinking a negative thought.

419. FUNDAMENTAL

- *a belief, skill, or component that is essential and basic*

DID YOU KNOW?

FUNDAMENTAL has its roots in the Latin word *fundamentum*, meaning "foundation." So a FUNDAMENTAL idea is the foundation upon which a theory or plan is built. For example, the belief that government should be based upon the consent of the people is a FUNDAMENTAL cornerstone of democracy.

420. SCENARIO

- *a sequence of possible events that may occur*

IN YOUR LIFE

Worst-case SCENARIOS are often used in strategic planning to help people prepare for unexpected emergencies. For example, what would you do if your college roommate played loud music, never studied, and partied all night? Since this SCENARIO often happens to college freshmen, it would be wise to develop a mental set of "just in case" contingency plans.

THE TOP FIFTY LEVEL 3 WORDS
PART 3

Chapter 40 is the third of our five-part series of chapters devoted to defining and illustrating the top fifty Level 3 words. Always remember that the hard questions are easy if you know the words

421. EMPATHY

- *great understanding of another person's feelings; great sympathy*

IN MY LIFE

Writing an SAT essay is not easy. I totally EMPATHIZE with students who feel a sense of nervous anticipation when the proctor finally says, "Open your test booklet to Section 1 and begin your essay." Like most of my students, I feel a sense of relief when I can think of two or three really good examples to illustrate my thesis.

422. PLAUSIBLE

- *believable; having a reasonable chance of something happening*

IN YOUR LIFE

Do you think the election of a female President of the United States in your lifetime is PLAUSIBLE? According to the Gallup Poll, that SCENARIO is not only PLAUSIBLE but likely. In 1955 just 52 percent of adults in the United States said that they would vote for a qualified woman for president. Today 92 percent of American adults say that they would vote for a qualified female presidential candidate.

423. HEYDAY

- *the peak of popularity and success of a movement, organization or person*

AP U.S. HISTORY

The late 1960s witnessed the HEYDAY of the hippie-led counterculture. Hippies believed that love was all America needed to end the Vietnam War and usher in a new era of peace and racial harmony. The Woodstock Festival in August 1969 marked the HEYDAY of the counterculture. Over 500,000 hippies watched 32 acts perform in a legendary outdoor concert promoted as "Three Days of Peace and Music."

424. INGENIOUS

- *a clever mix of creativity and inventiveness*

IN THE NEWS

In the fairy tale "Snow White and the Seven Dwarfs," the Wicked Queen uses a magic mirror to reveal who is "the fairest one of all." Now, thanks to the wizards at the New York Times Co. Research and Development Lab you too can own a "magic mirror." The Times' magic mirror is an INGENIOUS mix of sophisticated technology and basic human vanity. In addition to reflecting your image, the magic mirror can display a daily calendar, weather information, and news headlines. I wonder if it can also display an SAT vocabulary word-of-the-day. Now that would truly be INGENIOUS!

425. CONSPICUOUS

- *attracting attention by being unusual or very noticeable*

DID YOU KNOW?

Visitors who travel across the tropical savannas of Africa and Australia are surprised to see 25-foot-high sculpted hard earth mounds towering above the landscape. The mounds frequently resemble the towers of a castle and are often the region's most CONSPICUOUS natural feature. Believe it or not, the architects of these mounds are termites that are just 0.4 inches long. Relative to their small size, the termites construct the largest and by far the most CONSPICUOUS nests of any animal.

426. HIERARCHY

- *any system of persons, animals, or things that are ranked one above another*

DID YOU KNOW?

The mounds described in Word 425 house colonies that include millions of termites divided into a highly specialized HIERARCHY. Termite soldiers are armed with huge jaws and can emit a sticky toxic substance. The workers build the nest, produce food, cultivate fungi, and take care of the queen, eggs, and larvae. The queen is thirty times bigger than a worker. She lays eggs continuously, at a rate of about thirty per minute. The king is much smaller and mates with the queen for life.

427. EXASPERATE

- *to irritate; annoy; frustrate; VEX*

IN MY LIFE

No Jordan-Matthews High School student EXASPERATED my wife Susan more than Twig Wood. Twig employed an arsenal of excuses to explain his frequent absences from her class. Allegedly written by his mother, Twig's excuses ranged from "Twig, he have the toothache," to the classic "Twig, he have a little job to do." The notes were always signed, "Twig's mother, Lucille Wood." Although she was EXASPERATED at the time, Susan now fondly remembers Twig and his long list of grammatically incorrect but humorous excuses.

428. RESOLUTE

- *very determined and persistent; strong-minded*

MEET MY STUDENTS: MARC

Marc is an outstanding wrestler who refuses to quit. During one match he suffered a severe arm injury. Although he was forced to forfeit the match, Marc refused to become DISPIRITED (discouraged). Instead, he was RESOLUTE and vowed to return INVIGORATED (energized) and ready to go. Marc kept his promise and helped lead his team to a successful season.

429. MUNDANE

- *ordinary and commonplace*

IN THE NEWS

Amanda Knox was an American college student studying abroad who attracted world-wide attention when an Italian jury convicted her of murdering her roommate. But a second Italian jury overturned the verdict, allowing Amanda to return to her home in Seattle, Washington. After spending four years in a small concrete cell, Amanda yearned to enjoy the MUNDANE pleasures we take for granted. One of her first wishes, for example, was to sit on the green grass in her backyard.

430. SLOVENLY

- *characterized by being untidy in dress or appearance; messy and sloppy*

INSIDER INFO

Avoid confusing *SLOVENLY* with *CASUAL*. A SLOVENLY appearance would include wearing an unlaundered shirt and neglecting to shave for three days. For example, the cartoon character Homer Simpson is a SLOVENLY average guy who typically sits around in his underwear. In contrast, CASUAL would describe clothes you wear to an informal occasion like a backyard barbecue.

CHAPTER 41
THE TOP FIFTY LEVEL 3 WORDS
PART 4

Chapter 41 is the fourth of our five-part series of chapters devoted to defining and illustrating the top fifty Level 3 words. Always remember that the hard questions are easy if you know the words

431. DISPEL

- *to drive away or scatter; to remove*

IN YOUR LIFE

Many students believe that their college essay should focus on a lofty, "big" idea that will impress admissions officers. The College Board's authoritative guide book DISPELS this widespread but ERRONEOUS (wrong) idea. The College Board reminds students, "the greatest strength you bring to this essay is seventeen years or so of familiarity with the topic: YOU." Always remember that the key word in the Common Application essay prompt is "you"!

432. ADHERE

- *to follow closely; to stick with a policy or plan of action*

INSIDER INFO

The SAT word *ADHERE* is derived from a 15th-century French verb meaning "to stick." The same French verb also gives us the adjective *ADHESIVE* and the noun *ADHERENT*. All these words convey the quality of sticking with a plan or person. For example, if you ADHERE to a special diet, exercise program, or study plan, you stick with it. It is important to note that writers and artists can also ADHERE to a specific style. For example, the Harlem Renaissance author Zora Neale Hurston is known for her ADHERENCE to the use of authentic regional dialects to represent how her characters actually spoke.

433. TRIVIALIZE

- *to make TRIVIAL and thus insignificant; to minimize*

MEET MY STUDENTS: OLIVIA

Olivia loves to shop for clothes at Abercrombie & Fitch. However, when she recently returned a pair of jeans that had unexpectedly shrunk, the clerk questioned Olivia and seemed to minimize her complaint. Olivia stood her ground and displayed her formidable SAT vocabulary by telling the clerk, "You're TRIVIALIZING my complaint!" Although the clerk finally accepted the jeans, the incident left Olivia EXASPERATED (irritated) and angry. Vowing to take her business to Express, Olivia stormed out of the store.

434. NEGLIGENT

- *characterized by neglect and a careless lack of concern*

IN MY LIFE

Our first year of teaching at Jordan-Matthews High School presented my wife and me with a difficult problem. As graduation approached, the seniors at JM began to display the usual signs of senioritis by studying less and less. No senior was more NEGLIGENT in his work than Junior Hicks. He neglected to study for tests and failed to turn in required homework assignments. Junior's NEGLIGENT study habits brought him to the brink of failing both his required U.S. History and Senior English classes. If this happened, Junior would not graduate. See Word 435 to find out what happened!

435. ADEPT

- *demonstrating great skill in accomplishing a*
  task or in achieving a goal; ADROIT

IN MY LIFE

Junior panicked when my wife and I confronted him with his failing grades (see Word 434). After a long talk, he agreed to take make-up tests and turn in extra credit projects. Although Junior was not a good student, he was very ADEPT at charming his teachers. As a student in the Home Economics class, Junior had access to the school kitchen. Each day after school he delivered his extra credit projects and presented my wife and me with a special treat from the school kitchen. On one memorable occasion he presented my wife with a delicious vanilla ice cream sundae topped with whipped cream and a bright red cherry. Junior's ADEPT charm offensive worked. He pulled up his grades, barely passed his classes, and graduated with his classmates.

436. EMBELLISH

- *to enhance; to make more attractive with ornamentation*

INSIDER INFO
Note that the word *bell* is right in the middle of the word *EMBELLISH*. Bells are often used to decorate or EMBELLISH Christmas trees and other objects. So when you see the *bell* in *EMBELLISH*, think of ornaments used to enhance an object or even a story.

437. INSTILL

- *to gradually impart new values, attitudes, or skills*

IN YOUR LIFE
Religious leaders, parents, teachers, and coaches all attempt to INSTILL positive values and attitudes. For example, when coaches tell their players "No pain, no gain," they are attempting to INSTILL the importance of hard work and dedication.

438. EXACERBATE

- *to make worse; to aggravate a situation*

INSIDER INFO
EXACERBATE has appeared as a sentence completion answer on several recent tests. *EXACERBATE* is a negative word that always means "to make things worse." For example, the Boston Tea Party EXACERBATED tensions between the American colonists and the British.

439. IMPASSIONED

- *filled with passion and zeal; FERVENT*

AP U.S. HISTORY
On December 5, 1955, almost 7,000 African Americans crowded into the Holt Street Baptist Church to protest racial segregation on Montgomery city buses. They also came to listen to a speech by a young and untested minister named Dr. Martin Luther King, Jr. Dr. King urged the black community to continue its support for the bus boycott by saying, "There comes a time when people get tired of being trampled by the iron feet of oppression… We are determined here in Montgomery to work and fight until justice rushes down like water, and righteousness like a mighty stream." Dr. King's IMPASSIONED plea for justice GALVANIZED (electrified) the black community and marked his emergence as a national civil rights leader.

440. EUPHORIC

• *a feeling of great joy and overwhelming ELATION*

IN THE NEWS

Jack Andraka had a good reason to be proud and EUPHORIC. The Maryland teenager had just won the top award of $75,000 at the Intel Science and Engineering Fair for discovering an inexpensive and fast way to detect early-stage pancreatic cancer. When the Intel speaker announced his name, Jack reacted with unbridled joy as he ran to the stage to accept his award. Jack's EUPHORIC reaction quickly became a YouTube hit. You can see the video by searching for "Jack Andraka winning award." I promise that the video will leave you with an INDELIBLE (can't be erased) image of the meaning of EUPHORIC!

CHAPTER 42
THE TOP FIFTY LEVEL 3 WORDS
PART 5

Chapter 42 is the fifth of our five-part series of chapters devoted to defining and illustrating the top fifty Level 3 words. Always remember that the hard questions are easy if you know the words!

441. MOCK

- *to make fun of or mimic someone with contempt, ridicule, or DERISION*

INSIDER INFO

In the movie *The Life of Pi*, Piscine Molitor Patel is regularly MOCKED by classmates who call him "Pissing Patel." Piscine escapes this MOCKING by shortening his first name to Pi. SAT examples of MOCKING will probably be more SUBTLE and challenging than the humorous but blatant example in *The Life of Pi*. For example, on one recent critical reading passage, Mo is a Chinese professor who is jealous of Duncan, an idealistic young American English teacher. The passage concludes by telling us that "Mo did not make a comment to Duncan that did not include the word *kind*. 'If you would be so kind,' he said. 'Just a kindly reminder. How very kind of you,'" Mo uses the word *kind* as an exaggerated form of flattery intended to MOCK Duncan.

442. CREDIBLE

- *apparently reasonable; believable*

IN YOUR LIFE

Have you ever been late to school or to work? If so, did you make up a fake excuse to explain why you were late? If you do use a fake excuse, try to make it CREDIBLE. Saying that you were in a long line at Starbucks may be true, but your vice principal or boss may not find it CREDIBLE. The most widely used and therefore most CREDIBLE excuse is saying that you were stuck in heavy traffic.

443. DIVISIVE

- *creating disunity and dissension; POLARIZING*

AP U.S. HISTORY

The Kansas-Nebraska Act (1854) was one of the most fateful and DIVISIVE pieces of legislation in American history. The furor over the act broke the uneasy truce between the North and the South. It incited a bitter public outcry that PRECIPITATED (hastened) the DEMISE (death) of the Whig Party and emergence of the Republican Party.

444. HERALD

- *to praise or enthusiastically greet the arrival of someone or something*

INSIDER INFO

At one time, a HERALD was an official who announced important news. That is why newspapers such as the *International Herald Tribune* have *HERALD* in their names. Although *HERALD* can still refer to a person, it typically appears on the SAT as a verb meaning "to praise" or "greet enthusiastically." For example, Aung Sang Suu Kyi has been HERALDED by freedom-loving peoples around the world for her courageous advocacy of democratic reforms in Burma.

445. DEVOUR

- *to eat VORACIOUSLY; consume greedily*

POP CULTURE

In the television program *The Simpsons*, Homer has a RAVENOUS (insatiable) appetite and DEVOURS almost any food in sight. He particularly delights in DEVOURING doughnuts covered with pink icing and rainbow sprinkles. Come to think of it, I would love to DEVOUR one of Homer's favorite doughnuts!

446. SHIRK

- *to avoid or neglect one's assigned duties or responsibilities*

AP U.S. HISTORY

John F. Kennedy became President on an inauguration day filled with high excitement and drama. The new President recognized that the Soviet Union was an IMPLACABLE (relentless, unappeasable) foe that had to be contained. JFK boldly refused to SHIRK his responsibility to defend freedom "in its hour of maximum danger." Kennedy welcomed America's duty to "pay any price, bear any burden…to assure the survival and the success of liberty" at home and around the world.

447. TENACIOUS

- *stubborn and unyielding; not easily letting go or giving up; RESOLUTE*

MEET MY STUDENTS: JASON

Many of my students hope to take the SAT just once and then be "one and done." The SAT is a formidable test, however, that requires hard work and TENACITY. For example, Jason needed a 2300 to quality for a special program at an Ivy League college. The first two times he took the SAT, Jason scored a 2220 followed by a 2270. Although these were outstanding scores, Jason was TENACIOUS and refused to give up. He studied his vocabulary words, practiced writing essays, and focused on avoiding careless math mistakes. Jason's TENACITY paid off. He scored a 2320 and was accepted into the special program.

448. FEASIBLE

- *possible; capable of being achieved; VIABLE*

DID YOU KNOW?

Science fiction movies like *Back to the Future* regularly send characters backward and forward in time. But is time travel really FEASIBLE? According to Einstein, time travel is theoretically FEASIBLE if an object can travel faster than the speed of light. The problem, of course, is that nothing we know of can travel faster than light.

449. APPALL

- *to shock and outrage*

IN THE NEWS

On July 5, 2011, a Florida jury found Casey Anthony not guilty of murdering her two-year-old daughter. The verdict APPALLED many people who were convinced that the jury ignored evidence pointing to Anthony's guilt. Now REVILED (despised) as one of the most hated women in America, Anthony faces a PROBLEMATIC (unsettled) future as she lives in a secret location in Florida.

450. PERIPHERY

- *the outer boundary or fringe area of something;*
  MARGINAL and thus not part of the inner core

POP CULTURE

In the *Hunger Games* trilogy the Capitol is the political center of Panem. The city exercises absolute power over twelve surrounding districts. When the SAGA opens, Katniss Everdeen lives in District 12, an IMPOVERISHED (very poor) coal mining region located on the PERIPHERY of Panem. As the story unfolds, however, Katniss leads a rebellion that sparks a RESURGENCE (revival) of the once PERIPHERAL twelve districts.

CHAPTER 43
THE TOP THIRTY WORDS WITH MULTIPLE MEANINGS
PART 1

Many words in the English language have multiple meanings. For example, the word *BROAD* has fifteen different definitions! Most SATs contain one or two questions designed to test your knowledge of the less commonly known meanings of frequently used words. These questions are often the trickiest and most missed items on the test. Chapters 43–45 discuss thirty commonly tested words with multiple meanings. The definitions and examples all focus on how the word is typically tested on the SAT.

451. ORNATE
- *elaborately decorated; marked by a flowery writing style*

INSIDER INFO
ORNATE is usually used to describe the decoration of a building. For example, the Taj Mahal, Versailles Palace, and St. Peter's Cathedral all feature ORNATE decorations. *ORNATE* can also be used to describe a style of writing that relies upon flowery descriptions and elaborate rhetorical devices. For example, Charles Dickens was famous for his ORNATE style of writing.

452. AUSTERE
- *unadorned and plain; bare and SPARE*

INSIDER INFO
AUSTERE is usually used to describe the absence of decoration. For example, a high-security prison cell and a monk's chamber would both have AUSTERE furnishings. AUSTERE can also be used to describe a style of writing based upon the use of a few unadorned words or what the College Board test writers call "an economy of expression." For example, Ernest Hemingway was famous for his AUSTERE prose in works such as *The Old Man and the Sea*. Modern tweets also provide good examples of AUSTERE writing that use just 140 unadorned characters.

453. SPARE

- *lacking EMBELLISHMENT or ornamentation; a plain style of writing or decoration*

INSIDER INFO

What first comes to your mind when you hear the word *SPARE*? When asked this question, my students unanimously replied "extra," as in a SPARE tire. It is important to remember that the word *SPARE* can also be used to describe both a plain and unadorned style of writing and a work of art that lacks ornamentation. For example, SAT test writers often use the phrase "economy of expression" to indicate that a writer has a SPARE prose style. When describing a work of art, *SPARE* is often used as a synonym for *AUSTERE* (plain) or as an antonym for *ORNATE* (lavish).

454. ECONOMICAL

- *thrifty and frugal with money and with words; not wasteful*

INSIDER INFO

ECONOMICAL is most commonly used to describe consumers who are thrifty and do not waste money. For example, an ECONOMICAL shopper would take advantage of bargain sales. However, ECONOMICAL can also be used to describe thrifty writers who are SUCCINCT (concise) and thus do not waste words. On one test, for example, College Board test writers used Lucille Clifton as an example of a poet who employed an ECONOMICAL writing style to discuss feminist themes and her African American heritage.

455. CAPTURE

- *to attract and hold*

INSIDER INFO

SAT test writers know that *CAPTURE* usually means "to seize someone or something by force." But *CAPTURE* can also mean "to attract and hold someone's attention." Steve Jobs and Apple CAPTURED the public's imagination with a series of INNOVATIVE iPhones and iPads. A writer can also CAPTURE a reader's attention. For example, Zora Neale Hurston was a Harlem Renaissance novelist who skillfully used colloquial idioms to create authentic characters that CAPTURED her reader's imaginations.

456. CHANNEL

• *a pathway through which information is transmitted*

INSIDER INFO

The *Free Online Dictionary* lists thirteen different definitions of the word *CHANNEL*. For example, *CHANNEL* can refer to a body of water like the English CHANNEL or to a frequency band for the transmission and reception of electromagnetic signals. College Board test writers typically use *CHANNEL* to refer to a pathway through which information is transmitted. For example, billions of people around the world now use the Internet as a CHANNEL for the almost instantaneous sharing of ideas and news.

457. PEDESTRIAN

• *commonplace and unimaginative; CONVENTIONAL; BANAL*

INSIDER INFO

PEDESTRIAN is a classic example of a word with multiple meanings. In everyday language, it is a noun that describes a person traveling on foot. On the SAT, however, *PEDESTRIAN* is often used as an adjective to describe a person or performance that is ordinary and CONVENTIONAL. Test writers typically use *PEDESTRIAN* as a negative word to describe plays with uninspired acting and books with CONVENTIONAL plots.

458. LIBERAL

• *generous and plentiful*

INSIDER INFO

AP Government students will immediately define the term *LIBERAL* as "a person or politician who is left of center on the political spectrum." Don't expect the SAT to test your knowledge of controversial political terms. Instead, be prepared to know that *LIBERAL* can also mean generous and plentiful. For example, your mom will give you a LIBERAL helping of turkey on Thanksgiving, and a critic will hand out a LIBERAL dose of criticism to poets, playwrights, and architects.

459. ARREST

• *to check the expansion of something; to hold back*

INSIDER INFO

The word *ARREST* has a number of different meanings. Do not expect SAT test writers to be concerned with police ARRESTING criminals. Instead expect them to focus questions on ARRESTING the spread of a disease or ARRESTING the DELETERIOUS (harmful) effects of global warming.

460. BROAD

- *comprehensive; far-reaching*

IN YOUR LIFE

The *Free Online Dictionary* lists fifteen different definitions of *BROAD*, ranging from "wide" to "a slang word for a woman." Fortunately, SAT test writers will not expect you to know all of the different definitions of *BROAD*. Instead focus on the use of *BROAD* as a word meaning "comprehensive." For example, many college students take a BROAD range of courses.

CHAPTER 44
THE TOP THIRTY WORDS WITH MULTIPLE MEANINGS
PART 2

Most SATs contain one or two questions designed to test your knowledge of the less commonly known meaning of frequently used words. These questions are often the trickiest and most missed items on the test. Chapter 44 continues our discussion of thirty commonly tested words with multiple meanings. The definitions and examples all focus on how the word is typically tested on the SAT.

461. ODD
- *infrequent; irregular*

INSIDER INFO
What first comes to your mind when you hear the word *ODD*? Most high school math students probably think of integers that are not evenly divided by two, such as one, three, and five. Most everyday people probably think of *ODD* in the sense of being peculiar. As you have probably figured out, College Board test writers are not everyday people. They expect you to know that *ODD* also means "infrequent." For example, you might receive text messages from an old friend at ODD intervals.

462. SMART
- *elegant and stylish in manners or dress*

DID YOU KNOW?
Everyone knows that *SMART* is an easy Level 1 word meaning "intelligent." Yes, but very few SAT students also know that *SMART* means "elegant in manners or dress." For example, most high school girls would much rather wear a SMART dress to their prom than be seen in a DRAB and frumpy one.

463. LATITUDE

- *freedom from normal restraints and limitations*

INSIDER INFO

When most students hear the word *LATITUDE*, they first think of a geographic term referring to imaginary lines that are parallel to the equator. On the SAT, however, *LATITUDE* is typically used to describe freedom from normal restraints and limitations. For example, teachers can give their students wide LATITUDE in choosing topics for a term paper. In contrast, AUTOCRATIC (dictatorial) governments can severely restrict the LATITUDE given to their citizens.

464. DISCRIMINATING

- *characterized by selective judgment, especially in matters of taste*

INSIDER INFO

DISCRIMINATING is a very tricky word. Most students believe it is a negative word that describes the unfair treatment of a person or group on the basis of a prejudice. But *DISCRIMINATION* can also be a positive word that describes selective judgment, especially in matters of taste. SAT test writers typically use *DISCRIMINATING* as a synonym for *selective*. For example, sea otters are DISCRIMINATING eaters because they select only two or three types of prey from over thirty possible food sources. (Who says that you never learn new things on the SAT?)

465. COLD

- *lacking warmth or emotion; impersonal*

INSIDER INFO

What is the first thing you think of when you hear the word *COLD*? Most people probably think of either an annoying head COLD or a COLD snap in the weather. However, as you know, College Board test writers have a special PENCHANT (liking) for writing questions with uncommon uses of common words. Although it can be used to describe a viral infection or the weather, *COLD* can also be used to describe an impersonal lack of feeling. For example, Bharti Kirchner opens her novel *Darjeeling* by describing Manhattan's 52nd street as a "cold jumble of glass, concrete, chrome, and steel" that contrasted with the human warmth of the family-owned tea plantation in India where Aloka Gupta grew up. In this description, the word *COLD* means "impersonal," in the sense of showing no feeling.

466. DOCTOR

- *to falsify or alter; to tamper with*

POP CULTURE

The movie *Zero Dark Thirty* tells the story of the decade-long manhunt to find and eliminate terrorist leader Osama bin Laden. Although critics LAUDED (praised) the movie for its dramatic story, political and intelligence officials have criticized it for allegedly DOCTORING historic facts. For example, Senator John McCain complained that the film DOCTORS facts by suggesting that the use of torture played a crucial role in gathering intelligence that led to bin Laden's secret location in Pakistan.

467. ROUGH

- *approximate; not quite exact*

INSIDER INFO

ROUGH is a very versatile word with a number of commonly used meanings. For example, *ROUGH* can refer to a surface that is not smooth, a BOORISH (crude) manner of behaving, or a difficult experience. College Board test writers have recently used *ROUGH* to mean "approximate." For example, a ROUGH estimate of a statistic and a ROUGH sequence of events are not quite exact.

468. RESIGNATION

- *passive acceptance and submission*

INSIDER INFO

The word *RESIGNATION* has both an easy meaning, which most students know, and a very sophisticated meaning that most students don't know. *RESIGNATION* typically refers to the act of giving up or leaving a job. However, *RESIGNATION* can also refer to an attitude of passive acceptance. In a recent critical reading passage, the sentence "More silence, then a sigh" underscores a grandmother's sense of RESIGNATION about her inability to fully articulate her feelings. The word *sigh* conveys the grandmother's sense of RESIGNATION.

469. FURNISH

- *to provide something that is needed*

INSIDER INFO

The word *FURNISH* immediately calls to mind furniture. Thus we FURNISH a room by filling it with chairs and tables. But *FURNISH* is actually a versatile word that can be used to describe providing anything that is needed. For example, job applicants FURNISH answers to interview questions, and hosts FURNISH snacks for their guests. On a recent test, an employee was DISCONCERTED (unsettled) when his boss unexpectedly asked him to FURNISH a detailed report ahead of schedule.

470. FLAG

- *to experience a diminishing level of energy and attention; to become less intense*

INSIDER INFO

Everyone knows that a *FLAG* is a rectangular piece of cloth that contains a distinctive design used as a symbol, emblem, or signal. College Board test writers, however, often use *FLAG* as a verb to describe a person's diminishing level of energy. In one particularly tricky question, a student's attention never FLAGGED as she listened to a lengthy but fascinating lecture.

THE TOP THIRTY WORDS WITH MULTIPLE MEANINGS
PART 3

Most SATs contain one or two questions designed to test your knowledge of the less commonly known meaning of frequently used words. These questions are often the trickiest and most missed items on the test. Chapter 45 continues our discussion of thirty commonly tested words with multiple meanings. The definitions and examples all focus on how the word is typically tested on the SAT.

471. EXHAUSTIVE
• *careful and thorough; comprehensive*

IN MY LIFE
After earning a master's degree in sociology at Wake Forest University, I applied for a teaching position at Holmdel High School in New Jersey. The school was in the final stages of an EXHAUSTIVE search for a new history teacher. More than 600 people had already applied, and now it was my turn. I answered questions in a series of EXHAUSTIVE interviews that lasted all day. I even had to teach a demonstration lesson on the Civil War. Finally, at the end of a long and memorable day, the superintendent offered me a job. I was ECSTATIC, EXUBERANT, and ELATED (really happy)! My wife Susan and I left North Carolina and began a new life in New Jersey.

472. RETIRING
• *characterized by shy and modest behavior; SELF-EFFACING*

INSIDER INFO
RETIRING is a very tricky word. Everyone knows that when a person retires, he or she steps down from a job and doesn't intend to work anymore. But *RETIRING* can also be used to describe a person who is shy and modest. College Board test writers typically use *RETIRING* in sentence completion questions as a contrasting antonym with words such as *EXTROVERTED* (outgoing) and *controversial*.

473. TEMPER

- *to moderate or soften*

INSIDER INFO

TEMPER is typically associated with the emotion of anger. We try to control our TEMPER and usually regret it when we lose our TEMPER. Surprisingly, *TEMPER* can also mean "to moderate or soften" a feeling. On one sentence completion question, for example, a manager attempted to TEMPER, but not eliminate, the optimism of her overly ZEALOUS (very enthusiastic) sales force.

474. SHELVE

- *to put aside and postpone*

AP U.S. HISTORY

Lyndon B. Johnson began his presidency by promising to lead America on an IDEALISTIC quest to end racial segregation and wage war on poverty. The rising cost of the Vietnam War, however, forced LBJ to cut back and ultimately SHELVE many of his Great Society programs.

475. FASHION

- *to give something shape or form*

INSIDER INFO

Most people associate the word *FASHION* with trendy clothes and hip life styles. But clever College Board test writers know that *FASHION* can also mean "to give something shape or form." Over the years challenging sentence completion questions have asked students to realize that 18th-century artists FASHIONED a new artistic style and that contemporary Inuit sculptors are using traditional techniques to FASHION a modern cultural identity.

476. COMPROMISE

- *to expose to danger, suspicion, or disrepute*

POP CULTURE

American history students typically associate the word *COMPROMISE* with a middle ground where both sides make concessions. However, *COMPROMISE* can also mean "the act of exposing a person or organization to danger." In the movie *Skyfall*, for example, Patrice is a mercenary agent who has stolen a computer hard drive containing vital information about British agents placed undercover in terrorist organizations. If James Bond cannot recover it, the hard drive will COMPROMISE British intelligence activities around the world. Needless to say, no COMPROMISE is possible between Bond and Patrice's boss, the villainous cyberterrorist Silva.

477. COSMOPOLITAN

- *sophisticated and not limited by a narrow point of view;
  diverse and containing a variety of people*

INSIDER INFO

COSMOPOLITAN has two distinct definitions that are both tested in sentence completion questions. A COSMOPOLITAN person is sophisticated and not limited by a narrow, PROVINCIAL perspective. For example, the "Most Interesting Man in the World" commercials feature a COSMOPOLITAN man with a sophisticated knowledge of the world. In contrast, a COSMOPOLITAN place features a diverse and bustling population. New York City, Istanbul, and Hong Kong are all COSMOPOLITAN cities located at the crossroads of international trade.

478. PAROCHIAL

- *reflecting a narrow or limited point of view; PROVINCIAL*

INSIDER INFO

PAROCHIAL is derived from a Latin word meaning "of a parish." During the Middle Ages, a parish was a small section of a diocese that could support its own local church community. Today, *PAROCHIAL* is often used to refer to a church-supported school that provides both religious and CONVENTIONAL education. Do not expect to see this meaning of *PAROCHIAL* tested on your SAT. Instead, College Board test writers will focus on *PAROCHIAL* as a term used to describe a narrow or limited point of view. *PAROCHIAL* and its synonym *PROVINCIAL* are often used as antonyms of *COSMOPOLITAN* (Word 477).

479. TACKLE

- *to confront or take on a challenge*

IN THE NEWS

Jack Andraka is a Maryland teenager who won the top award at the 2012 Intel Science and Engineering Fair. (See Word 440 for Jack's EUPHORIC celebration.) Jack decided to TACKLE the problem of finding a way to detect pancreatic cancer after the disease claimed the life of his uncle. Jack contacted nearly 200 professors at Johns Hopkins University to ask for help with his project. He received almost 200 rejection letters. UNDAUNTED (not discouraged), Jack refused to quit and continued to TACKLE the problem of devising a new test for pancreatic cancer. To find out what happened, see Word 480.

480. YIELD

• *to produce or provide; to generate*

IN THE NEWS

Jack finally received a positive response from Dr. Anirba Maitra, Professor of Pathology and Oncology at Johns Hopkins School of Medicine. Supported by Dr. Maitra, Jack's research began to YIELD impressive results. Jack's novel ideas have YIELDED a faster, cheaper, and more accurate technique for detecting pancreatic cancer than today's standard diagnostic techniques. Jack's breakthrough method can also be used to detect ovarian and lung cancer.

CHAPTER 46
THE TOP TEN WORDS ABOUT KRISTEN STEWART & ROBERT PATTINSON

Kristen Stewart's cheating scandal generated intense media attention. Inquiring students want to know what happened. This chapter uses ten frequently used SAT vocabulary words to tell you all the news about K-Stew and R-Pattz.

481. CLANDESTINE &
482. SURREPTITIOUS

- *Both words describe FURTIVE activities and actions that are secret and hidden.*

POP CULTURE

The real-life romance between *Twilight* SAGA costars Kristen Stewart and Robert Pattinson captured the imagination of movie fans throughout the world. But fans were shocked when *Us Weekly* published pictures showing K-Stew having a CLANDESTINE romantic rendezvous with her *Snow White and the Huntsman* director, Rupert Sanders—a married father of two who is nineteen years older than Kristen. The pictures were taken by a photographer who SURREPTITIOUSLY followed Stewart and Sanders to a secluded place where they had what he called "a marathon make-out session."

483. REMORSEFUL &
484. CONTRITE

- *Both words describe feelings of regret and sorrow*

POP CULTURE

The pictures in *Us Weekly* forced Kristen to admit that she had indeed had a CLANDESTINE (secret) meeting with Rupert Sanders. Filled with REMORSE, K-Stew issued a public apology, declaring, "I'm deeply sorry for the hurt and embarrassment I've caused to those close to me and everyone that has been affected." The visibly CONTRITE actress then IMPLORED (begged) Pattinson to forgive her: "This momentary indiscretion has jeopardized the most important thing in my life, the person I love and respect the most, Rob. I love him. I love him. I'm so sorry."

485. SANCTUARY

- *a place where people go for peaceful tranquility and quiet introspection*

POP CULTURE

K-Stew's betrayal devastated R-Pattz. The *Twilight* star had believed that he and K-Stew were soulmates who would always be together. The MELANCHOLY (sad and depressed) star accepted Reese Witherspoon's invitation to stay at her secluded ranch in Ojai, northwest of Los Angeles. Reese's home served as a much-needed SANCTUARY where Rob reflected on what had happened.

486. IRE

- *an expression of strong anger*

POP CULTURE

While R-Pattz BROODED (dwelled anxiously) over what had happened to his seemingly perfect relationship, angry *Twilight* fans focused their IRE on Kristen. Angry fans branded her a "trampire" and refused to accept her public apology.

487. ANGUISH

- *a feeling of great distress, torment, and despair*

POP CULTURE

The apparent loss of R-Pattz and the IRE of her fans left K-Stew tortured by feelings of regret. Friends reported that the ANGUISHED star cried all night and was close to a total emotional meltdown.

488. ASSUAGE

- *to soothe, calm, and attempt to make less painful*

POP CULTURE

The guilt-ridden Kristen was determined to ASSUAGE Rob's pain and win back his trust. She bombarded Rob with phone calls and texts begging for forgiveness, swearing that her REMORSE was genuine, and promising that she would never betray his trust again. Kristen even openly wore a $40,000 locket Rob had previously given to her. It contained pictures of the couple and a Latin inscription that, when translated, reads, "Even if you can't see me, my love for you is always there."

489. RECONCILE

- *to restore a friendship or condition of harmony*

POP CULTURE

At first, RECONCILIATION between R-Pattz and K-Stew seemed impossible. Even though R-Pattz felt betrayed, he still loved Kristen and wanted to trust her. The two stars finally had a CLANDESTINE meeting, away from the prying cameras of intrusive paparazzi. Friends reported that "the frost between them is thawing." Within a short time the couple began appearing together in public, and their publicists confirmed that they had indeed RECONCILED.

490. PERSEVERE

- *to persist steadfastly, to hold on*

POP CULTURE

The scandal rocked Kristen's personal life and threatened to derail her acting career. But despite intense media attention, Kristen ultimately PERSEVERED. Fans accepted Kristen's apology and applauded when she and Rob appeared together for the opening of *Breaking Dawn—Part 2*. Universal Studios even announced that Kristen would appear in the sequel to *Snow White and the Huntsman*.

CHAPTER 47
THE TOP TEN WORDS ABOUT PSY AND GANGNAM STYLE

Psy and his music video "Gangnam Style" have become global sensations. But who is Psy, and what are the hidden messages in the "Gangnam Style" video? This chapter uses ten frequently tested SAT vocabulary words to answer these and other "Gangnam Style" questions.

491. VERVE

- *an energetic style that is FLAMBOYANT and full of vitality*

POP CULTURE

The music video "Gangnam Style" has transformed a previously unknown South Korean rapper into a global superstar. Psy is full of VERVE as he raps catchy rhymes and performs energetic horse-riding dance moves. Psy's unique combination of VERVE, attitude, and wit have helped turn the "Gangnam Style" video into a YouTube sensation that has received over one billion views. We agree (for now) with an EXUBERANT (very enthusiastic) liker who proclaimed, "Psy is boss!"

492. FRIVOLOUS VERSUS
493. TRENCHANT

- *FRIVOLOUS describes behavior that is silly and not serious.
  In contrast, TRENCHANT describes observations that
  are penetrating, incisive, and sharply perceptive.*

POP CULTURE

At first glance, "Gangnam Style" is a LIGHTHEARTED (carefree) and FRIVOLOUS (silly) video that displays Psy as he dances his way through a HODGEPODGE (jumble) of seemingly disconnected misadventures. Beneath the surface, however, "Gangnam Style" is a TRENCHANT social commentary on life in the Gangnam district of Seoul, South Korea. Gangnam is the wealthiest and most COVETED (desired) place to live in Seoul. It is the home of fashionable boutiques, trendy clubs, and prestigious prep schools. Psy's TRENCHANT video exposes the love-hate relationship South Koreans have with the PRETENTIOUS (self-important) people who live, work, and play in Gangnam.

494. DILAPIDATED

- *run-down, decaying, and shabby*

POP CULTURE

Gangnam is now known for its trendy stores and wealthy residents. Surprisingly, less than thirty years ago Gangnam was an IMPOVERISHED (very poor) and NONDESCRIPT (lacking interesting features) area, best known for its DILAPIDATED apartment buildings and streets lined with MALODOROUS (foul-smelling) drainage ditches.

495. APPREHENSIVE

- *describes an uneasy feeling of anxiety and worry*

POP CULTURE

Gangnam's wealthy residents inspire feelings of both envy and APPREHENSION. Many traditional South Koreans are APPREHENSIVE that the district's obsession with materialism will erode their country's traditional values of hard work and sacrifice. Their uneasy feeling contributes to a national sense of AMBIVALENCE (mixed feelings) that Psy skillfully captures in his "Gangnam Style" video.

496. OSTENTATIOUS

- *marked by showy and often tasteless displays of wealth*

POP CULTURE

Gangnam is the wealthiest district in South Korea. This AFFLUENCE has created an OSTENTATIOUS look known as the "Gangnam style." The self-important people who live in Gangnam prize OSTENTATIOUS clothes and expensive jewelry purchased at posh boutiques. In his official making of the "Gangnam Style" video, Psy expresses his disgust for this OSTENTATIOUS display of material possessions when he disdainfully notes, "Human society is so hollow."

497. DERIDE

- *to ridicule and make fun of; treat with scorn; DEPRECATE*

POP CULTURE

In his song "Gangnam Style," Psy DERIDES vain people who mindlessly pursue symbols of material wealth. For example, the song's lyrics DERIDE the Gangnam obsession with expensive coffee shops. In Gangnam trendy women and men often scrimp on food so they can splurge on drinks at boutique coffee shops. In his song, Psy's character proudly boasts that he is a guy who is so rich that he can "one-shot his coffee before it even cools down." Naturally, Psy wants to meet "a classy girl who knows how to enjoy the freedom of a cup of coffee."

498. QUIRKY

- *characterized by ECCENTRIC habits and odd mannerisms; peculiar*

POP CULTURE

Psy is a stage name derived from the first three letters of the word *psycho*. Psy has always viewed himself as a QUIRKY outsider. Unlike most K-pop (Korean pop) performers, he is not handsome, tall, or muscular. Instead, the QUIRKY Psy describes himself as "a guy who has bulging ideas rather than muscles." Psy is a thoughtful recording artist who writes his own songs and choreographs his own videos. At the same time, however, the QUIRKY Psy boasts that he is "a guy who goes completely crazy when the right time comes."

499. SALIENT

- *standing out in an obvious way; noticeable and prominent*

POP CULTURE

In an interview on NBC's *Today Show*, Psy acknowledged that he is neither handsome nor muscular. He then paused and correctly noted the most SALIENT point about his current status: "But I'm sitting here." Psy is right. He has succeeded where the other K-pop superstars have failed. The 35-year-old rapper has become the first K-pop artist to successfully crack the LUCRATIVE (very profitable) American music market.

500. VANGUARD

• *the leading position in a trend or movement*

MEET MY STUDENTS: CHRISTIN

Christin is proud of her Korean heritage. She taught me how to pronounce Gangnam and also pointed out some of the hidden cultural points in the "Gangnam Style" video. The man in the bright yellow suit, for example, is actually a very popular South Korean comedian and TV personality. The beautiful redhead Psy meets on the subway is the leader of a very famous K-pop girl group named 4Minute. Christin predicts that Psy is in the VANGUARD of a wave of K-pop recording artists who are poised to invade the COVETED (desired) but ELUSIVE (hard to reach) American music market.

PART II

THE ESSENTIAL GUIDE TO SENTENCE COMPLETIONS

CHAPTER 48
INTRODUCING SENTENCE COMPLETIONS

Chapters 1–47 provide you with definitions and illustrations of 500 key words frequently tested on the SAT. These words will help you become a more articulate writer and speaker. They will also help you achieve a higher critical reading score.

Each SAT contains three sections devoted to critical reading. These sections include a total of nineteen sentence completion questions and 48 passage-based questions. Vocabulary plays a particularly important role in the challenging Level 4 and Level 5 questions. In many ways, the critical reading section can be viewed as a sophisticated vocabulary test.

Part II of *The Essential 500 Words* is designed to provide you with a comprehensive overview of sentence completion questions. Chapters 49–52 will explain and illustrate four basic types of sentence completion questions. Chapters 53–57 will provide you with five full sets of practice questions.

BASIC INFORMATION

Each SAT contains nineteen sentence completion questions. These sentences contain one or two blanks. Your task is to fill in the blanks with a word or set of words which best fits the meaning of the sentence as a whole. According to the College Board, sentence completion questions are designed to test your vocabulary and "your ability to understand how the different parts of a sentence fit logically together."

ORDER OF DIFFICULTY

Each critical reading section will begin with a set of either eight, six, or five sentence completion questions. The sentence completions are arranged in order of difficulty. The first question will be relatively easy, and the next questions will become increasingly difficult. Here's what to expect:

- In the set of eight sentence completions, numbers 1–3 are usually easy, numbers 4–5 are medium, and numbers 6–8 are hard.
- In the set of six sentence completions, numbers 1–2 are usually easy, numbers 3–4 are usually medium, and numbers 5–6 are usually hard.
- In the set of five sentence completions, number 1 is usually easy, numbers 2–3 are usually medium, and numbers 4–5 are usually hard.

THE GOLDEN RULE

College Board test writers can't just use any sentence and arbitrarily leave out a word. They must provide enough information to make the correct choice indisputably right and the incorrect choices indisputably wrong. This information takes the form of key words, phrases, and examples. The Golden Rule for answering sentence completions is: ALWAYS FIND THE KEY WORD, PHRASE, OR EXAMPLE. IT WILL LEAD YOU TO THE CORRECT ANSWER.

A SAMPLE QUESTION
Take a look at the sample sentence completion below, and select the missing word:

The textbook on African history provides a _____ treatment of a diverse subject.
(A) compassionate
(B) deceptive
(C) chaotic
(D) fascinating
(E) chronological

Which answer did you choose? Why? Are the other answers clearly incorrect?

In this example, all five of the answer choices could be correct. The textbook treatment of African history could be compassionate, deceptive, chaotic, fascinating, or chronological. The sentence doesn't provide us with enough information to determine the best answer. Now take a look at this version of our sample sentence completion question:

The textbook on African history provides a _____ treatment of a diverse subject; it carefully describes the sequential development of a complex series of events.
(A) compassionate
(B) deceptive
(C) chaotic
(D) fascinating
(E) chronological

Which answer did you choose this time? Why? The key phrase "the sequential development" tells you that the textbook's treatment of African history must be CHRONOLOGICAL. No other answer choice will fit this defining phrase.

Every sentence completion on the SAT will have a key word, phrase, or illustrative example that will lead you to the correct answer. Your prime directive is to identify the key word or phrase and then match it with the appropriate answer choice. Chapters 49–53 will examine and illustrate different types of key words that will help you answer sentence completion questions correctly.

THE IMPORTANCE OF SENTENCE COMPLETION QUESTIONS

The nineteen sentence completion questions comprise 28 percent of the 67 critical reading questions on your SAT. Although this is a significant percentage, the importance of sentence completion questions transcends their number.

It is important to remember that each set of sentence completion questions ends with 2–3 challenging Level 4 and 5 questions. As a result, the nineteen sentence completions typically generate 7–9 Level 4 and 5 questions. As a general rule, each SAT contains between fifteen and twenty Level 4 and 5 questions. Challenging sentence completion questions thus comprise between forty and fifty percent of the tough Level 4 and 5 questions on a given SAT.

Level 4 and 5 sentence completion questions can have a particularly significant impact on the critical reading scores of students aspiring to score above a 700. The October 2012 SAT, for example, contained seven Level 4 and 5 sentence completion questions. These questions all tested challenging vocabulary words that are in this book. A student who missed these seven questions and correctly answered all the remaining sixty critical reading questions would have received a score of 690. These seven Level 4 and 5 questions were thus worth a total of 110 points!

CHAPTER 49
DEFINITIONAL SENTENCE COMPLETIONS

In Chapter 48 you learned to analyze each sentence completion by first looking for key words, phrases, and examples. Now examine the following three sentence completion examples:

1. **Discussions at the town hall meetings were usually _____, focusing on solving practical community problems.**
   (A) subversive
   (B) acrimonious
   (C) soporific
   (D) pragmatic
   (E) eclectic

2. **Some of the guests were _____, speaking rudely to their host and generally displaying deplorable manners.**
   (A) uncouth
   (B) despondent
   (C) euphoric
   (D) earnest
   (E) candid

3. **President Coolidge presents a challenge to would-be biographers because he was both _____ and _____: he said very little and accomplished even less.**
   (A) overbearing .. prescient
   (B) taciturn .. ineffective
   (C) aloof .. productive
   (D) audacious .. incompetent
   (E) indefatigable .. energetic

What type of pattern do you think the key words and phrases in these three questions have in common? In each sentence, the key group of words is a definition. In Sentence 1, the key phrase "focusing on solving practical community problems" tells you that the answer is (D) PRAGMATIC (Word 4). In Sentence 2, the key phrases "speaking rudely" and "displaying deplorable manners" tell you that the answer is (A) UNCOUTH (Word 111). In Sentence 3, the key phrase "said very little" tells you that the answer to the first blank is (B) TACITURN (Word 284). The key phrase "accomplished even less" tells you that the answer to the second blank is (B) ineffective.

In all three of these definitional sentences, the key words and phrases are definitions. The answer is therefore a word that is defined or explained in the sentence.

PRACTICE EXAMPLES

The following ten examples will give you an opportunity to practice the skill of identifying key definitional words, phrases, and examples. They will also give you an opportunity to use words from Chapters 1–47.

1. Mayor Jenkins is one of the most _____ politicians in the state; he is never candid, frequently insincere, and always calculating.
   (A) bombastic
   (B) disingenuous
   (C) vacillating
   (D) dilatory
   (E) paradoxical

2. Nishant laughed exuberantly and embraced his teammates, so _____ was he about leading his team to victory in the fencing tournament.
   (A) forlorn
   (B) indifferent
   (C) disdainful
   (D) euphoric
   (E) wistful

3. Richard Serra, an influential modern sculptor, is best known for his _____ and _____ style that combined eccentric themes with controversial images that sparked heated public debates.
   (A) idiosyncratic .. contentious
   (B) naïve .. nuanced
   (C) bizarre .. conciliatory
   (D) insipid .. inscrutable
   (E) audacious .. prodigious

4. Popular in 18th century Paris, Rococo art was both _____ and _____: it emphasized elaborate decorations along with frivolous scenes of aristocrats at play.
   (A) pastoral .. somber
   (B) ornate .. superficial
   (C) stark .. cerebral
   (D) unadorned .. fickle
   (E) convoluted .. profound

5. Cortez, Pizarro, and other Spanish conquistadores coveted gold and silver, and with this _____ came a ruthless willingness to conquer the Aztec and Inca empires.
   (A) lethargy
   (B) altruism
   (C) avarice
   (D) prescience
   (E) prudence

6. Viruses are _____; they are found in almost every ecosystem on Earth and are the most abundant type of biological entity.
   (A) auspicious
   (B) audacious
   (C) ubiquitous
   (D) ravenous
   (E) meticulous

7. The committee's report was completely _____; it was filled with inaccurate facts, unfounded innuendoes, and biased sources.
   (A) verifiable
   (B) corroborated
   (C) infallible
   (D) erudite
   (E) erroneous

8. Many beneficial scientific breakthroughs began by chance with the _____ discovery of _____ finding that deviated from accepted patterns and thus could not be explained by existing theoretical models.

    (A) premeditated .. an atypical
    (B) inadvertent .. a conventional
    (C) fortuitous .. an anomalous
    (D) predictable .. a revolutionary
    (E) calculated .. a trivial

9. Critics denounced the company's president for his _____ policies that lacked foresight and failed to address important trends in consumer tastes.

    (A) histrionic
    (B) prolific
    (C) trenchant
    (D) sagacious
    (E) myopic

10. During his negotiations with the Senate over the League of Nations, Woodrow Wilson was both _____ and _____: he refused to compromise and displayed a disdainful attitude toward senators whom he viewed as inferior and unworthy.

    (A) obstinate .. affable
    (B) flexible .. cavalier
    (C) fastidious .. altruistic
    (D) intransigent .. overbearing
    (E) frank .. surreptitious

ANSWERS

1. B: The key definitional phrase "never candid, frequently insincere, and always calculating" leads you to a person who is dishonest and deceitful. The correct answer is therefore DISINGENUOUS (Word 232).

2. D: The key definitional phrase "laughed exuberantly and embraced his teammates" leads you to a person who is very happy. The correct answer is therefore EUPHORIC (Word 440).

3. A: The key definitional word "eccentric" leads you to IDIOSYNCRATIC (Word 213) for the first blank. The key definitional word "controversial" leads you to CONTENTIOUS (Word 258) for the second blank. The correct answer is therefore IDIOSYNCRATIC .. CONTENTIOUS.

4. B: The key definitional phrase "elaborate decorations" leads you to ORNATE (Word 451) for the first blank. The key definitional phrase "frivolous scenes" leads you to SUPERFICIAL (Word 304) for the second blank. The correct answer is therefore ORNATE .. SUPERFICIAL.

5. C: The key definitional phrase "coveted gold and silver" leads to a word that means "very greedy." The correct answer is therefore AVARICE (See Word 240).

6. C: The key definitional phrase "found in almost every ecosystem on Earth" indicates that you are looking for an answer that means "everywhere." The correct answer is therefore UBIQUITOUS (Word 217).

7. E: The key phrase "inaccurate facts, unfounded innuendoes, and biased sources" tells you that the report was inaccurate. The correct answer is therefore ERRONEOUS (Word 331).

8. C: The key definitional phrase "began by chance" leads you to either INADVERTENT (choice B) or FORTUITOUS (choice C). Since the finding "deviated from accepted patterns" and therefore "could not be explained by existing theoretical models," it would be atypical and thus ANOMALOUS (Word 19). The correct answer is therefore FORTUITOUS .. ANOMALOUS.

9. E: The key definitional phrase "lacked foresight" leads to a word that means "shortsighted." The correct answer is therefore MYOPIC (Word 224).

10. D: The key definitional phrase "refused to compromise" leads you to either OBSTINATE (choice A) or INTRANSIGENT (choice D). Since Wilson also "displayed a disdainful attitude," he was OVERBEARING. The correct answer is therefore INTRANSIGENT (Word 146) .. OVERBEARING (Word 377).

CHAPTER 50
CONTRAST SENTENCE COMPLETIONS

In Chapter 49 you learned that the key word or group of words in many sentence completion questions is a definition or explanation. Now read the following three sentence completions:

1. **The diplomat was not at all _____; on the contrary, he was a duplicitous person who could not be trusted.**
   (A) vivacious
   (B) unscrupulous
   (C) disingenuous
   (D) frank
   (E) slovenly

2. **The compromise proposal avoids _____; its appeal is instead to a new spirit of harmony.**
   (A) acrimony
   (B) novelty
   (C) austerity
   (D) amiability
   (E) credibility

3. **The participants in the study considered themselves _____, but in yielding to the wishes of the group they were assuming _____ values.**
   (A) cooperative .. communal
   (B) traditional .. orthodox
   (C) innovative .. conventional
   (D) egalitarian .. elitist
   (E) diligent .. industrious

What type of pattern do the key words and groups of words in these three sentences have in common? Each sentence contains a word or group of words that signals a change in direction. In Sentence 1, the phrase "on the contrary" signals that you are looking for an answer that is the reverse of "duplicitous." In Sentence 2, the phrase "is instead" signals that you are looking for an answer that is the reverse of "harmony." In Sentence 3, the word "but" signals that you are looking for a pair of opposites.

"On the contrary," "is instead," and "but" are all reversal words that alert you to expect a contrast or change of direction in the sentence. The list below includes the most common reversal words used in SAT contrast sentence completion questions:

- BUT
- IN CONTRAST TO
- ON THE CONTRARY
- INSTEAD OF
- ALTHOUGH
- HOWEVER
- NEVER
- NEVERTHELESS
- YET
- NOT KNOWN FOR
- PARADOXICALLY

Sentences containing reversal words are called *contrast sentences*. In this type of sentence completion, the answer will be a word that contrasts with the key word or group of words. For example, in the three sentences above FRANK (Word 7) contrasts with duplicitous, ACRIMONY (Word 346) contrasts with harmony, and INNOVATIVE (Word 88) and CONVENTIONAL (Word 2) make up a contrasting pair of antonyms. Note that CONVENTIONAL is supported by the definitional phrase "yielding to the wishes of the group."

PRACTICE EXAMPLES

The following ten practice examples will give you an opportunity to practice the skill of identifying key contrast words and phrases. They will also give you an opportunity to use words from Chapters 1–47.

1. Akhil was not _____ and instead preferred to participate in team sports and join a variety of social clubs.
   (A) shrewd
   (B) ebullient
   (C) impulsive
   (D) aloof
   (E) venal

2. Ernest Hemingway's distinctive writing style was characterized by a simplicity of expression, _____ sentence structure that contrasted with the elaborate and often _____ prose of 19th-century British writers.
   (A) a subservient .. docile
   (B) a verbose .. succinct
   (C) a varied .. eclectic
   (D) a spare .. ornate
   (E) a mundane .. mediocre

3. As a civilization, the ancient Greeks were full of contradictions: _____ and yet prizing utility, egalitarian and yet sometimes prone to _____ philosophies.
   (A) pragmatic .. communal
   (B) expedient .. autocratic
   (C) sensible .. reciprocal
   (D) aesthetic .. elitist
   (E) empathetic .. democratic

4. Madison's surprisingly _____ explanation contrasted with her usual _____ manner of speaking.
   (A) succinct .. loquacious
   (B) garrulous .. verbose
   (C) brusque .. curt
   (D) candid .. forthright
   (E) disingenuous .. deceptive

5. Although the speaker was in fact quite perturbed by the rowdy crowd, she managed to remain outwardly _____.
   (A) unflappable
   (B) agitated
   (C) irascible
   (D) disconcerted
   (E) apprehensive

6. Kurt's dispassionate and objective explanation sharply contrasted with his usual _____ point of view.
   (A) soporific
   (B) biased
   (C) provisional
   (D) disinterested
   (E) pristine

7. Nothing in Anchal's speech was _____: instead she recited carefully documented facts and recounted carefully rehearsed anecdotes.
   (A) succinct
   (B) coherent
   (C) objective
   (D) corroborated
   (E) extemporized

8. Never _____, Rebecca instead treated everyone she knew with respect and and as an equal.
   (A) indomitable
   (B) cavalier
   (C) quixotic
   (D) laconic
   (E) conspicuous

9. Some people alternate between contrasting temperaments; either they are _____ or they are _____.
   (A) haughty .. imperious
   (B) eccentric .. idiosyncratic
   (C) compliant .. submissive
   (D) overwrought .. histrionic
   (E) somber .. lighthearted

10. Never _____, Zack was instead a _____ person whose **effervescent personality enlivened school parties.**

    (A) capricious .. mercurial
    (B) despondent .. morose
    (C) altruistic .. magnanimous
    (D) obstinate .. recalcitrant
    (E) reticent .. gregarious

ANSWERS

1. D: The reversal phrase "and instead" signals that you are looking for an answer that contrasts with participating in team sports and and joining a variety of social clubs. Akhil would not be ALOOF, because an ALOOF person prefers to be detached from groups. The correct answer is therefore ALOOF (Word 373).

2. D: The reversal phrase "contrasted with" signals that you will be looking for a pair of antonyms. The phrase "a simplicity of expression" will lead you to "a SPARE sentence structure." This would contrast with the "elaborate" and therefore "ORNATE prose of 19th-century British writers." The correct answer is therefore SPARE (Word 453) .. ORNATE (Word 451).

3. D: The key phrase "full of contradictions" alerts you to look for a pair of antonyms. The first blank must be filled with a word that is the opposite of "prizing utility." The second blank must be filled with a word that is the opposite of "egalitarian." The correct answer is therefore AESTHETIC (Word 1) .. ELITIST (Word 193).

4. A: The reversal phrase "contrasted with" alerts you to look for a pair of opposites. Only answer choice A meets this test. The correct answer is therefore SUCCINCT (Word 16) .. LOQUACIOUS (Word 149).

5. A: The reversal word "although" alerts you to look for an answer that contrasts with the key word "perturbed." The correct answer is therefore UNFLAPPABLE (Word 172).

6. B: The reversal phrase "sharply contrasted with" alerts you to look for an answer that contrasts with a "dispassionate and objective explanation." The correct answer is therefore BIASED (Word 48).

7. E: The reversal word "instead" alerts you to find an answer that contrasts with reciting "carefully documented facts" and recounting "carefully rehearsed anecdotes." The correct answer is therefore EXTEMPORIZED (Word 283).

8. B: The reversal word "instead" alerts you to find an answer that contrasts with treating people "with respect as an equal." The correct answer is therefore CAVALIER (Word 131).

9. E: The reversal phrase "alternate between contrasting temperaments" alerts you to look for a pair of opposites. The correct answer is therefore SOMBER (Word 409) .. LIGHTHEARTED (Word 59).

10. E: The reversal word "instead" alerts you to find an answer for the first blank that contrasts with the answer for the second blank. A person who has an "effervescent personality" that enlivens school parties would be GREGARIOUS. In contrast, a person who is RETICENT would not have this characteristic. The correct answer is therefore RETICENT (Word 10) .. GREGARIOUS (Word 323).

CHAPTER 51
USING POSITIVE AND NEGATIVE WORDS TO SOLVE SENTENCE COMPLETION QUESTIONS

SAT sentence completion questions frequently use challenging vocabulary words and complex sentence structures. As a result, even the best students are not always sure of the answer to each question.

If you are having trouble answering a sentence completion question, don't give up. There are effective strategies you can use to eliminate distracters and focus in on the correct answer.

A STRATEGY FOR USING POSITIVE AND NEGATIVE WORDS

Suppose a friend said to you, "I don't recommend the video game, it is too complicated and ____." What word would you put in the missing blank? Words like violent and boring quickly come to mind. Why is that? Why don't words like interesting and entertaining come to mind?

The answer of course, is that your friend specifically said, "I don't recommend the video game." As a result, you expect to hear negative words to complete the statement. If your friend had said, "I strongly recommend the video game," you would expect to hear positive words to explain this statement.

Like your everyday conversations, SAT sentence completion questions often use positive and negative words. Knowing this can help you master some of the test's toughest sentence completion questions. Here is a three-step strategy for using positive and negative words:

1. First, use contextual clues to determine if the missing word (or words) is most likely a positive word or a negative word. A positive word is one with good connotations, while a negative word is one with bad connotations. As you determine the meaning of the sentence, write a positive sign (+) in the blank if it requires a positive word or a negative sign (−) if it requires a negative word.

2. Second, write a positive or negative sign next to each of the answer choices.

3. Third, match the symbols you placed in the sentence blanks with the symbols you placed beside the choices.

CASE EXAMPLES

Let's apply this three-step procedure to the following two case examples:

1. Climatologists have long warned that global warming will have _____ effect, raising sea levels, flooding coastal areas, and endangering arctic wildlife.
    (A) an auspicious
    (B) an exhilarating
    (C) an uplifting
    (D) a deleterious
    (E) a lucrative

STEP 1:
Use contextual clues to determine if the missing word is positive or negative. This sentence clearly calls for a negative word, since climatologists are warning that global warming will lead to a series of negative consequences. Therefore place a (−) sign in the blank.

STEP 2:
Write a positive or negative symbol beside each of the answer choices:

(A) AUSPICIOUS means "favorable" and is thus a positive word.
(B) EXHILARATING means "refreshing and exciting" and is thus a positive word.
(C) UPLIFTING means "elevating to a higher social or moral level" and is thus a positive word.
(D) DELETERIOUS means "very harmful" and is thus a negative word.
(E) LUCRATIVE means "profitable" and is thus a positive word.

STEP 3:
Find answer choices that match your sentence symbols. Since you are looking for a negative answer, you can eliminate answer choices (A), (B), (C), and (E). The correct answer is (D) DELETERIOUS (Word 101).

2. During the late 1940s, the theories published by William Foote Whyte on the social structure of an Italian street gang were dismissed or even _____, but now they are _____ and unanimously praised by sociologists.

    (A) derided .. lauded
    (B) celebrated .. circumvented
    (C) refuted .. bemoaned
    (D) revered .. truncated
    (E) scorned .. neglected

STEP 1:

Use contextual clues to determine if the missing words are positive or negative. This sentence clearly calls for a strong negative first word since Whyte's theories were originally "dismissed." The second blank, however, clearly calls for a positive word, since Whyte's theories are now "unanimously praised by sociologists." Therefore, place a (–) sign in the first blank and a (+) sign in the second blank.

STEP 2:

Write positive and negative symbols beside each answer choice:

(A) DERIDE means "to treat with scorn" and is thus a negative word. LAUD means "to praise" and is thus a positive word.
(B) CELEBRATE means "to rejoice" and is thus a positive word. CIRCUMVENT means "to go around or bypass something" and thus can be either a positive or a negative word.
(C) REFUTE means "to prove that something is false" and thus can be either a positive or a negative word. BEMOAN means "to express disapproval or regret" and is thus a negative word.
(D) REVERE means "to show great respect" and is thus a positive word. TRUNCATE means "to cut short" and thus can be either a positive or a negative word.
(E) SCORN means "to express open dislike" and is thus a negative word. NEGLECT means "to pay little or no attention to" and is thus a negative word.

STEP 3:

Find answer choices that match your sentence symbols. Since you are looking for a negative–positive combination, you can eliminate choices (B), (C), (D), and (E). The correct answer is (A) DERIDED (Word 497) .. LAUDED (Word 398).

PRACTICE EXAMPLES

The following ten examples will give you an opportunity to practice the skill of using positive and negative words to answer sentence completion questions. They will also give you an opportunity to practice using words from Chapters 1–47.

1. Although it had been promoted as the plane of the future, the new airliner proved to be a _____: it cost too much, leaked oil, and had faulty lithium ion batteries.
   (A) a landmark
   (B) a fiasco
   (C) a triumph
   (D) a colossus
   (E) an anachronism

2. Investigators uncovered the politician's _____ when a hidden surveillance camera recorded him accepting bribes from a local businessman seeking special favors.
   (A) probity
   (B) charisma
   (C) venality
   (D) forbearance
   (E) idiosyncrasies

3. Chadni's _____ behavior had its usual _____ effect on her colleagues, who put aside their differences and reached a reasonable compromise.
   (A) conciliatory .. salutary
   (B) quirky .. soporific
   (C) earnest .. adverse
   (D) lighthearted .. autocratic
   (E) belligerent .. elusive

4. Critics called the new play bland because its plot was _____ and its poorly executed dialogue relied upon repetitious and mindless _____.
   (A) hackneyed .. platitudes
   (B) innovative .. redundancies
   (C) discerning .. anecdotes
   (D) scintillating .. allusions
   (E) trite .. subtleties

5. Although President Harding was personally honest, the Teapot Dome scandal tarnished his reputation and ultimately ____ his presidency.
   (A) bolstered
   (B) dignified
   (C) redeemed
   (D) discredited
   (E) rejuvenated

6. Recent promising advances have led proponents of renewable energy sources to predict confidently that solar panel technology will soon enter a new and more _____ phase of development.
   (A) ominous
   (B) perplexing
   (C) contentious
   (D) auspicious
   (E) inscrutable

7. Tyler's _____ was the inverse of his sister's _____: he was tolerant and generous while she was vengeful and unforgiving.
   (A) munificence .. benevolence
   (B) vivacity .. lethargy
   (C) diffidence .. prudence
   (D) ineptitude .. dexterity
   (E) magnanimity .. vindictiveness

8. The unruly students were not merely scolded, they were _____ during a lengthy _____ by their irate vice-principal.
   - (A) extolled .. eulogy
   - (B) excoriated .. rebuke
   - (C) extrapolated .. manifesto
   - (D) exonerated .. pronouncement
   - (E) expunged .. tribute

9. The skillful store manager was able to _____ the irate customer by offering her a sincere apology and a valuable gift certificate.
   - (A) exasperate
   - (B) mollify
   - (C) stigmatize
   - (D) admonish
   - (E) confound

10. Although the new high-speed rail line met with _____ from passengers, it also had its _____ who protested that it was very expensive to build and operate.
   - (A) acclaim .. critics
   - (B) derision .. detractors
   - (C) approbation .. proponents
   - (D) accolades .. benefactors
   - (E) enmity .. zealots

ANSWERS

1. B: The sentence calls for a strong negative answer since it lists three negative characteristics of the new airliner. Answers (A) and (C) can be eliminated because they are positive words. Answer (D) can be eliminated because a colossus is a huge object. Answer (E) can be eliminated because an anachronism (Word 212) is a person, event, or object that is chronologically out of place. The correct answer is therefore (B) since a FIASCO is a disaster (See Word 316).

2. C: The sentence calls for a negative word, since the hidden camera recorded the politician accepting bribes. Answers (A), (B), and (D) can all be eliminated since they are positive words. Answer (E) can be eliminated since an idiosyncrasy (Word 213) is an eccentric behavior. The correct answer is therefore (C), because VENALITY describes behavior that is corrupt and dishonest (Word 210).

3. A: The sentence calls for two positive words since Chadni's behavior caused her colleagues to "put aside their differences" and reach "a reasonable compromise." Answers (B), (C), (D), and (E) can all be eliminated because they contain at least one negative word. The correct answer is therefore (A) since CONCILIATORY (Word 253) means "willing to make concessions" and SALUTARY (Word 266) means "beneficial."

4. A: The sentence calls for two negative words, because the critics called the play "bland" and criticized the dialogue for being "repetitious and mindless." Answers (B), (C), (D), and (E) can all be eliminated since they contain at least one positive word. The correct answer is therefore (A) since HACKNEYED (Word 168) means "trite" and PLATITUDE (Word 167) means "commonplace, unoriginal, and mindless."

5. D: The sentence calls for a negative word that contrasts with the positive word "honest." Answers (A), (B), (C), and (E) can all be eliminated because they are positive words. The correct answer is therefore (D) since DISCREDIT (Word 376) means "to cast doubt on the reputation of a person."

6. D: The sentence calls for a positive word, since "promising advances" have led proponents of renewable sources of energy to confidently predict that panel technology will soon enter a new phrase of development. Answers (A), (B), (C), and (E) can all be eliminated, because they are negative words. The correct answer is therefore (D) since AUSPICIOUS means "favorable" (Word 301).

7. E: The sentence calls for a pair of antonyms, featuring a positive first word that is compatible with "tolerant and generous" and a negative second word that is compatible with "vengeful and unforgiving." Answers (C) and (D) can be eliminated since diffidence is a negative trait that means "lacking self-confidence," and ineptitude is a negative trait that means "lacking skill." Answer (A) can be eliminated since both munificence and benevolence are positive words meaning "generous" and "kind" respectively. Answer (B) can be eliminated because vivacity means "full of life" and lethargy means "lazy." Although vivacious is a positive trait and lethargy is a negative trait, these words are not supported by the definitional phrases in the sentence. The correct answer is therefore (E) since MAGNANIMITY (Word 181) means "generous" and VINDICTIVENESS (Word 182) means "vengeful and unforgiving."

8. B: The sentence calls for a pair of negative words, since the irate (angry) vice-principal strongly scolded the "unruly students." Answers (A), (D), and (E) can all be eliminated because they contain positive words. Answer (C) can be eliminated because extrapolate means "to project" and a manifesto is a public declaration of beliefs. The correct answer is therefore (B) because EXCORIATE (Word 154) means "to harshly denounce" and REBUKE (Word 378) means "to reprimand."

9. B: The sentence calls for a positive word that is consistent with using a "sincere apology and a valuable gift certificate" to placate the irate customer. Answers (A), (B), (D), and (E) can all be eliminated because they are negative words. The correct answer is therefore MOLLIFY (See Word 3), meaning "to calm or lessen."

10. A: The sentence calls for a positive first word and a negative second word that describes a person who protests that the high-speed rail line is too expensive. Answers (B) and (E) can be deleted since derision (ridicule) and enmity (animosity) are both negative first words. Answers (C) and (D) can be deleted since proponents and benefactors are both positive second words. The correct answer is therefore (A), because ACCLAIM (Word 398) means "to praise" and a CRITIC is someone who expresses dissatisfaction.

CHAPTER 52

ANSWERING THE MOST CHALLENGING SENTENCE COMPLETION QUESTIONS

The most challenging sentence completion questions are easy to find. They always appear at the end of each of the three sets of sentence completion questions. You can expect to have seven to nine challenging sentence completion questions worth over 110 points of your critical reading score.

CHARACTERISTICS OF CHALLENGING SENTENCE COMPLETION QUESTIONS

Challenging Level 4 and 5 sentence completions are easier to find than to answer. What characteristic features make these questions so difficult? Their degree of difficulty is based upon two key factors:

1. CHALLENGING VOCABULARY
Level 4 and 5 sentence completion questions contain a number of difficult vocabulary words. These challenging words are used in both the answer choices and in the sentence. In order to successfully answer these tough questions, you must have a strong vocabulary. Chapters 18–27 define and illustrate 100 Level 5 words. Chapters 28–37 define and illustrate 100 Level 4 words.

2. COMPLEX SENTENCE STRUCTURE
The most challenging sentence completion questions employ a combination of definitions, contrast words, and positive and negative vocabulary. In addition, recent tests have included questions asking you to determine the logical connection between the answer choices. For example, you may be asked to find a cause-and-effect relationship between key words in the sentence and the answer choices.

CASE EXAMPLE 1: CHALLENGING VOCABULARY

EAGER TO AVOID APPEARING FRENETIC AND PROVINCIAL, PRANAY CULTIVATED A PUBLIC PERSONA THAT MADE HIM APPEAR TO BE BOTH _____ AND _____.

   (A) imperturbable .. cosmopolitan
   (B) imperious .. tenacious
   (C) brusque .. ostentatious
   (D) unflappable .. parochial
   (E) overwrought .. urbane

Pranay wants to avoid appearing frenetic (wildly excited) and provincial (limited and narrow). You must therefore find a pair of positive answers that contrast with these two negative traits. Answer choice D is a possibility, since unflappable (calm and poised) is a positive antonym of frenetic. You must eliminate (D), however, since parochial is a negative synonym of provincial. Answer choices (B), (C), and (E) can all be eliminated because they contain negative first words that are not antonyms of frenetic. The correct answer is therefore (A), since IMPERTURBABLE (Word 171) is a positive word that contrasts with frenetic and COSMOPOLITAN (Word 477) is a positive word that contrasts with provincial.

CASE EXAMPLE 2: COMPLEX SENTENCE STRUCTURE

THE TEACHER WARNED HER STUDENTS THAT THE AP PREP BOOK WAS TOO _____ TO HELP THEM PREPARE FOR THE EXAM, GIVEN ITS _____ TREATMENT OF A COMPLEX SUBJECT.

   (A) coherent .. disjointed
   (B) superficial .. cursory
   (C) encyclopedic .. narrow
   (D) methodical .. haphazard
   (E) unsophisticated .. shrewd

This sentence asks you to find a pair of words that are logically connected. For example, you can eliminate (A) because a prep book that is too coherent or organized would not offer a disjointed or unconnected treatment of a complex subject. Choices (C), (D), and (E) can all be eliminated for the same reason. Encyclopedic does not imply narrow, methodical does not imply haphazard, and unsophisticated does not imply shrewd. Only (B) provides a pair of logically related words. A teacher would warn her students to avoid a SUPERFICIAL (Word 304) prep book because it would provide a CURSORY (Word 281) treatment of a complex subject.

PRACTICE EXAMPLES

The following ten examples will give you an opportunity to practice the skill of answering challenging sentence completion questions. They will also give you an opportunity to practice using vocabulary words from Chapters 1–47.

1. A long week of demanding homework assignments, challenging tests, and grueling soccer practices drained Lindsay's energy: she felt to _____ to do anything but sleep.
   (A) resilient
   (B) galvanized
   (C) enervated
   (D) unfettered
   (E) unnerved

2. Recent advances in solar technology indicate that energy independence is feasible, but environmentalists are quite _____ in their public statements, mindful of prior claims that proved _____.
   (A) impulsive .. ephemeral
   (B) audacious .. illusory
   (C) equivocal .. prescient
   (D) jovial .. irrevocable
   (E) prudent .. erroneous

3. Professor Duncan has a well-deserved reputation as _____: he disdains tradition and regularly attacks cherished beliefs.
   (A) a dilettante
   (B) a zealot
   (C) a demagogue
   (D) an iconoclast
   (E) a progenitor

4. Although Navajo sand paintings have been created for centuries, their artistic merits remain _____ because they have always been _____ works of art that medicine men promptly destroy.
   (A) enigmatic .. indelible
   (B) authenticated .. elusive
   (C) conclusive .. therapeutic
   (D) beguiling .. futile
   (E) uncorroborated .. ephemeral

5. The comedian is _____ by nature: he has a penchant for displaying a disrespectful attitude in situations that call for a serious response.
   (A) flippant
   (B) wistful
   (C) prudent
   (D) jovial
   (E) didactic

6. The new sales manager was not at all _____; on the contrary she was co-operative, open-minded, and always willing to listen.
   (A) peremptory
   (B) pragmatic
   (C) docile
   (D) conciliatory
   (E) shrewd

7. Fortunately, the committee's confidence in their appointee's abilities was _____: an investigation uncovered her participation in several _____ business ventures.
   (A) justified .. unsavory
   (B) vindicated .. lucrative
   (C) warranted .. unscrupulous
   (D) reciprocated .. licentious
   (D) premature .. exemplary

8. The shy and _____
behavior of the platypus accounts for
the _____ of confirmed
observations about its life cycle in the
wild.
  (A) gregarious .. dearth
  (B) reticent .. confluence
  (C) retiring .. paucity
  (D) mercurial .. plethora
  (E) contentious .. coherence

9. The Internet embodies
_____ inquiry, since the
system encourages free and open access
to a vast trove of facts, opinions, and
images.
  (A) specialized
  (B) impeded
  (C) unfettered
  (D) frenzied
  (E) coerced

10. The fable of Arachne centers on a human's
_____, the overweening
pride that makes a mortal believe she can
defeat a goddess.
  (A) hubris
  (B) diffidence
  (C) histrionics
  (D) duplicity
  (E) versatility

ANSWERS

1. C: The key word "drained" leads you to a word that means "to feel mentally and physically weakened." The correct answer is therefore ENERVATED (Word 271).

2. E: The sentence asks you to find a pair of words that are logically connected. Logically, the environmentalists would be very careful or PRUDENT (Word 76), because they are mindful that prior claims proved to be wrong or ERRONEOUS (Word 331).

3. D: The key definitional phrase "disdains tradition and regularly attacks cherished beliefs" leads you to describe Professor Duncan as an ICONOCLAST (Word 85).

4. E: This sentence asks you to find a pair of words that are logically connected. Logically, the artistic merits of Navajo sand paintings must remain unproven or UNCORROBORATED (Word 113) and therefore EPHEMERAL (Word 230) since the medicine men promptly destroy them.

5. A: The key definitional phrase "a penchant for displaying a disrespectful attitude in situations that call for a serious response" leads you to describe the comedian as someone who has a FLIPPANT (Word 63) nature.

6. A: The key reversal phrase "on the contrary" tells you to look for an answer that is the opposite of the key definitional phrase "co-operative, open-minded, and always willing to listen." The correct answer is therefore PEREMPTORY (Word 20).

7. B: This sentence asks you to find a pair of words that are logically connected. The key word "fortunately" signals that both answers will be positive words. The correct answer is therefore VINDICATED (Word 350) .. LUCRATIVE (Word 415).

8. C: This sentence asks you to find a pair of words that are logically connected. The key word "shy" will lead you to either reticent or retiring for the first blank. Shy and retiring behavior will logically lead you to paucity or shortage of confirmed observations. The correct answer is therefore RETIRING (Word 472) .. PAUCITY (Word 384).

9. C: The key definitional phrase "free and open access" leads you to describe the Internet as a system that embodies UNFETTERED (Word 112) inquiry.

10. A: The key definitional phrase "overweening pride" leads you to conclude that the fable of Arachne centers on a human's HUBRIS (Word 130).

CHAPTER 53

SENTENCE COMPLETIONS
PRACTICE SETS 1-3

Try to recall a situation in which you were performing under the pressure of a ticking clock. Athletes, entertainers, and writers often have to "beat the clock," "keep a schedule," and "make a deadline." The pressure builds whenever you feel like you don't have enough time to do what you are capable of doing. Learning how to handle time pressure requires practice, patience, and confidence.

The SAT will require you to perform well while working at a brisk pace. Students aspiring for top scores should strive to answer all or almost all the sentence completion questions. The vocabulary chapters, strategies, and practice exercises you have completed so far are designed to enable you to master even the most challenging sentence completion questions. Each of the three SAT critical reading sections will begin with a set of either eight, six, or five sentence completion questions. You should spend an average of about forty seconds on each sentence completion question. This means devoting about five minutes to the set of eight questions, four minutes to the set of six questions, and about 3.5 minutes to the set of five questions. This pace is designed to leave you with ample time to complete the critical reading passages.

SENTENCE COMPLETION PRACTICE SET 1— GROUP OF EIGHT

Directions: Mark the answer for each of the following eight sentence completion questions. Try to complete the entire set in five minutes. When you have finished, use the space provided to record how long you took to complete the set and how many questions you answered correctly.

1. Jean Piaget has _____ the study of cognitive development by fundamentally altering the way people think about how infants and children understand the world.
   (A) readjusted
   (B) revolutionized
   (C) discredited
   (D) coveted
   (E) hindered

2. Each painting for the Picasso exhibit was carefully selected and then _____ according to a carefully designed chronological and thematic pattern.
   (A) muddled
   (B) abandoned
   (C) renounced
   (D) ignored
   (E) positioned

3. Attending support groups can have _____ effect: they help people heal personal troubles and restore psychological health.
   (A) a deleterious
   (B) a therapeutic
   (C) a counterproductive
   (D) a perplexing
   (E) an unusual

4. Many club members report feeling _____ after participating in strenuous exercise workouts with physical trainer Marc Vindas, but he, in contrast, is _____.
   (A) fatigued .. indefatigable
   (B) diminished .. shriveled
   (C) resplendent .. radiant
   (D) uncommunicative .. taciturn
   (E) replenished .. rejuvenated

5. West African folklore consists of _____ mix that includes a wide range of songs, legends, and oral histories.
   (A) an eclectic
   (B) an inscrutable
   (C) an egregious
   (D) a bland
   (E) a homogeneous

6. Although he was very modest about his achievements, Kavin was not a _____; he was in fact an accomplished chess player.
   (A) misanthrope
   (B) pundit
   (C) heretic
   (D) connoisseur
   (E) neophyte

7. The governor's term in office was marked by _____ as he became entangled in a series of _____ and disgraceful scandals.
   (A) approbation .. seminal
   (B) idealism .. divisive
   (C) rectitude .. appalling
   (D) ignominy .. esteemed
   (E) chicanery .. venal

8. Karl's behavior was so
_____ that it offended
many club members: few people liked him
because he was _____ and
arrogant.
- (A) deplorable .. affable
- (B) exemplary .. amiable
- (C) cavalier .. overbearing
- (D) conciliatory .. despotic
- (E) execrable .. egalitarian

TIME: _____

NUMBER CORRECT: _____

SENTENCE COMPLETION PRACTICE SET 1— GROUP OF SIX

Directions: Mark the answer for each of the following six sentence completion questions. Try to complete the entire set in four minutes. When you have finished, use the space provided to record how long you took to complete the set and how many questions you answered correctly.

1. In contrast to Abhin's
_____ response, Helen
delayed completing the questionnaire and
thus did not receive an interview.
- (A) hesitant
- (B) monotonous
- (C) irrelevant
- (D) prompt
- (E) argumentative

2. Art and literature _____
during the European Dark Ages:
modern historians have noted
_____ of creative
endeavors.
- (A) retreated .. an abundance
- (B) unfolded .. an absence
- (C) languished .. a rebirth
- (D) stagnated .. a dearth
- (E) flourished .. paucity

3. The purpose of the arbiter's mission was
to mediate the dispute by helping labor
and management _____
their differences.
- (A) reconcile
- (B) exacerbate
- (C) prolong
- (D) ignore
- (E) deprecate

4. Francis Parkman's monumental seven-
volume history of the European
colonization of North America featured
_____ narrative style that
included elaborate descriptions of people,
places, and events.
- (A) an unadorned
- (B) an ornate
- (C) an evenhanded
- (D) an oversimplified
- (E) an incoherent

5. Fatigued from the start, the athlete
became even more _____
as the strenuous game continued.
- (A) inscrutable
- (B) enervated
- (C) taciturn
- (D) indulgent
- (E) officious

6. Outraged Church officials accused the
heretic of being _____
because he was a morally unprincipled
person who would never reform his
_____ lifestyle.
- (A) an iconoclast .. virtuous
- (B) a hedonist .. righteous
- (C) a toady .. laudable
- (D) a raconteur .. unorthodox
- (E) a reprobate .. depraved

TIME: _____

NUMBER CORRECT: _____

SENTENCE COMPLETION PRACTICE SET 1— GROUP OF FIVE

Directions: Mark the answer for each of the following five sentence completion questions. Try to complete the entire set in 3.5 minutes. When you have finished, use the space provided to record how long you took to complete the set and how many questions you answered correctly.

1. The presidency of James Monroe is often called "the Era of Good Feelings" because it was a _____ period that was relatively free of controversy.
   (A) heterogeneous
   (B) skeptical
   (C) chaotic
   (D) tranquil
   (E) contentious

2. While everyone agrees that the President and Congress should work together, this _____ vanishes once the politicians confront contentious political issues.
   (A) consensus
   (B) analogy
   (C) speculation
   (D) metaphor
   (E) allusion

3. The landlord complained that the negligent tenant abandoned his apartment and left it in _____ condition: the paint was peeling off the walls and the pipes were encrusted with rust.
   (A) pristine
   (B) tolerable
   (C) dilapidated
   (D) enhanced
   (E) punctilious

4. The group responded to Srishti's _____ story with tearful support that verged on becoming _____.
   (A) poignant .. maudlin
   (B) ominous .. lighthearted
   (C) wistful .. callous
   (D) uplifting .. disdainful
   (E) beguiling .. indifferent

5. Bismarck unified Germany by intimidation and _____, not by encouragement and _____.
   (A) persuasion .. coaxing
   (B) compromise .. conciliation
   (C) conjecture .. fidelity
   (D) rumination .. nostalgia
   (E) coercion .. cajolery

TIME: _____

NUMBER CORRECT: _____

PRACTICE SET 1—ANSWERS
GROUP OF EIGHT

1. B: The key definitional phrase "fundamentally altering" leads you to a word that describes a significant change. The correct answer is therefore REVOLUTIONIZED.

2. E: The key phrases "carefully selected" and "carefully designed" lead you to a word that means "placed." The correct answer is therefore POSITIONED.

3. B: The key definitional phrase "help people heal" indicates that you want a positive word that means "to heal" or "to help." The correct answer is therefore THERAPEUTIC.

4. A: The key reversal phrase "in contrast" indicates that you want a pair of antonyms. Only choice (A) meets this criterion. The correct answer is therefore FATIGUED .. INDEFATIGABLE (Word 262).

5. A: The key definitional phrase "mix that includes a wide range" leads you to a word that means "varied." The correct answer is therefore ECLECTIC (Word 202).

6. E: The reversal word "not" indicates that you are looking for a word that means the opposite of "an accomplished chess player." The correct answer is therefore NEOPHYTE (Word 94).

7. E: This sentence asks you to find a pair of words that are logically connected. The key phrase "disgraceful scandals" tells you to look for a pair of related negative words. Only answer (E) meets these criteria. The correct answer is therefore CHICANERY (Word 211) .. VENAL (Word 210).

8. C: The sentence asks you to find a pair of words that are logically connected. They key words "offended" and "arrogant" tell you to look for negative answers that mean "arrogant." The correct answer is therefore CAVALIER (Word 131) .. OVERBEARING (Word 377).

GROUP OF SIX

1. D: The key reversal phrase "in contrast to" tells you to look for an answer that means the opposite of "delayed." The correct answer is therefore (D) PROMPT.

2. D: This sentence asks for you to find a pair of words that are logically connected. The correct answer is therefore STAGNATED .. a DEARTH (Word 384).

3. A: The key definitional word "mediate" tells you that the arbiter is trying to help labor and management find a solution to their dispute. The correct answer is therefore the positive word RECONCILE (WORD 489).

4. B: The key definitional word "elaborate" tells you to look for an answer that means "embellished." The correct answer is therefore ORNATE (Word 451).

5. B: The key word "fatigued" and the key phrase "even more" tells you to look for an answer that means "very tired." The correct answer is therefore ENERVATED (Word 271).

6. E: The key definitional phrase "morally unprincipled person" tells you to look for a very negative word for the first blank. The second word must then be a logical characteristic of this "morally unprincipled person." The correct answer is therefore REPROBATE (Word 82) .. DEPRAVED.

GROUP OF FIVE

1. D: The key definitional phrase "relatively free of controversy" tells you to look for an answer that means "calm." The correct answer is therefore TRANQUIL.

2. A: The key definitional phrase "everyone agrees" tells you to look for an answer that means "general agreement." The correct answer is therefore CONSENSUS.

3. C: The key word "negligent" and the deteriorating condition of the paint and pipes tell you to look for a negative answer that means "run-down." The correct answer is therefore DILAPIDATED (Word 397).

4. A: The sentence asks you to find a pair of words that are logically connected. The first word must describe a story that would bring the group to tears. The second word must describe a state of excess emotion. The correct answer is therefore POIGNANT (Word 368) .. MAUDLIN (Word 139).

5. E: The sentence asks you to find a first word that is consistent with "intimidation" and a second contrasting word that is consistent with "encouragement." The correct answer is therefore COERCION (Word 189) .. CAJOLERY (Word 190).

SENTENCE COMPLETION PRACTICE SET 2— GROUP OF EIGHT

Directions: Mark the answer for each of the following eight sentence completion questions. Try to complete the entire set in five minutes. When you have finished, use the space provided to record how long you took to complete the set and how many questions you answered correctly.

1. **Unable to discover why the riot began, police investigators filed a tentative report stating that the causes were still** _____.
   (A) unresolved
   (B) irrefutable
   (C) definitive
   (D) compelling
   (E) consolidating

2. **The** _____ **of an ancient streamed on the surface of Mars** _____ **the long-standing scientific hypothesis that water once freely flowed on the now arid planet.**
   (A) uncovering .. discredits
   (B) discovery .. confirms
   (C) revelation .. disguises
   (D) absence .. verifies
   (E) existence .. contradicts

3. **The conference commissioner surprised sports fans by publicly arguing that athletic programs become too competitive when excessive** _____ **compromises a college's academic mission.**
   (A) outrage
   (B) nationality
   (C) moderation
   (D) compassion
   (E) rivalry

4. Whereas Colin's work bristles with
_____ rage against all
humanity, Devon's novels are more
_____ and good-natured.
   - (A) pleasing .. gracious
   - (B) cynical .. callous
   - (C) misguided .. erroneous
   - (D) surly .. sullen
   - (E) misanthropic .. genial

5. When autumn arrives in New Mexico
visitors are greeted everywhere they look
by bright golden-yellow chamisa flowers,
as this previously _____
shrub suddenly seems to be
_____.
   - (A) indefatigable .. rejuvenated
   - (B) infinitesimal .. pervasive
   - (C) resplendent .. somber
   - (D) inconspicuous .. ubiquitous
   - (E) indigenous .. exotic

6. Although scientists have proposed
a number of theories to explain the
extinction of the dinosaurs, definitive
answers to this puzzle remain
_____.
   - (A) indisputable
   - (B) elusive
   - (C) corroborated
   - (D) sufficient
   - (E) infallible

7. The normally _____
diplomat was uncharacteristically
_____ when negotiating a
treaty with the defeated nation.
   - (A) churlish .. brusque
   - (B) meticulous .. painstaking
   - (C) haughty .. cavalier
   - (D) intransigent .. adamant
   - (E) magnanimous .. vindictive

8. Some viruses including those causing
AIDS and viral hepatitis are hard to target
because they are _____,
and thus able to change and evade most
immune responses.
   - (A) protean
   - (B) immutable
   - (C) cerebral
   - (D) incontrovertible
   - (E) paradoxical

TIME: _____

NUMBER CORRECT: _____

SENTENCE COMPLETION PRACTICE SET 2 – GROUP OF 6

Directions: Mark the answer for each of the following 6 sentence completion questions. Try to complete the entire set in 4 minutes. When you have finished use the space provided to record how long you took to complete the set and how many questions you answered correctly.

1. The editor rejected the investigative report as _____ because it relied too heavily on undocumented allegations.
   - (A) crucial
   - (B) fundamental
   - (C) innovative
   - (D) laudable
   - (E) inadequate

2. The young child is prone to emotional excess: he can be alarmingly _____ one moment and utterly _____ the next.
   - (A) haughty .. imperious
   - (B) despondent .. euphoric
   - (C) diffident .. aloof
   - (D) lighthearted .. jovial
   - (E) capricious .. fickle

3. There is little chance of _____ in _____ society in which entrepreneurs are encouraged to create new products and ways of doing things.
   - (A) partisanship .. a static
   - (B) boredom .. a moribund
   - (C) serenity .. a mundane
   - (D) stagnation .. an innovative
   - (E) excess .. an ingenious

4. Compiled by experts with _____ standards of excellence, the research report is so _____ that it leaves no part of the issue unexamined.
   - (A) egregious .. exalted
   - (B) precise .. nonchalant
   - (C) exacting .. meticulous
   - (D) painstaking .. dilapidated
   - (E) negligent .. comprehensive

5. The critic's _____ review of the new play demonstrates her keen insight into the drama's nuanced themes.
   - (A) confounding
   - (B) discerning
   - (C) flippant
   - (D) dilatory
   - (E) superficial

6. Elizabeth was a _____ person who often made foolish gaffes that underscored her lack of maturity.
   - (A) flamboyant
   - (B) precocious
   - (C) ethereal
   - (D) puerile
   - (E) charismatic

TIME: _____

NUMBER CORRECT: _____

SENTENCE COMPLETION PRACTICE SET 2 – GROUP OF 5

Directions: Mark the answer for each of the following 5 sentence completion questions. Try to complete the entire set in 3.5 minutes. When you have finished use the space provided to record how long you took to complete the set and how many questions you answered correctly.

1. The smart phone is a _____ device that enables users to send text messages, photograph friends, and access the Internet.
   - (A) fragile
   - (B) specialized
   - (C) versatile
   - (D) appalling
   - (E) chaotic

2. As Shelley aged, financial setbacks and personal betrayals turned her once unbridled spirit of youthful _____ into a guarded and often _____ outlook on people.
   - (A) exuberance .. euphoric
   - (B) skepticism .. ambivalent
   - (C) sentimentality .. sanguine
   - (D) contrition .. expectant
   - (E) optimism .. cynical

3. The indignant microbiologist _____ the critic's charge that she had used fallacious data, citing the fact that her experiment had been replicated numerous times by _____ scientists.
   - (A) reiterated .. unbiased
   - (B) rebutted .. impartial
   - (C) corroborated .. partisan
   - (D) eschewed .. venal
   - (E) reaffirmed .. incredulous

4. Some of the party guests were unquestionably _____ , speaking rudely to their host and generally exhibiting _____ manners.
   - (A) boorish .. crude
   - (B) uncouth .. impeccable
   - (C) candid .. urbane
   - (D) cosmopolitan .. opportunistic
   - (E) unassuming .. condescending

5. Although Isaac Asimov was renowned as a _____ author who published over 500 books, he was also a trenchant thinker whose futuristic stories offered _____ insights into the enduring dilemmas of human nature.
   - (A) prodigious .. pedestrian
   - (B) prolific .. incisive
   - (C) sporadic .. penetrating
   - (D) copious .. perilous
   - (E) sparing .. implausible

TIME: _____

NUMBER CORRECT: _____

PRACTICE SET 2 – ANSWERS
GROUP OF 8

1. A: The key definitional phrases "unable to discover why" and "tentative report" lead you to a word that means undetermined. The correct answer is therefore UNRESOLVED.

2. B: This sentence asks you to find a pair of words that are logically connected. The correct answer is therefore DISCOVERY .. CONFIRMS.

3. E: The key definitional phrases "too competitive" and "excessive" tell you to look for a strong word that means highly competitive. The correct answer is therefore RIVALRY.

4. E: The key reversal word "whereas" tells you to look for a pair of antonyms. The first word must be consistent with the definitional phrase "rage against all humanity" and the second word must be consistent with the definitional phrase "good-natured." The correct answer is therefore MISANTHROPIC (Word 92) .. GENIAL (see Word 418).

5. D: The key reversal phrase "as this previously" tells you to look for a pair of antonyms. The key definitional phrase "greeted everywhere" tells you that the second word must mean widespread. Both pervasive (Choice B) and UBIQUITOUS (Choice D) meet this test. However, infinitesimal means very small and thus does not fit the first blank. The correct answer is therefore INCONSPICUOUS (Word 425) .. UBIQUITOUS (Word 217).

6. B: The key reversal word "although" tells you to look for a word that is opposed to the key definitional phrase "definitive answers." The correct answer is therefore ELUSIVE (Word 403).

7. E: The key words "normally" and "uncharacteristically" tell you to look for a pair of antonyms. The correct answer is therefore MAGNANIMOUS (Word 181) .. VINDICTIVE (Word 182).

8. A: The key definitional phrase "able to change and evade" tells you to look for a word that means variable. The correct answer is therefore PROTEAN (Word 125).

GROUP OF 6

1. E: The key word "rejected" and the key phrase "relied too heavily on undocumented allegations" tell you to look for a negative word that explains why the editor refused to accept the report. The correct answer is therefore INADEQUATE.

2. B: The key phrases "one moment" and "the next" tell you to look for a pair of antonyms that describe "emotional excesses." The correct answer is therefore DESPONDENT (Word 103) .. EUPHORIC (Word 440).

3. D: The sentence asks you to find a pair of words that are logically connected. The second word must be consistent with the definitional phrase creating "new products and ways of doing things." The correct answer is therefore STAGNATION .. INNOVATIVE (see Word 88).

4. C: The key phrases "standards of excellence" and "leaves no part of the issue unexplained" tell you to look for a pair of positive words that mean very thorough. The correct answer is therefore EXACTING (see Word 147) .. METICULOUS (Word 148).

5. B: The key definitional phrase "keen insight" tells you to look for a word that means very perceptive. The correct answer is therefore DISCERNING (Word 17).

6. D: The key definitional phrase "lack of maturity" tells you to look for a word that means very immature. The correct answer is therefore PUERILE (Word 290).

GROUP OF 5

1. C: The sentence asks you to find an adjective to describe the word "device." The sentence then lists three positive uses of smart phones. You can conclude that the smart phone is capable of performing many tasks. The correct answer is therefore VERSATILE.

2. E: The sentence asks you to find a pair of antonyms to describe the change in Shelley's outlook on life. The first word must be consistent with "unbridled spirit" and the second word must be consistent with "guarded." The correct answer is therefore OPTIMISM .. CYNICAL (see Word 64).

3. B: This sentence asks you to find a pair of words that are logically connected. The first word must be consistent with the fact that the microbiologist is "indignant." The second word must be consistent with the fact that she defends herself by citing experiments that "had been replicated numerous times." The correct answer is therefore REBUTTED (Word 43) .. IMPARTIAL.

4. A: The sentence asks you to find a pair of logically connected negative words that describe guests who speak "rudely to their host." The correct answer is therefore BOORISH (see Word 111) .. CRUDE (see Word 111).

5. B: The sentence asks you to find a first word that is consistent with the fact that Asimov "published over 500 books" and a second word that is consistent with the definitional word trenchant (see Word 493). The correct answer is therefore PROLIFIC (Word 137) .. INCISIVE.

SENTENCE COMPLETION PRACTICE SET 3 – GROUP OF 8

Directions: Mark the answer for each of the following 8 sentence completion questions. Try to complete the entire set in 5 minutes. When you have finished use the space provided to record how long you took to complete the set and how many questions you answered correctly.

1. The author _____ the widely held view that nuclear power is too risky, arguing that it offers America's best hope to reduce its expensive dependence upon imported oil.
    (A) reciprocates
    (B) abridges
    (C) concedes
    (D) underscores
    (E) disputes

2. The new President quietly sought his predecessor's _____, noting that his counsel in foreign affairs could prove to be invaluable.
    (A) advice
    (B) misconceptions
    (C) transgressions
    (D) distortions
    (E) euphemisms

3. Determined to avoid becoming _____ and predictable, the young fashion designer always attempts to add an element of _____ to his new wardrobes.
    (A) reliable .. tradition
    (B) conventional .. surprise
    (C) erratic .. caprice
    (D) elaborate .. complexity
    (E) predetermined .. monotony

4. While the new proposal to set aside land for a public park is hailed by its _____ as a much needed benefit for the community, its _____ argue that the park will raise taxes by restricting much needed residential development.

    (A) supporters .. advocates
    (B) adversaries .. critics
    (C) antagonists .. zealots
    (D) pundits .. benefactors
    (E) proponents .. detractors

5. Never _____, Anjali was a _____ person whose effervescent personality always enlivened school parties.

    (A) somber .. despondent
    (B) capricious .. whimsical
    (C) obstinate .. stubborn
    (D) reticent .. gregarious
    (E) affable .. cordial

6. The discovery of an effective malaria vaccine was not the result of a single scientific breakthrough, but rather the _____ of a number of research findings.

    (A) confluence
    (B) combustion
    (C) antagonism
    (D) suspension
    (E) repudiation

7. Angry investors denounced the company's president for rigidly following _____ plans that lacked foresight and failed to address important new trends in consumer taste.

    (A) prescient
    (B) trenchant
    (C) myopic
    (D) sagacious
    (E) coherent

8. Experienced political scientists expressed a particularly unfavorable opinion of the novice pundit because her blogs were _____ and _____: they lacked depth and were filled with sarcastic asides.

    (A) provocative .. meditative
    (B) craven .. derogatory
    (C) superficial .. caustic
    (D) subtle .. disingenuous
    (E) profound .. sardonic

TIME: _____

NUMBER CORRECT: _____

SENTENCE COMPLETION PRACTICE SET 3 – GROUP OF 6

Directions: Mark the answer for each of the following 6 sentence completion questions. Try to complete the entire set in 4 minutes. When you have finished use the space provided to record how long you took to complete the set and how many questions you answered correctly.

1. Government regulators charged that banks had engaged in _____ practices by deliberately misleading investors about the true value of their real estate holdings.
   (A) deceptive
   (B) nostalgic
   (C) laudable
   (D) credible
   (E) vital

2. Alaina was a person characterized by _____: she continued to live without hope after suffering many personal losses.
   (A) ambivalence
   (B) lightheartedness
   (C) pessimism
   (D) moderation
   (E) extravagance

3. Kandinsky's series of abstract "Compositions" are _____ in the history of Western art because they had no artistic _____.
   (A) singular .. fallacies
   (B) routine .. peers
   (C) unique .. antecedents
   (D) unsurpassed .. strengths
   (E) obsolete .. predecessors

4. Lincoln quickly discovered that the Southern secessionists were _____ extremists who stubbornly refused to compromise on the issue of extending slavery into the new western territories.
   (A) jovial
   (B) evenhanded
   (C) tenacious
   (D) irresolute
   (E) intrepid

5. Psy invokes the vibrant spirit of K-pop music with great _____ by exhibiting an energetic style that is exuberant and full of vitality.
   (A) empathy
   (B) verve
   (C) reciprocity
   (D) deceit
   (E) decorum

6. It is odd that an architect who once claimed to be _____ now designs such consistently _____ buildings.
   (A) an innovator .. novel
   (B) an iconoclast .. pedestrian
   (C) an optimist .. exuberant
   (D) a maverick .. idiosyncratic
   (E) a pioneer .. unconventional

TIME: _____

NUMBER CORRECT: _____

SENTENCE COMPLETION PRACTICE SET 3 – GROUP OF 5

Directions: Mark the answer for each of the following 5 sentence completion questions. Try to complete the entire set in 3.5 minutes. When you have finished use the space provided to record how long you took to complete the set and how many questions you answered correctly.

1. Owls have the unique and essential ability to rotate their heads 270 degrees in each direction, an _____ trait that enables them to spot prey and avoid predators.
   - (A) unpredictable
   - (B) detrimental
   - (C) incidental
   - (D) indispensible
   - (E) ineffectual

2. Nothing in Anid's speech was _____: he skillfully used short but essential personal _____ to illustrate key points.
   - (A) salient .. sagas
   - (B) exemplary .. allusions
   - (C) supercilious .. hyperboles
   - (D) superfluous .. anecdotes
   - (E) innocuous .. platitudes

3. Rithvik's essays are considered both _____ and _____: they are filled with obscure references and valuable instructional tips.
   - (A) recondite .. didactic
   - (B) arcane .. convoluted
   - (C) succinct .. edifying
   - (D) verbose .. bombastic
   - (E) abstruse .. confounding

4. President Nixon's conduct in the Watergate scandal was so _____ that it tarnished his presidency and brought him great personal dishonor.
   - (A) autonomous
   - (B) circuitous
   - (C) inconspicuous
   - (D) ambiguous
   - (E) ignominious

5. In the age of texting, handwritten letters are rapidly becoming _____: antiquated practices from the pre-smart phone era.
   - (A) enigmatic
   - (B) anachronisms
   - (C) nuanced
   - (D) egregious
   - (E) sedentary

TIME: _____

NUMBER CORRECT: _____

PRACTICE SET 3 – ANSWERS GROUP OF 8

1. E: The author clearly disagrees with the "widely held view that nuclear power is too risky." The correct answer is therefore DISPUTES.

2. A: The key definitional word "counsel" leads you to a positive word that means guidance. The correct answer is therefore ADVICE.

3. B: The sentence asks you to find a pair of antonyms to describe the young fashion designer. The first word must be consistent with "predictable" and the second word must offer a contrast. The correct answer is therefore CONVENTIONAL (Word 2) .. SURPRISE.

4. E: The sentence asks you to find a pair of people who have contrasting views about setting aside land for a public park. The key word "hailed" tells you that the first person will support the park. As a result, the second word must describe a person who is critical of the new park. The correct answer is therefore PROPONENTS (Word 89) ..DETRACTORS.

5. D: The key reversal word "never" tells you to find a pair of antonyms. The second word must be consistent with the key definitional phrase "effervescent personality always enlivened school parties." The correct answer is therefore RETICENT (Word 10) .. GREGARIOUS (Word 323).

6. A: The key reversal word "but" tells you to find a word that is the opposite of a "single" cause. The correct answer is therefore CONFLUENCE (Word 255).

7. C: The key definitional phrase "lacked foresight" tells you to look for a negative word that means shortsighted. The correct answer is therefore MYOPIC (Word 224).

8. C: The sentence asks you to find a first word that is consistent with the definitional phrase "lacked depth" and a second word that is consistent with the definitional phrase "filled with sarcastic asides." The correct answer is therefore SUPERFICIAL (Word 304) .. CAUSTIC (Word 68).

GROUP OF 6

1. A: The key definitional phrase "deliberately misleading" tells you to look for a negative word that means dishonest. The correct answer is therefore DECEPTIVE.

2. C: The key definitional phrase "live without hope" tells you to look for a negative word that means gloomy. The correct answer is therefore PESSIMISM.

3. C: The sentence asks you to find a pair of words that are logically connected. The correct answer is therefore UNIQUE .. ANTECEDENTS (Word 408).

4. C: The key definitional phrase "stubbornly refused to compromise" tells you to look for a word that means determined to hold on to a position. The correct answer is therefore TENACIOUS (Word 447).

5. B: The key definitional word "vibrant" and the key definitional phrase "exuberant and full of vitality" tell you to look for a word that means great energy. The correct answer is therefore VERVE (Word 491).

6. B: The reversal phrase "it is odd" tells you to look for a pair of words in which the second word is an adjective that is not a characteristic of the first word. The correct answer is therefore ICONOCLAST (Word 85) .. PEDESTRIAN (Word 457).

GROUP OF 5

1. D: The key phrase "unique and essential ability" tells you to look for a word that means vital. The correct answer is therefore INDISPENSIBLE.

2. D: The key phrase "short but essential personal" tells you to look for a second word that means a brief story. The reversal phrase "nothing in" tells you to look for a word that is the opposite of essential. The correct answer is therefore SUPERFLUOUS (Word 385) .. ANECDOTES (Word 21).

3. A: The key definitional phrase "filled with obscure references" tells you to look for a first word that means knowledge that is difficult to understand. The key definitional phrase "valuable instructional tips" tells you to look for a second word that means to enlighten. The correct answer is therefore RECONDITE (Word 160) .. DIDACTIC (Word 53).

4. E: The key phrases "tarnished the presidency of" and "great personal dishonor" tell you to look for a word that means great public shame. The correct answer is therefore IGNOMINIOUS (Word 231).

5. B: The key definitional phrase "antiquated practices" tells you to look for a word that describes a practice that is not in the proper time. The correct answer is therefore ANACHRONISMS (Word 212).

PART III

THE ESSENTIAL GUIDE TO PASSAGE-BASED VOCABULARY QUESTIONS

CHAPTER 54
INTRODUCING CRITICAL READING PASSAGES AND QUESTIONS

Chapters 1–47 provide you with definitions and illustrations for 500 key words frequently tested on the SAT. These words will help you become a more articulate writer and speaker. They will also help you achieve a higher critical reading score.

Each SAT contains three sections devoted to critical reading. These sections include a total of nineteen sentence completion questions and 48 passage-based questions. Vocabulary plays a particularly important role in the challenging Level 4 and Level 5 questions. In many ways, the critical reading section can be viewed as a sophisticated vocabulary test.

The critical reading passages and questions on the SAT are designed to measure your abilities as a critical reader. It is important to remember that good readers, like good scientists, writers, and athletes, got that way through practice and hard work.

The "best" approach to reading any material depends on the purpose for which you are reading it. When you take the SAT, you are reading strictly for the purpose of answering 48 passage-based questions. This special purpose requires a variety of unique strategies.

Part III of *The Essential 500 Words* is not designed to provide you with a comprehensive overview for all the passage-based questions. Instead, we will focus on the questions that rely upon a knowledge of *The Essential 500 Words*. Chapter 54 will begin our presentation by discussing key points about critical reading passages and passage-based questions. Chapters 55–58 will explain and illustrate questions that rely upon vocabulary paraphrasing, rhetorical devices, the author's attitude, and vocabulary-in-context. Chapter 59 will provide you with a comprehensive review of these critical reading skills.

THREE TYPES OF PASSAGES

Each SAT contains seven critical reading passages that can be assigned to one of the following three categories:

1. SHORT PASSAGES

Each test contains two short paragraph-length passages. Each of these passages contains ten to fifteen lines and is followed by two questions.

2. LONG PASSAGES

Each test contains three long passages that range from fifty to ninety lines in length. The passages are typically followed by six, nine, or thirteen questions.

3. PAIRED OR DUAL PASSAGES

Each SAT contains two paired or dual passages. The paired passages focus on a related topic. The authors of these passages support, oppose, and sometimes complement each other. The short paired passages are just two paragraphs long and are followed by four questions. The long paired passages contain ninety lines and are followed by thirteen questions.

THREE TYPES OF QUESTIONS

Most SAT passage-based questions can be assigned to one of the following three categories:

1. GENERAL QUESTIONS

General questions test your overall understanding of a passage. They usually ask you to
- identify the main idea, theme, or purpose of a passage
- distinguish the author's attitude, tone, or mood

2. VOCABULARY–IN–CONTEXT QUESTIONS

These questions ask you to infer the meaning of a word or short phrase from its context.

3. SPECIFIC QUESTIONS

These questions ask you about a specific paragraph, sentence, or phrase. Specific questions comprise over two-thirds of all passage-based questions. There are two basic types of specific questions:
- Literal comprehension questions ask you about facts or points directly stated in the passage. The correct answer is usually a restatement or paraphrasing of words found in the text of the passage.
- Extended reasoning questions ask you to draw inferences or conclusions from information stated in the passage. Typical extended reasoning questions ask you to understand the implications of what is stated, follow the logic of an argument, and evaluate the author's assumptions.

ORDER OF DIFFICULTY

As you have seen, sentence completion questions are presented in order of difficulty. In contrast, passage-based questions are NOT presented in order of difficulty. As a result, you may find that the first two questions are very difficult. Don't despair! Every passage is followed by easy, medium, and hard questions.

Passages, like the questions, will also vary in difficulty. As a general rule two of the seven passages will be relatively easy, three will be medium, and two will be challenging. However, the degree of difficulty of a passage is subjective and will vary from reader to reader. For example, students who enjoy science may find a difficult science passage easy and an easy social science passage quite challenging.

TIME ALLOCATION

The critical reading passages require time and concentration. As a general rule you should allow about seventy seconds for each passage-based question. One way to quickly compute how much time you need for a passage is to add the number 2 to the total number of questions following a passage. For example, you should allocate fifteen minutes to a paired passage that contains thirteen questions.

BASIC STRATEGIES FOR ATTACKING THE PASSAGES

Many students expect to read a passage and then quickly answer all the questions. They then become frustrated when this strategy doesn't work. Don't allow yourself to become frustrated. Reading SAT passages requires a sound strategy. Here are seven keys to developing a successful strategy for attacking critical reading passages:

1. ALWAYS READ THE INTRODUCTORY BLURB

Most critical reading passages begin with an italicized blurb. Don't skip these brief but vital paragraphs. The blurb sets the stage for the passage. For example, in fictional passages the blurb identifies the principle characters and succinctly explains how they are related.

2. DON'T READ THE QUESTIONS FIRST

On some tests it might be a good idea to read the questions first. However, this common sense approach is not an effective strategy for the SAT. Many SAT passages contain 9 to 13 questions. Reading these questions first will overwhelm your short term memory and waste valuable time. Reading the questions first really means that you have to read questions twice, which will take far too much time. There are 48 critical reading questions on the SAT. Don't turn them into 96.

3. READ A PARAGRAPH AND THEN ANSWER THE QUESTIONS

The overwhelming majority of SAT passage-based questions are micro questions that are rooted in specific lines within a specific paragraph. Take advantage of these line references by first reading a paragraph and then answering the questions that are rooted in that paragraph. This "back-and-forth" strategy is focused and efficient.

4. ANSWER THE MAIN IDEA QUESTIONS LAST

Many SAT passages will begin with a main idea question. Do not let these questions tempt you into reading the entire passage. Instead, simply skip these macro questions and answer them last. Remember, when you complete the "back-and-forth" method you will have read the entire passage and will then be prepared to answer all the general questions.

5. DIVIDE AND CONQUER THE PAIRED PASSAGES

On first glance a paired passage may look twice as hard as a single passage. Fortunately, appearances are deceiving. There is no reason for you to be worried. The best way to approach a paired passage is to cut it down to size by utilizing the following four step "divide and conquer" strategy:

• First, glance at the questions and label them P1 (for Passage 1), P2 (for Passage 2), or B (for Both).
• Second, read Passage 1 and then answer the Passage 1 questions.
• Third, read Passage 2 and then answer the Passage 2 questions.
• Fourth, now that you have read both passages attack the Both questions. It is important to note that test writers often place two or even three Both questions at the beginning of the question sequence. This tactic is designed to tempt you into first reading both passages. Don't fall for this trick!

6. DON'T STUDY THE PASSAGES

SAT critical reading passages are not homework assignments. The passages will not be snatched from you when you get to the questions. So don't try to memorize specific information such as names and dates. Remember, the questions only draw from a relatively small percentage of the information in a typical passage.

7. DON'T GIVE UP

Many students report feeling lost and bored as they work on critical reading passages. Don't expect to enjoy each SAT passage. The passages are not intended to entertain you; they are intended to evaluate your critical reading skills. The critical reading passages are the ultimate test of your indomitable will. Stay mentally alert and don't quit. Remember, your job is to get a feel for the passage so you can answer the questions and earn points.

CHAPTER 55
CRITICAL READING
» RECOGNIZING A PARAPHRASE

Carefully examine the following pairs of phrases:

COLUMN A
Overpowering and threatening
Vast and infinite
Unable to agree
Widespread appeal

COLUMN B
Overwhelming and intimidating
An immense expanse
A lack of consensus
Pervasive attention

What relationship does each pair of phrases have in common? Each phrase in COLUMN B is a paraphrase or rewording of a phrase in COLUMN A. We frequently use paraphrasing in our everyday conversations. For example, if your best friend misses a class, you would help him or her by paraphrasing key points from the lesson.

THE GOLDEN RULE

Many passage-based questions ask you to understand information presented in the passage. The correct answer is often a paraphrase or restatement of words found directly in the text. A correct answer is thus based upon what is stated in the passage. When answering passage-based questions always remember this Golden Rule: AN ANSWER IS AN ANSWER BECAUSE IT HAS SUPPORT IN THE PASSAGE. This support will take the form of key words, phrases, and examples. Never go outside the passage to find support for your answers.

CASE EXAMPLES

Knowing how to identify a paraphrase is an important skill for answering passage-based questions. Always match your answers with key material contained in the passage. The following three examples are designed to introduce you to the skill of recognizing a paraphrase.

1. **The sheer novelty of the first talking pictures mesmerized audiences, but their vapid content and banal dialogue dismayed critics.**

    Which of the following best describes how audiences responded to the first talking pictures?
    (A) outrage
    (B) disappointment
    (C) indifference
    (D) ambivalence
    (E) fascination

    The question asks you how audiences responded to the first talking movies. According to the passage, the audiences were "mesmerized" by the new invention. The key word "mesmerized" will lead you to the positive answer choice (E) FASCINATION. Note that if the question had asked you how the critics responded to the talking pictures the word "dismayed" would have led you to the negative answer choice (B) DISAPPOINTMENT.

2. **A good investigative reporter must ask probing and even embarrassing questions. Like the great muckrakers in the early 1900s, a journalist must dispute accepted facts and argue with officials who attempt to conceal the truth.**

    The "officials" (line 5) would most likely describe the narrator as
    (A) genial
    (B) profound
    (C) contentious
    (D) charismatic
    (E) misunderstood

The question asks you how the "officials" would most likely describe the narrator. According to the passage, narrator would "dispute" facts and "argue" with officials. These key words will lead you to choice (C) CONTENTIOUS (Word 258). Note that this is a Level 5 question because it contains difficult vocabulary. However, if you have mastered *The Essential 500 Words* in Chapters 1 – 47 then this question should have been easy. This underscores an important paradox – on the SAT the hard questions are easy if you know the vocabulary!

3. **I don't know why I thought your Mama Day would be a big, tall woman. From the stories you told about your clashes with her, she had loomed that way in my mind. Hard. Strong. Yes, it definitely showed in the set of her shoulders. But she was barely five feet and could have been snapped in the middle with one good-sized hand…"I'm Mama Day to some, Miss Miranda to others. You decide what I'll be to you." That type of straightforward honesty would cheapen anyone returning less than the same.**
    (from *Mama Day* by Gloria Naylor)

    Lines 1 – 13 characterize Mama Day as being
    (A) decrepit and even senile
    (B) vigorous but also duplicitous
    (C) diminutive and supercilious
    (D) forceful and forthright
    (E) brusque and aloof

Questions 1 and 2 asked you to match key words from a passage with a single-word answer choice. In contrast, Question 3 asks you to match key words from a passage with two-word answer choices. It is very important to understand that both words must be supported by the passage. A favorite test writer trick is to provide you with an answer choice in which one of the words is supported by the passage while the second word is unsupported. For example, in choice (C) Mama Day is diminutive or small but she is not supercilious or arrogant. Mama Day is best described as FORCEFUL because she is "Hard" and "Strong" and FORTHRIGHT because of her "straightforward honesty."

PRACTICE EXAMPLES

The following 10 examples are designed to give you an opportunity to practice the skill of identifying answers that paraphrase words found directly in the text. Circle the correct answer.

1. Today, standing at the base of the Great Pyramid at Giza, millions of awed tourists have asked themselves: "How could this mountain of stone have been built by people who had not even begun to use the wheel?" Each perfectly cut stone block weighs at least 2.5 tons. Some weigh 15 tons. More than 2 million of these blocks are stacked with precision to a height of 481 feet. The entire structure covers more than 13 acres.

   The author's description emphasizes the Great Pyramid's
   (A) aesthetic beauty
   (B) impressive size
   (C) diverse functions
   (D) economic importance
   (E) isolated location

2. Coach McClamrock's rules were as fixed as the laws of physics. And they were clearly spelled out.

   Coach McClamrock's rules are described as
   (A) immutable and punitive
   (B) elusive and unpredictable
   (C) biased and scholarly
   (D) unvarying and definitive
   (E) superfluous and universal

3. Ninety-five percent of Greenland is covered by ice. Towns and villages cling to the coastline; at their backs loom glaciers a thousand meters thick: gleaming, white, blue, clear, transparent ice.
   (from *Frozen Earth* by Doug Macdougall)

   Which of the following words best describe the towns and villages?
   (A) wretched and forlorn
   (B) defiant and truculent
   (C) imperturbable and incomprehensible
   (D) volatile and frivolous
   (E) exposed and vulnerable

4. As the first female Hispanic judge in a small Georgia town, Ms. Hernandez made certain that she rendered her decisions in a calm, unvarying voice, since opinions tentatively offered were usually questioned. If she chose to talk to the press at all she made sure that she was both clear and succinct. She didn't want to be either misquoted or interrupted.

   As described in lines 1 – 9, Ms. Hernandez's manner of speaking is best characterized as
   (A) oddly melancholy
   (B) intentionally incoherent
   (C) carefully calculated
   (D) overtly hostile
   (E) noticeably irreverent

5. Although Mr. Myers rarely smiled, he was both compassionate and considerate of others. However, his lofty bearing and reserved temperament left many with the erroneous impression that he was cold and detached.

   Mr. Myers manner is best described as
   (A) sympathetic but aloof
   (B) imperious but jovial
   (C) surreptitious and beguiling
   (D) sarcastic and flippant
   (E) prudent and impulsive

6. Art historian Marilyn Stokestad argues that in all of known history only three major artists appeared on the scene by themselves: 14th century Renaissance artist Giotto, 17th century Baroque artist Caravaggio, and 20th century Cubist artist Picasso. Every other artist was part of a movement or a specific style.

The passage indicates that Giotto, Caravaggio, and Picasso are best viewed as
  (A) artistic anomalies
  (B) inspired dilettantes
  (C) rival contemporaries
  (D) precocious novices
  (E) benevolent mentors

7. I realized from the beginning that Mr. Williams was a natural teacher. But he was not a great educator in any conventional sense. Of course he had a deep understanding of all the seminal words of American literature. But he also had an intuitive grasp of his teenage students. He repeatedly demonstrated an uncanny ability to link our lives to great works of literature. And most of all, he was a talented raconteur who enthralled us with his personal anecdotes.

As explained by the narrator, Mr. Williams is best described as
  (A) genial but soporific
  (B) redundant but taciturn
  (C) visceral but reticent
  (D) erudite but superficial
  (E) gifted but unorthodox

8. The ancient Sumerians worshipped over 3,000 different gods. Archaeologists speculate that the Sumerians created clay dolls of their gods to help their children learn how to identify their various deities. The dolls thus functioned as learning tools and not as venerated sacred objects.

According to the passage, archaeologists speculate that the Sumerians used clay dolls of their gods as
  (A) didactic tools
  (B) revered idols
  (C) frivolous toys
  (D) nostalgic relics
  (E) popular heroes

9. I grew up on what seemed at the time like the edge of the world – in a remote corner of northeastern Tennessee. Our humble home had few books or magazines, and no television. Apart from a few people who occasionally visited Johnson City, virtually nobody we knew travelled outside our county. We lived in a closed society that thought of itself as self-sufficient.

The author characterizes the environment in which he grew up as
  (A) bohemian and quirky
  (B) provincial and autonomous
  (C) peripheral but scintillating
  (D) pastoral but chaotic
  (E) drab but unique

10. When *Luncheon on the Grass* by Edouard Manet was first exhibited at the 1863 Salon des Refuses in Paris it created a sensation. The painting was both embraced and reviled. Outraged critics accused Manet of deliberately provoking a scandal. But his small group of avant-garde defenders lauded the work as a groundbreaking challenge to the rigid conventions of academic art. Today, *Luncheon on the Grass* is widely acclaimed as the first modern painting and Manet is recognized as the first modern artist.

The passage indicates that in 1863 *Luncheon on the Grass* was met with
(A) universal praise
(B) unquestioning derision
(C) perfunctory queries
(D) measured assessments
(E) antithetical judgments

The painting *Luncheon on the Grass* is best described as
(A) an egregious error in judgment
(B) a watershed event in Western art
(C) a provocative but fleeting work of art
(D) a pioneering work that appealed to traditionalists
(E) a diversion from the historic events taking place in Paris in 1863

ANSWERS

1. B: The author emphasizes the Great Pyramid's vast weight and size by telling us that the structure is 481 feet high and covers 13 acres. These details support (B) IMPRESSIVE SIZE.

2. D: The passage tells us that Coach McClamrock's rules were "fixed" and "clearly spelled out." These key words support (D) UNVARYING and DEFINITIVE. It is interesting to note that the passage does support immutable or unchanging in choice (A). However, the passage does not support describing the rules as punitive or punishing.

3. E: According to the passage the "towns and villages cling to the coastline" while enormous glaciers "loom" above them. The key words "cling" and "loom" indicate that the towns and villages occupy an unprotected and thus (E) EXPOSED and VULNERABLE position along the coastline. The passage does not support wretched (pitiful) and forlorn (despondent); defiant (rebellious) and truculent (belligerent); imperturbable (calm) and incomprehensible (bewildering); or volatile (very changeable) and frivolous (silly).

4. C: The passage provides a great deal of information to support describing Ms. Hernandez's manner of speaking as (C) CAREFULLY CALCULATED. For example, her decisions are not "tentative." In addition, Judge Hernandez always makes sure that her interaction with the press is "both clear and succinct" and therefore not careless or impromptu. As a person who carefully calculates her words, Judge Hernandez does not want to be "either misquoted or interrupted."

5. A: The key words "compassionate," "considerate," and "reserved" all support choice (A) SYMPATHETIC but ALOOF (Word 373). Although imperious in choice (B) is supported by Mr. Myers' "lofty bearing" there is no evidence to support describing him as jovial or humorous.

6. A: This passage tells us that Giotto, Caravaggio, and Picasso are all atypical because they each "appeared on the scene by themselves." They are therefore artistic ANOMALIES (Word 19) since "every other artist was part of a movement or a specific style."

7. E: The key phrases "natural teacher," "deep understanding," and "talented raconteur" all support GIFTED in choice (E). The key phrase "not a great educator in any conventional sense" supports the second word UNORTHODOX in choice (E). Mr. Williams is therefore best described as GIFTED but UNORTHODOX (Word 163).

8. A: The key phrase "learning tools" supports describing the clay dolls as DIDACTIC (Word 53) tools. You can eliminate choice (B) because the dolls were not used as venerated or revered objects.

9. B: The key phrases "remote corner" and "closed society" both support PROVINCIAL (see Word 478). This is further supported by the fact that the author's home had "few books or magazines, and no television." In addition, very few people travelled outside the author's home county. The author concludes by saying that the people believed they were "self-sufficient." This clearly supports the second word in choice (B) AUTONOMOUS or self-reliant.

10. E: The passage tells us that *Luncheon on the Grass* was both "embraced and reviled." It is important to note that embraced is a positive word. In contrast, reviled is a very negative word that means to scorn or denounce. This pair of antonyms clearly supports choice (E) ANTITHETICAL (Word 11) judgments.
B: The passage underscores the importance of *Luncheon on the Grass* by concluding that it is "the first modern painting." This clearly supports calling the work "a WATERSHED (Word 216)

event in Western art." Note that the first part of choice (D) "a pioneering work" is correct. However, the second part of this answer "that appealed to traditionalists" is incorrect. Be alert for answers that are half true and half false. Test writers often use this trick to lure students into choosing a wrong answer.

CHAPTER 56
CRITICAL READING – IDENTIFYING RHETORICAL DEVICES

What do the terms SIMILE, PARADOX, and PARALLEL STRUCTURE have in common? All three are rhetorical devices that you have probably studied in your language arts and literature classes. All three are frequently tested in SAT passage-based questions. And finally, all three are discussed and illustrated in Chapter 3 of this book.

In recent years College Board test writers have begun to ask more and more rhetorical device questions. These questions are not difficult if you have a full command of the key rhetorical devices discussed and illustrated in Chapters 3 and 4. This chapter is designed to give you an opportunity to apply these terms to passage-based questions.

CASE EXAMPLES

Knowing how to identify rhetorical devices is an important skill for achieving a high critical reading score. The following three examples are designed to introduce you to how rhetorical devices are used in SAT passages and questions.

1. **The apple-green Cadillac with the white vinyl roof and Florida plates turned into Brewster like a greased cobra.**
   (from *The Women of Brewster Place* by Gloria Naylor)

   Lines 1 – 3 make use of which of the following rhetorical devices?
   (A) Simile
   (B) Understatement
   (C) Satire
   (D) Irony
   (E) Paradox

   Lines 1 – 3 contain a very vivid SIMILE (Word 23) that compares a Cadillac to a "greased cobra." SIMILES are one of the most frequently tested rhetorical devices. Always remember that a SIMILE is often introduced by the words "like" or "as."

2. **Uncle Amos stood out splendidly above all my uncles because he did not stand out at all. That was his distinction. He was the averagest man I ever knew.**
   (from *My Average Uncle Amos* by Robert P. T. Coffin)

   The statement in lines 1 – 3 ("Uncle Amos .. all") is an example of
   (A) a metaphor
   (B) a euphemism
   (C) a paradox
   (D) an understatement
   (E) an irony

   The statement in lines 1 – 3 is an excellent example of a PARADOX (Word 26). The author uses a contradictory statement to illustrate a truth about his uncle. Always remember that a PARADOX is based upon a contradiction.

3. **I have the right to education. I have the right to play. I have the right to sing. I have the right to talk. I have the right to go to market. I have the right to speak up. (from a 2011 interview with Malala Yousufzai)**

   Lines 1 – 4 ("I have .. up") are notable chiefly for their use of
   (A) hyperbole
   (B) understatement
   (C) paraphrase
   (D) vignette
   (E) parallel structure

   Malala's eloquent statement uses PARALLEL STRUCTURE (Word 30) to underscore her passion and commitment to the cause of women's rights in Pakistan. Malala's repetition of the phrase "I have the right to" provides a particularly powerful example of PARALLEL STRUCTURE. It is important to point out that College Board test writers sometimes use REPETITION as an answer choice instead of PARALLEL STRUCTURE. Don't let this confuse you. The two terms are equivalent.

PRACTICE EXAMPLES

The following 10 examples are designed to give you an opportunity to practice the skill of identifying rhetorical devices. Circle the correct answer.

1. **New York City is an ever-changing kaleidoscope of revealing human interactions. For example, I once stood in a long line at a popular Central Park vending stand. A well-known celebrity saw the line and walked around to the back of the cart where I heard him ask if he could avoid the line. When the vendor refused, the pompous celebrity indignantly asked, "Don't you know who I am?" Like a true Jacksonian democrat, the egalitarian vendor replied, "Of course! But you still gotta wait in line!"**

This passage makes use of which of the following rhetorical devices?
   I.   Metaphor
   II. Allusion
   III. Anecdote

   (A) I only
   (B) II only
   (C) I and II only
   (D) II and III only
   (E) I, II, and III

2. **Nobody else could see much of anything through this telescope, nor did I have a great deal of initial success, lacking experience as I did – and having been a bit unnerved when, on one of my first attempts to use the thing, I looked through its four-power finder scope and was confronted by the grotesquely magnified image of a flying cockroach who had just landed on the tube and was scurrying away.**
   (from *Seeing in the Dark* by Timothy Ferris)

This paragraph makes use of which rhetorical device?
   (A) A witty lampoon
   (B) A hypothetical conjecture
   (C) An obscure allusion
   (D) A humorous anecdote
   (E) A dramatic hyperbole

3. **Countless suspicious eyes followed Dorothea Lange as she entered a sprawling cardboard slum that its Depression-era residents called a "Hooverville." As she approached a homeless woman the famed photographer asked, "How are you today?" The destitute but proud woman looked Lange directly in the eye and said, "Let me give you a tour of my cardboard palace."**

The homeless woman's use of the word "palace" (line 10) is best characterized as
   (A) anecdotal
   (B) belligerent
   (C) ironic
   (D) conditional
   (E) neighborly

4. **Uhmma's hands are as old as sand. They have always been old, even when they were young. In the mornings, they would scratch across our sleeping faces as she smoothed our foreheads, our cheeks, and tell us quietly, Wake up. Time for school.**
   (from *A Step From Heaven* by An Na)

The paragraph makes use of which of the following rhetorical devices?
   I.   Simile
   II. Understatement
   III. Paradox

   (A) I only
   (B) II only
   (C) I and II only
   (D) I and III only
   (E) II and III only

5. The question "Why have there been no great women artists?" is simply the top tenth of an iceberg of misinterpretation and misconception; beneath lies a vast dark bulk of shaky ideas about the nature of art and its situational concomitants, about the nature of human abilities in general and of human excellence in particular, and the role that the social order plays in all this.
(from *Why Have There Been No Great Women Artists* by Linda Nochlin)

The iceberg (line 3) functions as
   (A) a satirical commentary
   (B) an apt metaphor
   (C) a subtle understatement
   (D) a personal anecdote
   (E) an extended allegory

6. Menhaden have always been an integral, if unheralded, part of America's history. This was the fish that Native Americans taught the Pilgrims to plant with their corn. This was the fish that made larger-scale agriculture viable in the eighteenth and early nineteenth centuries for those farming the rocky soils of New England and Long Island. As the industrial revolution transformed the nation, this was the fish whose oil literally greased the wheels of manufacture, supplanting whale oil as a principal industrial lubricant and additive by the 1870s.
(from *The Most Important Fish in the Sea: The Menhaden and America* by H. Bruce Franklin)

Lines 3 – 11 are notable for their use of
   (A) repetition
   (B) outrageous hyperbole
   (C) symbolic motifs
   (D) play on words
   (E) parenthetical expression

7. Marine biologist Sara Gottlieb, author of a groundbreaking study on menhaden's filtering capability, compares their role with the human liver's: "Just as your body needs its liver to filter out toxins, ecosystems also need those natural filters." Overfishing menhaden, she says, "is just like removing your liver."
(from *The Most Important Fish in the Sea: The Menhaden and America* by H. Bruce Franklin)

Sara Gottlieb makes use of which of the following rhetorical devices?
   (A) Analogy
   (B) Allusion
   (C) Personification
   (D) Euphemism
   (E) Hyperbole

8. I remember the walk we took one morning… About halfway down the beach there was a tall wooden platform shaped like a castle turret. During the summer months lifeguards stood up there and kept an eye on the swimmers…I simply couldn't believe that I was about to move to a place where there was no ocean… Because the ocean had always been there, in good times as well as the bad times of my life…the tide rising and falling just as it always did, no matter what and it seemed to me that even if you weren't actively letting your emotions ride its surface, the ocean still went on giving you something, teaching you some sort of lesson.
(from *Goodbye Tsugumi* by Banana Yoshimoto)

The author makes use of which of the following rhetorical devices?
   I. Analogy
   II. Figurative language
   III. Personification

   (A) I only
   (B) II only
   (C) I and II only
   (D) I and III only
   (E) II and III only

9. It's April 1979, and I'm standing in a crowded living room on the Upper Westside, sipping wine and surveying the surroundings. The room, modest except for the walls lined with magisterial bookshelves – this is mostly a literary, or at least a writing crowd – is buzzing with the noise of animated group-talk… In the group next to me, the subject of discussion is X, a well-known writer and literary critic whose opinions, in the opinion of this group, are terribly wrong. "The man has a regrettable penchant for Saul Bellow. It's his Achilles heel," a short, pudgy man pronounced with languid deliberation.
(from *Lost in Translation* by Eva Hoffman)

The passage makes use of which of the following rhetorical devices?
(A) Literary allusion
(B) Hyperbole
(C) Qualification
(D) Rebuttal
(E) Paradox

10. The sightseer (at the Grand Canyon) may be aware that something is wrong. He may simply be bored; or he may be conscious of the difficulty: that the great natural wonder yawning at his feet somehow eludes him. The harder he looks at it the less he can see. It eludes everybody.
(from *The Message in the Bottle* by Walter Percy)

The passage includes an example of which rhetorical device?
(A) Extended anecdote
(B) Dramatic foil
(C) Humorous caricature
(D) Paradox
(E) Euphemism

ANSWERS

1. E: In order for METAPHOR to be the correct answer the author must compare two unrelated objects. The opening sentence meets this test by comparing New York City to "an ever-changing kaleidoscope." In order for ALLUSION to be the correct answer there must be a reference to a historical or literary person or place. The passage meets this test when the author calls the vendor "a true Jacksonian democrat." This is an ALLUSION to the value President Andrew Jackson placed on the importance of common man. In order for ANECDOTE to be the correct answer there must be a short story intended to illustrate a key point. The story about the street vendor meets this test by illustrating the egalitarian nature of contemporary American social norms. The correct answer is E since the passage includes a METAPHOR (Word 24), ALLUSION (Word 33), and ANECDOTE (Word 21).

2. D: In order for ANECDOTE to be the correct answer there must be a short, personal story that illustrates a key point. The description in this passage meets both of these tests. The story is short, personal, and it illustrates the author's lack of initial success. The correct answer is therefore ANECDOTE (Word 21). Note that by College Board standards this is a humorous story!

3. C: In order for IRONY to be the correct answer the author must say one thing while implying something else. The homeless woman's use of the word "palace" meets this test. A palace is a large opulent building. In contrast, the woman actually lives in a cardboard shack. The correct answer is therefore IRONIC (Word 28).

4. D: In order for SIMILE to be the correct answer the author must use like or as to compare two unlike things. The description in line 1 meets this test since Uhmma's hands are compared to sand. In addition, the passage contains a PARADOX since the author describes

Uhmma's hands as being "old, even when they were young." This contradictory statement expresses a truth about Uhmma. The correct answer is therefore SIMILE (Word 23) and PARADOX (Word 26).

5. B: In order for METAPHOR to be the correct answer the author must compare two unrelated objects without using like or as. The author uses the iceberg as a METAPHOR for a huge mass of "misinterpretation and misconception." The correct answer is therefore AN APT METAPHOR (Word 24).

6. A: In order for REPETITION to be the correct answer the author must repeat words and phrases that are similar in meaning and structure. The author's repetition of the phrase "This was the fish" meets this test. The correct answer is therefore REPETITION. Note that PARALLEL STRUCTURE (Word 30) would also have been a correct answer.

7. A: In order for ANALOGY to be the correct answer an author must compare an unfamiliar idea or object with a familiar one. Sara Gottlieb's quote meets this test by comparing the menhaden's filtering function with the human liver's filtering function. The correct answer is therefore ANALOGY (Word 36).

8. E: In order for FIGURATIVE LANGUAGE to be the correct answer an author must use either a SIMILE or a METAPHOR or both. The author meets this test by comparing the "tall wooden platform" to a "castle turret." In addition, the author uses PERSONIFICATION by giving the ocean the human ability to teach a lesson. The correct answer is therefore FIGURATIVE LANGUAGE (See Words 23 and 24) and PERSONIFICATION (Word 25).

9. A: In order for LITERARY ALLUSION to be the correct answer the passage must include a direct reference to an author, work of literature, or literary figure. The passage meets this test by referring to both the well-known twentieth century author Saul Bellow and the legendary Greek hero Achilles. The correct answer is therefore LITERARY ALLUSION (Word 337).

10. D: In order for PARADOX to be the correct answer the passage must include a contradictory statement that expresses a truth. The sentence, "The harder he looks at it the less he can see," meets this test. The correct answer is therefore PARADOX (Word 26).

CHAPTER 57

CRITICAL READING – IDENTIFYING AN AUTHOR'S ATTITUDE, TONE, AND MOOD

Take a close look at the following list of words. What do they all have in common?

- HAPPINESS
- SADNESS
- FEAR
- ANGER
- SURPRISE
- DISGUST

Each of these words describes a different mood. A MOOD is a predominant emotion. If you are with a friend, how can you determine if he or she is angry or happy? In our everyday conversations, we pay close attention to a person's tone of voice and body language. For example, a person who is angry will often raise his or her voice and frown.

Interpreting a person's mood requires good human relation skills. Interpreting a writer's mood requires a good vocabulary and good critical reading skills. Each author has an ATTITUDE, or state of mind, toward the subject he or she is writing about. While authors cannot literally frown or smile at the reader, they can reveal their attitudes by the descriptive phrases and examples they use.

ATTITUDE, MOOD, AND TONE QUESTIONS

SAT test writers often ask you to determine an author's attitude, mood, or tone. These questions are easy to spot. Here are examples of the formats used on typical tests:

- The author's attitude toward X is best described as
- The author's tone in the passage is best described as
- The tone of lines xx – yy is best described as
- The author uses the word _____ to express
- The author's attitude toward X changed from _____ to _____
- Compared to the tone of Passage 1, the tone of Passage 2 is more _____

THE IMPORTANCE OF USING POSITIVE AND NEGATIVE WORDS

In Chapter 51 you learned how to use positive and negative words to help you answer sentence completion questions. The same skill can help you master attitude, tone, and mood questions. Since most of these questions direct you to a sentence or paragraph, always carefully examine these lines for positive and negative words and phrases. Positive words and phrases indicate that the author approves a person, place, or idea. Negative words and phrases indicate that the author disapproves of a person, place, or idea. Once you have gained a sense of whether the author is positive or negative about a subject delete the choices that do not reflect this view. Chapters 6 – 8 define and illustrate 30 key attitude, tone, and mood words.

CASE EXAMPLES

Knowing how to identify an author's attitude, tone, and mood is an important skill for achieving a high critical reading score. The following two examples are designed to illustrate how key words can completely change an author's attitude toward a subject.

1. **For as long as I can remember, in our town people idolized Coach J. D. Harris and spoke about him with awe and respect. Both his former and current players praise Coach Harris' dedication, work ethic, and ability to inspire his teams to perform at a championship level.**

   According to the narrator, the town's attitude toward Coach Harris is best characterized as
   (A) indifferent
   (B) disdainful
   (C) adulatory
   (D) amused
   (E) ambivalent

   The narrator uses a number of positive words to describe how the town views Coach Harris. For example, he is an "idolized figure" who is spoken of with "awe and respect." In addition, his players all consistently praise Coach Harris. These positive descriptive words all support ADULATORY (Word 401) as the correct answer to this question.

2. **For as long as anyone can remember, Coach J.D. Harris has been a controversial figure in our town where he is spoken about with both awe and jealousy. Both his former and current players praise Coach Harris' determination, work ethic, and ability to inspire his teams to perform at a championship level. However, former assistant coaches describe Coach Harris as vain, autocratic, and willing to do anything to win.**

   According to the narrator, the town's attitude toward Coach Harris is best characterized as
   (A) indifferent
   (B) disdainful
   (C) adulatory
   (D) amused
   (E) ambivalent

   Note that the narrator now tempers his portrayal of how the town views Coach Harris. For example, he is now described as a "controversial figure" who is spoken of with both "awe and jealousy." While Coach Harris' players continue to praise his performance, his assistant coaches have a negative view. They describe Coach Harris as "vain" and "autocratic." Taken together, these mixed views support AMBIVALENT (Word 71) as the correct answer to this question.

PRACTICE EXAMPLES

The following 10 examples are designed to give you an opportunity to practice the skill of identifying an author's attitude, tone, and mood. Circle the correct answers,

1. On October 4, 1957 the Soviet Union stunned the world by launching Sputnik, the first human-made satellite to orbit the Earth. The American public worried about what this ominous event meant and impatiently waited to see how President Eisenhower would respond.

   The American public's attitude toward the launch of Sputnik can best be described as
   (A) energized
   (B) belligerent
   (C) skeptical
   (D) apprehensive
   (E) despondent

2. The director's meticulous attention to plot, dialogue, and costume are among the highlights of a brilliant film that clearly establish Sanjana Mehta as a rising star in the film industry.

   The tone of the sentence is best described as
   (A) scathing
   (B) effusive
   (C) cryptic
   (D) maudlin
   (E) exasperated

3. Jazz is filled with eccentrics – idiosyncratic people with odd habits and prickly personalities. Jelly Roll Morton, however, is at the head of the pack. A boaster, con man, liar, gambler, he nonetheless possessed a winning charm and a high musical intelligence. He claimed to have invented jazz and, like the boxer Muhammad Ali, insisted that he was its greatest practitioner, but in his music he was both honest and deadly serious. (from The Great Jazz Artists, by James Lincoln Collier)

The author's attitude toward Jelly Roll Morton is best described as
   (A) open disdain
   (B) undisguised envy
   (C) evenhanded respect
   (D) nostalgic regret
   (E) amused skepticism

4. There is only one way to shield the United States from the deleterious effects produced by our national addiction to fossil fuels. We must launch a sustained program to develop such green alternatives as wind and solar power. Such a farsighted policy will yield numerous benefits. It will end our dangerous dependence upon importing oil from nations that are often hostile to our national interest. It will also spur economic growth by creating new industries and new jobs.

   The tone of lines 1 – 13 ("There is .. jobs") is best described as
   (A) unequivocal
   (B) impartial
   (C) resigned
   (D) triumphant
   (E) whimsical

5. The Anasazi, or Ancient Ones, lived in the valleys and canyons of the American Southwest. Like other people in pre-Columbian America, the Anasazi did not have horses, mules, or the wheel. Instead, they relied on human labor to quarry sandstone from the canyon walls and move it to the site. Skilled builders then used a mud-like mortar to construct walls up to five stories high.

   The author's overall tone in lines 1 – 10 ("The Anasazi .. high") is best described as
   (A) disdainful and judgmental
   (B) brooding and distant
   (C) bewildered and incredulous
   (D) concerned and inquisitive
   (E) objective and scholarly

6. Almost 200,000 Jews managed to survive the horrors of the Nazi death camps. Many clung to life so that they could bear witness to what had happened. The survivors' efforts were not in vain. When a Nazi commander named Adolf Eichman was asked about his hideous deeds, he replied, "I will obey, obey, obey." The Holocaust demonstrated that evil orders must never be obeyed and that the values of tolerance and respect for others must be preserved.
(from *World History Perspectives on the Past* by Larry Krieger)

The author's tone in the final sentence ("The Holocaust .. preserved") is best characterized as
  (A) condescending
  (B) sardonic
  (C) dismissive
  (D) intrigued
  (E) didactic

7. Growing up in the Lower East Side of New York City I experienced a jarring juxtaposition of cultures. At school I learned about my new American homeland and its democratic government. But when the final bell rang, the densely packed streets and impersonal playgrounds became my new classrooms. I quickly learned to avoid the suspicious eyes of vigilant shopkeepers watching for young shoplifters. I was wary of both worlds. I knew the Gettysburg Address by heart and I also knew how to read and understand the silent language of the street. I soon became someone else. It wasn't hard to imagine that great dangers lay ahead.

The author's overall attitude toward the Lower East Side is best described as
  (A) unalloyed fear
  (B) weary cynicism
  (C) cautious unease
  (D) cheerful optimism
  (E) studied neutrality

8. The belief that teenagers will inevitably succumb to peer pressure is both widespread and erroneous.

The tone of this statement is best described as
  (A) caustic
  (B) dismayed
  (C) emphatic
  (D) ambivalent
  (E) apologetic

9. I thought about my late husband as I sat beneath our favorite tree. I am sure I had a soft, distant smile on my face as I remembered our shared dreams. We always imagined a happy retirement blessed with good health. But then cancer took away our future and I am left with a slow and painful dance with grief.

The narrator's mood in lines 1 – 6 ("I thought .. health") is best characterized as
  (A) wistful
  (B) lighthearted
  (C) exasperated
  (D) morose
  (E) nonchalant

10. Margaret Miller always liked to pretend that she would do poorly on our calculus tests. She insisted that she didn't understand the material and was sure to fail the next big test. Of course, when no one was looking, Margaret was hard at work studying. In addition to our textbook, she studied several prep books and even hired a tutor from the local community college. When the test day finally arrived, Margaret was fully prepared. I glanced at her during the test and what do you know – her fingers effortlessly hit the buttons on her expensive calculator and the correct answer miraculously flashed on her screen. Needless to say, Margaret modestly attributed her high score to good luck.

In context, which best describes the author's tone in the final two sentences ("I glanced .. luck")?
(A) empathetic
(B) measured
(C) confounded
(D) sardonic
(E) laudatory

ANSWERS

1. **D:** The American public's attitude toward the launch of Sputnik is defined by the key words "worried" and "impatiently." These words will lead you to select an answer that conveys a feeling of unease and misgiving. The correct answer is therefore APPREHENSIVE.

2. **B:** The tone of this sentence is conveyed in the series of positive words that the author uses to describe Sanjana's work. The key words "meticulous" "brilliant," and "a rising star" all convey a feeling of lavish and unrestrained praise. The correct answer is therefore EFFUSIVE (Word 209).

3. **C:** The author's attitude toward Jelly Roll Morton is complex. On the one hand, he lists a series of negatives that include describing Morton as "a boaster, con man, liar, gambler." However, these negative traits are balanced by the author's list of positive characteristics that include "a winning charm," and "high musical intelligence." The author thus provides an EVENHANDED (Word 75) description of Jelly Roll Martin. The author's concluding statement that "in his music he was both honest and deadly serious" conveys the author's concluding attitude of respect. The correct answer is therefore EVENHANDED RESPECT.

4. **A:** The author's tone is clearly established in the first five words when he confidently asserts, "There is only one way.." This sense of strong conviction establishes a tone that is UNEQUIVOCAL (Word 274).

5. **E:** The author uses a straightforward presentation of facts to establish an overall tone that is impartial, academic, and learned. The correct answer is therefore OBJECTIVE AND SCHOLARLY (Word 58).

6. **E:** The author's final sentence is intended to convey an important message about refusing to obey evil orders while also defending the values of "tolerance and respect for others." The correct answer is therefore DIDACTIC (Word 53).

7. C: The author succinctly summarizes his attitude toward the Lower East Side's "jarring juxtaposition of cultures" when he declares, "I'm wary of both worlds." The key word "wary" tells us that the author is cautious. His final acknowledgement that "great dangers lay ahead" expresses his sense of unease. The correct answer is therefore CAUTIOUS UNEASE.

8. C: The author unambiguously declares that the widespread belief that teenagers "will inevitably succumb to peer pressure" is "erroneous." The author's forceful statement conveys a feeling of great conviction. The correct answer is therefore EMPHATIC (Word 54).

9. A: The narrator's overall mood is complex and nuanced. Although she is clearly very sad, the narrator is not MOROSE or deeply depressed. As she reflects on the passing of her husband the narrator is neither lighthearted (Word 59) nor exasperated (Word 427). The key phrase "I had a soft, distant smile on my face" supports the view that her overall mood is sadly thoughtful. The correct answer is therefore WISTFUL (Word 73).

10. D: The author prepares us for his final two sentences by stating that Margaret "liked to pretend that she would do poorly in calculus." However, while no one was looking, Margaret SURREPTITIOUSLY (Word 482) studied prep books and even hired a personal tutor. These CLANDESTINE (Word 481) activities helped prepare Margaret to achieve a high score on her calculus test. Given this context, it comes as no surprise that the author mocks Margaret's "effortless" performance and false modesty. SARDONIC (Word 62) best captures the author's very sarcastic tone.

CHAPTER 58

CRITICAL READING – ANSWERING VOCABULARY–IN–CONTEXT QUESTIONS

Many words in the English language have multiple meanings. For example, the Free Online Dictionary lists 7 different definitions or uses of the word common. Possible definitions of common include: shared (common interests), widespread (a common saying), ordinary (a common person), coarse (common manners), familiar (a common sight), plain (a common face), and frequent (a common occurrence).

When a word has many different meanings, how do you know which one the author is using? The intended meaning clearly depends upon the context in which the word is being used. For example, what does the word common mean within the context of this sentence: "She didn't see herself as a hero but simply as a common citizen." Since the author tells us that the woman didn't see herself as a hero, we are looking for a definition of common that means the opposite of hero. Within the context of this sentence, common means ordinary.

VOCABULARY–IN–CONTEXT QUESTIONS

College Board test writers are well aware of the large number of common words that have uncommon definitions. Recent tests have included more and more questions designed to test your knowledge of these words. Chapters 43 – 45 define and illustrate 30 key multiple meaning words.

Vocabulary-in-context questions are specifically designed to test your ability to use contextual clues to determine the meaning of a word or phrase with multiple meanings. Your SAT will include 3 – 5 vocabulary-in-context questions. Fortunately, these questions are very easy to spot. Here are the two most frequently used question stems:

- In line 15 the word "common" most nearly means
- In context, the phrase "XYZ" is best understood to mean

A CASE EXAMPLE

Read the following paragraph and then answer the accompanying vocabulary-in-context question:

In 1492, two complex but totally different cultures collided. Europeans believed that land could be bought, sold, and divided. In contrast, Native Americans viewed land as a common resource that, like water and air, could be used by everyone.

In line 3, "common" most nearly means
(A) coarse
(B) plain
(C) frequent
(D) familiar
(E) shared

All vocabulary-in-context questions provide a line reference. Your first step is to use this reference to go back to the passage and locate the appropriate sentence. It is wise to read both the sentence you are referred to and the ones that precede and follow it. This will provide you with a more complete context.

Vocabulary-in-context questions are very similar to sentence completion questions. As you have learned, each sentence completion question contains a key word or phrase that will lead you to the correct answer. The same principle applies to vocabulary-in-context questions. In the example above, Native Americans are described as viewing land as a "common resource" that "could be used by everyone." In contrast, Europeans "believed that land could be bought, sold, and divided." Native Americans viewed land as a resource that should be shared by everyone. Although choices (A), (B), (C), and (D) are all possible meanings of common, none of them is supported by contextual clues in the passage. Choice (E) is therefore the correct answer.

In this example, all of the answer choices are different definitions of the word common. It is important to remember that vocabulary-in-context answer choices can also include unrelated words. Don't let unrelated words fool you. They are distractors and should be deleted.

PRACTICE EXAMPLES

Read each of the following 10 paragraphs. Then use the contextual clues to determine the best answer for each question. Circle the correct answer.

1. There is only one way to shield the United States from the deleterious effects produced by our national addiction to fossil fuels. We must launch a sustained program to develop such green alternatives as wind and solar power. Such a farsighted policy will yield numerous benefits. It will end our dangerous dependence upon importing oil from nations that are often hostile to our national interests. It will also spur economic growth by creating new industries and new jobs.

In line 8, "yield" most nearly means
(A) surrender
(B) concede
(C) produce
(D) collapse
(E) retain

2. In 1883, Paul Gauguin left his family and a comfortable job to pursue a career as an artist. Gauguin promptly abandoned traditional paintings for what he called his "savage instinct." Seeking pure sensation untainted by decadent French civilization, Gauguin spent the final ten years of his life in Tahiti. He lived in a native hut and painted vividly colored, symbolic works that drew their inspiration from Tahitian carvings and customs.

In line 10, "drew" most nearly means
(A) sketched
(B) lured
(C) derived
(D) pumped out
(E) repelled

3. In Stanley Milgram's famous series of experiments on obedience his naïve subjects were innocent of the experiment's true purpose. Milgram cleverly told them that he was testing the effects of punishment on learning and memory. In reality, Milgram was testing factors that promote obedience to a person who is perceived as a legitimate authority figure.

In line 3, "innocent" most nearly means
(A) blameless
(B) unaware
(C) trusting
(D) unsullied
(E) harmless

4. Sonia Sotomayor is the first Hispanic and the third woman appointed to the United States Supreme Court. In her book *My Beloved World*, Sotomayor recounts her life from growing up in a crime-ridden Bronx housing project to attending Yale Law School and serving on the nation's highest court. Although her family lacked many material comforts, Sotomayor's home was always rich in love and understanding.

In line 10, "rich" most nearly means
(A) wealthy
(B) splendid
(C) filling
(D) deep
(E) abundant

5. Creating a world history textbook proved to be a difficult and often arduous undertaking. My first step was to write down a preliminary list of topics and then quickly group them into a rough chronological sequence. My editor promptly ordered me to reduce the list to 36 chapters, one for each week of the school year.

In line 5, "rough" most nearly means
   (A) rugged
   (B) harsh
   (C) untamed
   (D) boorish
   (E) approximate

6. A massive wave of "new" immigrants from southern and eastern Europe began to pour into American cities during the 1890s. They soon received a cold reception from unsympathetic Americans who kept their distance from the alien newcomers and their strange customs. One Italian saying expressed the sense of disillusionment felt by many immigrants: "I came to America because I heard the streets were paved with gold. When I got here, I found out three things: First, the streets weren't paved with gold; second, they weren't paved at all; and third, I was expected to pave them."

In line 4, "cold" most nearly means
   (A) impersonal
   (B) freezing
   (C) stale
   (D) unconscious
   (E) animated

7. Lyndon Johnson was one of the most influential Senate majority leaders in American history. Standing six foot three, the tall Texan dominated any room he entered. Johnson demonstrated great skill in the give and take needed to reach an agreement. People called his legendary ability to persuade Senators to support his bills, "the Johnson treatment." The Johnson treatment included a liberal use of flattery supplemented with generous special favors.

In line 10, "liberal" most nearly means
   (A) freethinking
   (B) tolerant
   (C) broad
   (D) plentiful
   (E) progressive

8. The kidnapping of Charles Lindbergh, Jr., the son of the world famous aviator Charles Lindbergh, was one of the most highly publicized crimes in the twentieth century. The 20-month-old infant was abducted from his family home near Hopewell, New Jersey on the evening of March 1, 1932. After an exhaustive investigation that took over two years, authorities arrested Bruno Hauptmann. A solid body of circumstantial evidence linked Hauptmann to the crime convincing jurors to find him guilty. However, Hauptmann never confessed and proclaimed his innocence until his execution on April 3, 1936.

In line 11, "solid" most nearly means
   (A) substantial
   (B) unbroken
   (C) rugged
   (D) uniform
   (E) unanimous

9. Mr. Hosokawa chose Rusalka as a measure of his respect for Miss Coss. It was the centerpiece of her repertoire and would require no extra preparation on her behalf, a piece that surely would have been in her program had he not requested it...He simply wanted to hear her sing Rusalka while standing close to her in a room. (from Bel Canto by Ann Patchett)

In line 1, "measure" most nearly means
(A) dimensions
(B) quantity
(C) plan
(D) indicator
(E) procedure

10. In his book *Cyber War*, government security expert Richard A. Clarke defines cyberwarfare as "actions by a nation-state to penetrate another nation's computers or networks for the purposes of causing damage or disruption." Clarke warns that China, Russia, and North Korea are devoting significant resources to preparing for cyber attacks against vulnerable American transportation, financial, and utility networks. At a major security conference he called upon the President and Congress to develop a broad plan to protect these vital U.S. facilities from hostile cyber attacks.

In line 14, "broad" most nearly means
(A) focused
(B) comprehensive
(C) open
(D) deep
(E) roomy

ANSWERS

1. C: The passage tells you that an energy policy based on green alternatives "will yield numerous benefits." The next two sentences then describe some of these benefits. Given this context, you can conclude that YIELD (Word 480) has a meaning that is similar to create. The correct answer is therefore PRODUCE.

2. C: The passage tells you that Gauguin "abandoned traditional paintings." Instead he spent his final year in Tahiti where he drew his inspiration from local carvings and customs. Given this context, you can conclude that DREW has a meaning that is the opposite of "abandoned" and is consistent with obtained. The correct answer is therefore DERIVED.

3. B: The passage tells you that Milgram's "naïve subjects were innocent" of the real purpose of his experiments. Instead of revealing the truth, Milgram told his subjects that the experiment was about "the effects of punishment on learning and memory." Given this context, you can conclude that INNOCENT has a meaning that is consistent with being naïve or not properly informed. The correct answer is therefore UNAWARE.

4. E: The passage tells you that although Sotomayor's family "lacked many materials comforts" it "was always rich in love and understanding." The key reversal word "although" tells you to look for a meaning of RICH that contrasts with "lacked." Given this context, you can conclude that RICH has a meaning that is the opposite of "lacked" and is consistent with full. The correct answer is therefore ABUNDANT.

5. E: The passage tells you that after writing "a preliminary list of topics" the narrator quickly grouped them in "a rough chronological sequence." The key phrase "quickly grouped" tells you to look for a meaning of ROUGH (Word 467) that is similar in meaning to nearly accurate. Given this context, the correct answer is therefore APPROXIMATE.

6. A: The passage tells you that the new immigrants "received a cold reception from unsympathetic Americans who kept their distance from the alien newcomers and their strange customs." The key phrases "unsympathetic Americans" and "kept their distance" tell you that the immigrants did not receive a warm welcome. Given this context, you can conclude that COLD (Word 465) has a meaning similar to detached and distant. The correct answer is therefore IMPERSONAL.

7. D: The passage tells you that the "Johnson treatment included a liberal use of flattery supplemented with generous special favors." The key word "generous" tells you that Lyndon Johnson made great use of flattery. Given this context, you can conclude that LIBERAL (Word 458) has a meaning similar to extensive. The correct answer is therefore PLENTIFUL.

8. A: The passage tells you that a "solid body of circumstantial evidence linked Hauptmann to the crime." The key word "circumstantial" tells you that the evidence involved at least some conjectures. In addition, Hauptmann always maintained his innocence. Given this context, you can conclude that SOLID has a meaning that is similar to considerable. The correct answer is therefore SUBSTANTIAL.

9. D: The passage tells you that "Mr. Hosokawa chose Rusalka as a measure of his respect for Miss Coss." The passage concludes by telling you that Mr. Hosokawa "wanted to hear her sing Rusalka while standing close to her in a room." The key phrase "standing close to her in a room" demonstrates Mr. Hosokawa's great respect for Miss Coss. Given this context, you can conclude that MEASURE has a meaning that is similar to point to or show. The correct answer is therefore INDICATOR.

10. B: The passage tells you that security expert Richard A. Clarke warns that hostile cyber attacks could threaten vulnerable American "industrial, financial, and governmental targets." Clarke has therefore called upon the President and Congress to develop "a broad plan to protect vital facilities." Given this context, you can conclude that BROAD (Word 460) has a meaning that is similar to extensive. The correct answer is therefore COMPREHENSIVE.

CHAPTER 59
CRITICAL READING – PRACTICE SETS 1 – 2

Critical reading passages and questions pose a major challenge for most students. The difficult Level 4 and 5 questions usually contain challenging vocabulary words. Chapters 55 – 58 introduce and illustrate key types of passage-based questions that rely on your ability to use and apply the key vocabulary words from Chapters 1 – 47.

This chapter is designed to give you an opportunity to practice your critical reading skills. Each of the following two practice sets contains 5 passages and 10 passage-based questions. Try to complete each set in less than 15 minutes.

CRITICAL READING PRACTICE SET 1: PASSAGES AND QUESTIONS

PASSAGE 1

To the modern reader the complex rules of etiquette that precisely regulated Louis XIV's life at the Versailles Palace appear to be a ridiculous and comical waste of time. But Louis knew better. The King explained that, "The people over whom we reign, being unable to apprehend the basic reality of things, usually derive their opinion from what they can see with their eyes." Louis was insightful. In France, "the basic reality of things" was that Louis XIV ruled as an absolute monarch by divine right. Unlike the King of England, Louis exercised an undisputed monopoly over all the power of the French government. Viewed from this perspective, the daily rituals at Versailles were an accurate visual display of the power and grandeur of the French monarchy.

1. **The passage suggests that the royal ceremonies at Versailles were best viewed as**
    (A) opulent but frivolous
    (B) haughty and impromptu
    (C) exacting and revealing
    (D) intricate but ultimately confounding
    (E) deceitful and recklessly decadent

2. **The author's general attitude toward Louis XIV is best described as one of**
    (A) guarded skepticism
    (B) righteous indignation
    (C) complete indifference
    (D) pragmatic recognition
    (E) subtle sarcasm

PASSAGE 2

The hallmark of the Hollywood superhero movie is a comic book hero who possesses a distinctive power. A spate of recent superhero movies included a Norse god who wields a cosmic hammer (**Thor**), a man in a pulsating lime-green bodysuit who sculpts objects made from his mind entirely of light (**The Green Lantern**), and a bionically enhanced paramilitary stoic who protects himself with an impenetrable shield (**Captain America: The First Avenger**). The backstories that power superhero movies are becoming increasingly repetitive and banal. We seem to be watching the same stories over and over again. Of course, given Hollywood's long-standing penchant for profits over artistic creativity this comes as no surprise.

3. The author characterizes the recent group of Hollywood superhero movies as
    (A) provocative and contentious
    (B) versatile and omnipotent
    (C) redundant and pedestrian
    (D) unique and eclectic
    (E) belligerent and nuanced

4. The author's tone in the final sentence ("Of course .. surprise") can best be described as
    (A) perplexed and nonchalant
    (B) disdainful and sardonic
    (C) exasperated and incredulous
    (D) emphatic but triumphant
    (E) ambivalent but optimistic

PASSAGE 3

"Archana, I'm really apprehensive about leaving home and going to a college in the South. The people are so different in that part of the country. I'll never fit in. And I'll miss the Rocky Mountains. They are always in the background towering above the Plains. I should stay home in Boulder."

Archana did not appreciate my litany of complaints. "You're a spoiled brat!" she scornfully upbraided. Archana sounded irate and she was. "Madison, you've led a sheltered life here in the Boulder bubble. It's time for you to go out and experience a new place and meet new people."

5. In line 5, "appreciate" most nearly means
   (A) rise in value
   (B) feel indebted to
   (C) highly rate
   (D) openly welcome
   (E) partially underestimate

6. Which of the following best characterizes the tone of Archana's statement in line 5 ("You're a .. brat")?
   (A) A mild rebuke
   (B) A supportive admonition
   (C) A welcome verification
   (D) An unalloyed compliment
   (E) An indignant reprimand

7. Archana would most likely characterize Madison as
   (A) romantic yet timid
   (B) perceptive yet dilatory
   (C) naïve and provincial
   (D) sensible and pragmatic
   (E) ambitious but duplicitous

PASSAGE 4

Aloka Gupta gazed down from the window of her apartment at the gray-brown bustle of Manhattan's Fifty-Second Street, her thoughts turning to her childhood home and the family-owned tea plantation in Darjeeling. The cold jumble of glass, concrete, chrome, and steel before her now stood in cruel contrast to the allure of that idyllic time…As she turned away, the final divorce papers, legal-sized and officiously stamped with the seal of the state of New York and the day's date, stared accusingly from the top of her writing desk. (from *Darjeeliing* by Bharti Kirchner)

8. Aloka Gupta's mood in lines 1 – 4 ("Aloka Gupta … time") is best characterized as a mix of
    (A) reflection and nostalgia
    (B) apprehension and heartlessness
    (C) prudence and caution
    (D) elation and mirth
    (E) rejection and disdain

9. Lines 4 – 7 ("As she … desk") are noteworthy for their use of which of the following rhetorical devices?
    (A) simile
    (B) rebuttal
    (C) paradox
    (D) parallel structure
    (E) personification

PASSAGE 5

Margaret Miller always liked to pretend that she would do poorly on our calculus tests. She insisted that she didn't understand the material and was sure to fail the next big test. Of course, when no one was looking, Margaret was hard at work studying. In addition to our textbook, she had several prep books and even hired a tutor from the local community college. When the test day finally arrived, Margaret was fully prepared. I glanced at her during the test and what do you know – her fingers effortlessly hit the buttons on her expensive calculator and the correct answer miraculously flashed on her screen. Needless to say, Margaret modestly attributed her high score to good luck.

10.The description of Margaret Miller in lines 1 – 8 ("Margaret Miller … luck") depicts her as
   (A) nonchalant and obstreperous
   (B) diffident and maudlin
   (C) studious and aloof
   (D) forthright and shrewd
   (E) disingenuous and resourceful

CRITICAL READING PRACTICE SET 1: ANSWERS

1. C: The passage tells you that the rules of etiquette at Versailles were "complex," "precise," and "an accurate visual display." These key words support choice (C) EXACTING (Word 148) and REVEALING.

2. D: The author begins by stating that modern readers view Louis XIV and his rules of etiquette as "a ridiculous and comical waste of time." The author then explains that Louis XIV used the daily rituals to display "the power and grandeur of the French monarchy." This argument supports an answer that is consistent with a practical acknowledgement. The correct answer is therefore choice (D) PRAGMATIC (Word 4) RECOGNITION.

3. C: The author describes the recent group of superhero movies as "increasingly repetitive and banal." He then reinforces this view by writing that "We seem to be watching the same stories over and over again." The key phrases "repetitive" and "over and over again" support REDUNDANT. The key word "banal" supports PEDESTRIAN. The correct answer is therefore choice (C) REDUNDANT and PEDESTRIAN (Word 457).

4. B: The author prepares you for his final sentence by using negative words and phrases to describe the recent group of Hollywood superhero movies. Given this context, you should look for a negative pair of answers that convey a tone of contempt and sarcasm. The correct answer is therefore DISDAINFUL (Word 66) and SARDONIC (Word 62).

5. D: The passage tells you that Archana "scornfully upbraided" Madison for her "litany of complaints." Given this context, you can conclude that APPRECIATE has a meaning that is similar to receive. The correct answer is therefore (D) OPENLY WELCOME.

6. E: Archana's tone is forceful and unequivocal. The key phrase "scornfully upbraid" and the key word "irate" both convey Archana's feeling of outrage and disapproval. The correct answer is therefore (E) an INDIGNANT (Word 61) REPRIMAND (see Word 378).

7. C: Archana concludes by telling Madison that it is time for her to leave the "Boulder bubble" and experience new places and new people. We can conclude that Archana believes that Madison is leading an overly sheltered life. This supports choice (C) NAÏVE (Word 183) and PROVINCIAL (see Word 478).

8. A: The key phrases "gazed down" and "her thoughts turning to" tell you that Aloka Gupta's mood is quietly thoughtful. She is thinking about the "idyllic" times she enjoyed at her family's "tea plantation in Darjeeling." These key phrases convey a mood of thoughtfully longing for something in the past. The correct answer is therefore (A) REFLECTION (Word 77) and NOSTALGIA (Word 13).

9. E: In order for PERSONIFICATION to be the correct answer there must be an inanimate object that is given human characteristics. Lines 4 – 7 meet both of these tests. The divorce papers are given the human characteristic of staring "accusingly" at Aloka Gupta. The correct answer is therefore (E) PERSONIFICATION (Word 25).

10. E: The key phrase "liked to pretend" establishes that Margaret Miller is a deceptive person who is creating the false impression that she doesn't "understand the material" and will "fail the next big test." In reality, Margaret is a very shrewd and enterprising person who has purchased prep books and also "hired a tutor." These key facts support a negative first word that is consistent with being deceptive and a positive second word that is consistent with being shrewd and enterprising. The correct answer is therefore (E) DISINGENUOUS (Word 282) and RESOURCEFUL (see Word 365).

PRACTICE TEST 2

PASSAGE 6

According to a widespread but mistaken popular belief, Shakespeare's London was a golden age of culture and sophistication. In reality, a small army of vagabonds and criminals prowled the city's narrow streets and preyed on unlucky residents. The city's criminal population kept its jailors and executioners very busy. Judges had very little latitude in handing out punishments. London's harsh criminal code demanded that jailors cut off a thief's right ear. Executioners also had much to do. Over 200 crimes in Shakespeare's London were punishable by death. Some 800 English citizens were hung every year. The most notorious criminals and traitors were decapitated and had their heads placed on pikes at the entrance to London Bridge as a grim warning to other lawbreakers.

11. According to the author, the popular view of Shakespeare's London is
   (A) ubiquitous and logical
   (B) resilient and reverent
   (C) pervasive but erroneous
   (D) localized but misinformed
   (E) cavalier but overwrought

12. In line 5, the word "latitude" most nearly means
   (A) liberty
   (B) space
   (C) compass
   (D) restriction
   (E) sobriety

13. London's criminal code during the Age of Shakespeare is best described as
   (A) embryonic
   (B) draconian
   (C) cosmopolitan
   (D) theatrical
   (E) benevolent

PASSAGE 7

On February 15, 2013 an asteroid with the seemingly harmless name of 2012 DA14 passed within 17,200 miles of the Earth's surface. The asteroid is about 150 feet in diameter and has a mass estimated at about 143,000 tons. But don't be fooled by 2012 DA14's deceptively small size. According to NASA astronomer Don Yeomas, "Should an object that size hit Earth, it would cause a blast with the energy equivalent of about 2.4 million tons – or 2.4 megatons – of TNT explosives, more than 180 times the power of the atomic blast that leveled Hiroshima."

Yeomas and his colleagues at NASA believe that we should take the threat of an asteroid striking Earth very seriously. Scientists speculate that about 65 million years ago an asteroid 6 miles in diameter collided with Earth and killed the dinosaurs and most large vertebrates. Fortunately, we have the technology to prevent such a catastrophe from happening again. NASA could send a specially armed spacecraft to crash into the asteroid and deflect its trajectory. It appears that the dinosaurs became extinct because they didn't have a space program to protect them.

14. The author's tone in the last sentence ("It appears ... them") can best be described as
    (A) a rueful confession
    (B) a resentful accusation
    (C) a nostalgic rumination
    (D) a grudging admission
    (E) a wry aside

15. Compared to paragraph 1, paragraph 2 is primarily focused on
    (A) an objective description
    (B) a scholarly counterargument
    (C) a vehement plea
    (D) a hypothetical scenario
    (E) a flippant anecdote

PASSAGE 8

British archaeologist Howard Carter discovered the entrance to Pharaoh Tutankhamen's tomb on November 26, 1922. Carter had indeed found the tomb but it took several years of meticulous work to locate the royal mummy. The young pharaoh's burial chamber lay behind yet another sealed door. When that door was opened, Carter's electric lamp revealed a breathtaking sight – a large, box-shaped shrine of gilded wood that filled the entire room. Nested within the large shrine were three smaller ones, and within the smallest shrine was a great stone coffin.

Carter's crew of workers used a rope and tackle to slowly hoist the heavy lid off the coffin. From inside, a golden face looked up at them through deep blue eyes of precious stones. Resting lightly on this gleaming mask was a fragile wreath of flowers placed by Tutankhamen's young widow. Carter later wrote that, "Among all that regal splendor, that royal magnificence there was nothing so beautiful as those few withered flowers. They told us what a short period 3,300 years really was."

16. The author characterizes Carter's work as
    (A) arduous and futile
    (B) painstaking and exacting
    (C) dilatory and unparalleled
    (D) clandestine and inconclusive
    (E) compassionate and exasperating

17. The wreath of flowers (lines 10 – 13) is best described as
    (A) a watershed event in the history of ancient Egypt
    (B) a perplexing clue that remains an unsolved mystery
    (C) an impediment that forced Carter to curtail his investigation
    (D) an evocation that connects the past with the present
    (E) a radiant symbol of Tutankhamen's power and wealth

PASSAGE 9

Dr. Kreskey dominated the Bell Laboratory during a period of exhilarating scientific discoveries and demoralizing budget cuts. Everyone had an opinion about "the boss." To his admirers, Dr. K was a leader of unquestioned integrity, sincere dedication, and lofty standards of excellence. To his critics, Dr. K was a humorless and imperious tyrant who stubbornly insisted that his vision was best for the organization. In spite of his faults, Dr. Kreskey nevertheless had a knack for instilling an invincible sense of professional pride into each research scientist. For example, whenever he evaluated a new project, Dr. K would convince himself, and us, that it was "the greatest idea since Einstein."

18. The author's overall attitude toward Dr. Kreskey is best described as one of
    (A) intense consternation
    (B) professional admiration
    (C) private indignation
    (D) public bewilderment
    (E) secret disillusionment

19. Which of the following best describes how Dr. Kreskey's critics viewed his style of leadership?
    (A) He was a supercilious leader who was oddly irresolute.
    (B) He was an earnest leader who displayed great personal rectitude.
    (C) He was an egalitarian leader who advocated misguided policies.
    (D) He was a despotic leader who compromised his principles.
    (E) He was a domineering leader who was overbearing and obstinate.

PASSAGE 10

Qigong is an integrated mind-body healing method that has been practiced with remarkable results in China for thousands of years. The Chinese have long treasured qigong for its effectiveness both in healing and in preventing disease. More recently they have used it in conjunction with modern medicine to cure cancer immune system disorders and other life-threatening conditions. (from *The Way of Qigong* by Kenneth S. Cohen)

20. According to the passage, the goal of qigong is to create
    (A) a harmonious unity
    (B) an incongruent hodgepodge
    (C) an autonomous superstructure
    (D) an emergency stopgap
    (E) a dissonant conflation

CRITICAL READING PRACTICE SET 2: ANSWERS

11. C: According to the author, the popular view that Shakespeare's London was a "golden age of culture and sophistication" is both "widespread" and "mistaken." The key word "widespread" will support either UBIQUITOUS (Word 217) in choice (A) or PERVASIVE (see Word 217) in choice (C). The key word "mistaken" does not support LOGICAL in choice (A). However, it does support ERRONEOUS (Word 331) in choice (C). The correct answer is therefore choice (C) PERVASIVE (see Word 217) but ERRONEOUS (Word 331).

12. A: The passage tells you that judges had "very little latitude in handing out punishments." Instead, London had a "harsh criminal code" that required severe punishments for specific crimes. Given this context, you can conclude that LATITUDE (Word 463) has a meaning that is consistent with freedom of action. The correct answer is therefore (A) LIBERTY.

13. B: The key word "harsh" tells you to look for an answer that means very severe. The correct answer is therefore (B) DRACONIAN (Word 135).

14. E: The last sentence is a witty departure from the main body of the passage. The statement provides an excellent example of a dry sense of humor. The correct answer is therefore (E) a WRY (Word 173) ASIDE.

15. D: Paragraph 1 provides an objective fact-filled discussion of asteroid 2012 DA14. In contrast, paragraph 2 shifts the discussion by using the key phrases "we should take," "Scientists speculate that," and "NASA could send," The key words "should," "speculate," and "could" all support the author's shift to a more speculative discussion. The correct answer is therefore (D) a HYPOTHETICAL SCENARIO.

16. B: The passage tells you that it took Carter "several years of meticulous work" to locate Pharaoh Tutankhamen's royal mummy. The key word METICULOUS (Word 148) will lead you to an answer that means very precise and careful. The correct answer is therefore (B) PAINSTAKING (Word 147) and EXACTING (see Word 147).

17. D: The "wreath of flowers" clearly touched Carter. He writes that even "among all that regal splendor" the withered flowers "told us what a short period 3,300 years really was." The wreath thus had the power to call forth a vivid memory. The correct answer is therefore (D) an EVOCATION (Word 302) that connects the past with the present.

18. B: The author begins by comparing the attitudes of Dr. Kreskey's admirers with those of his critics. Not surprisingly, the admirers use positive words to describe Dr. K, while the critics use a series of negative words. The author's attitude is contained in the final two sentences of the passage. While acknowledging that Dr. K has faults, the author praises him for "instilling an invincible sense of professional pride into each research scientist." This achievement supports an answer that expresses a positive attitude. The correct answer is therefore (B) PROFESSIONAL ADMIRATION.

19. E: Dr. Kreskey's critics describe him as "humorless," "imperious," and stubborn. These negative answers will enable you to delete the positive words in choices (B) and (C) and focus on choices (A), (D), and (E). The key to finding the correct answer is to look at the second part of each of these answer choices. You can delete (A) because Dr. Kreskey was not "oddly irresolute" and (D) because Dr. Kreskey did not compromise his principles. Only choice (E) is fully supported by the passage. According to his critics, Dr. K was a domineering leader who was OVERBEARING (Word 377) and OBSTINATE (see Word 145).

20. A: According to the passage, qigong is an "integrated mind-body healing method." The key phrase "integrated mind-body" leads you to look for an answer that is consistent with an agreeable blend. The correct answer is therefore (A) a HARMONIOUS unity.

APPENDIX:
THE TOP 30 SAT ROOTS

You have now learned over 500 high-frequency SAT vocabulary words. This Appendix is designed to further AUGMENT your SAT LEXICON by teaching you 30 of the most frequently used roots and 94 words derived from them. A root is a word or word element from which other words are formed. Learning roots will give you insights into unfamiliar words that will enable you to answer difficult questions. For example, one Level 4 question asked students to read the following sentence and determine how the narrator viewed Lewis' hand: "I watched his hand rather than the location, for it seemed to have power over the terrain." Knowing that the root POTEN means power will enable you to connect the passage word "power" with the correct answer OMNIPOTENT meaning all-powerful.

1. ACRI AND ACER:

- *Latin roots that mean SHARP, VERY BITTER*
ACUTE – very sharp, as a keen insight
ACUMEN – mental sharpness, keenness
ACERBIC – characterized by a bitter, cutting tone
EXACERBATE – to make something very bitter; to worsen
ACRIMONIOUS – filled with bitterness and strong resentment; rancorous in tones

2. AMICUS:

- *a Latin root meaning FRIEND*
AMICABLE – characterized by or showing friendliness
AMITY – friendly relations between people or countries
AMIABLE – good-natured and friendly; affable

3. BELLI:

- *a Latin root meaning WAR*
REBELLION – an uprising that leads to war
ANTEBELLUM – before the war, especially the American Civil War
BELLIGERENT – waging war and thus inclined to fight
BELLICOSE – warlike; favoring war to settle a dispute

4. CHRON:

- *a Greek root meaning TIME*
CHRONOLOGY – the story of events in time
CHRONICLE – a record of events in order of time
CHRONIC – a condition, habit, or disease that occurs all the time
ANACHRONISM – an event placed out of its proper time

5. CLUD AND CLUS:

- *Latin roots meaning CLOSE, SHUT*
EXCLUDE – to shut out
CONCLUSION – the close or end of a story
PRECLUDE – to exclude or shut out beforehand;
to prevent because of preexisting conditions
RECLUSIVE – describes someone who prefers to shut out and
therefore retire from the rest of the world

6. CRED:

- *a Latin root meaning BELIEF*
CREDIBLE – capable of being believed; plausible
CREED – a formal system of beliefs
CREDIBILITY – the quality of being believable; trustworthy
CREDULOUS – disposed to believe too readily;
tending to believe something with little evidence
DISCREDIT – to cause to be disbelieved or distrusted

7. DEMOS:

- *a Greek root meaning PEOPLE*
DEMOGRAPHY – the study of vital statistics about people
DEMAGOGUE – a leader who uses passionate speeches to agitate the people

8. FID:

- *a Latin root meaning TRUST, FAITH*
FIDELITY – to faithfully perform one's duties and obligations
CONFIDENT – a person you can trust completely
DIFFIDENT – lacking faith or confidence in oneself
PERFIDIOUS – to show disloyalty and treachery

9. FLU:

- *a Latin root meaning TO FLOW*
FLUENT – able to speak readily; the words literally flow out of your mouth
CONFLUENCE – to flow together
MELLIFLUOUS – to literally flow like honey and thus to be sweet and
flowing like a lullaby
SUPERFLUOUS – to flow above in the sense of exceeding what is necessary

10. GREG:

- *a Latin root meaning FLOCK or HERD; in English
  the root GREG means GROUP*
CONGREGATE – to flock together in a group
SEGREGATE – to separate the flock into different groups
GREGARIOUS – living in flocks or herds and therefore very sociable
EGREGIOUS – standing out from the herd in the negative sense of
being extraordinarily bad
AGGREGATE – to gather different groups into a whole new flock or total

11. LOQU:

- *a Latin root meaning TALK*
  LOQUACIOUS – very talkative
  LOCUTION – a word or expression that is used by a particular person or group; a style of speaking

12. LUC AND LUMEN:

- *Latin roots meaning LIGHT*
  LUCID – filled with light and thus very clear
  ELUCIDATE – to bring into the light and thus clarify
  LUMINOUS – bathed in light; glowing

13. MORI:

- *a Latin root meaning to DIE or DEATH*
  MORIBUND – near death; stagnant
  MOROSE – very despondent and gloomy

14. MORPH:

- *a Latin root meaning SHAPE or FORM*
  AMORPHOUS – lacking shape or form
  ANTHROPOMORPHIC – taking human shape

15. MUT:

- *a Latin root meaning CHANGE*
  MUTATE: to undergo a great change
  IMMUTABLE – not able to be changed

16. NOV:

- *a Latin root meaning NEW*
  NOVEL – new and unusual
  NOVICE – a person who is new at an occupation; a beginner
  INNOVATE – to introduce new ideas; methods, or products
  INNOVATOR – a person who introduces new ideas, methods, or products
  RENOVATE – to restore or make new again

17. ONUS:

- *a Latin word meaning BURDEN*
  ONEROUS – very burdensome
  EXONERATE– to be freed from a burden; to be free from blame

18. PACIS:

- *a Latin word meaning PEACE*
PACIFY – to bring peace to; to calm or soothe
PACIFISM – a doctrine that opposes war and the use of military force
PACIFIST – a person who opposes war or the use of physical force to settle disputes

19. PAR:

- *a Latin root meaning EQUAL*
PARITY – equality in amount, value, or status
DISPARITY– an inequality in age, rank, income, or treatment
DISPARATE – entirely dissimilar; completely unequal

20. PATHOS:

- *a Greek root meaning FEELING*
APATHY – to show no feeling or emotion
ANTIPATHY – to show feelings against someone or something
EMPATHY– to share strong feelings with someone;
to feel as one would in another's place; great sympathy
EMPHATIC (WORD 27) – to express very strong feelings about
someone or something; great conviction

21. PLAC:

- *a Latin root meaning CALM*
PLACID – to be outwardly calm and composed
PLACATE– to calm someone down especially by appeasing or yielding concessions
COMPLACENT – to be so calm as to be self-satisfied or smug
IMPLACABLE – cannot be calmed down and therefore relentless

22. POTEN:

- *a Latin root meaning POWERFUL*
OMNIPOTENT – all-powerful
POTENTATE – a very powerful person

23. PUG:

- *a Latin root meaning FIST*
PUGILIST – a professional boxer
PUGNACIOUS – literally someone who is eager to use his or her fists
and therefore quick to fight; combative
IMPUGN – to use one's verbal fists in the sense of challenging, questioning
or criticizing the accuracy or honesty of someone

24. QUIESCERE:

- *a Latin word meaning QUIET*
QUIESCENT – quiet and still
ACQUIESCENT – quietly accepting something

25. SCRIB:

- *a Latin root meaning WRITE*
CIRCUMSCRIBE – literally to write around in the sense of limiting or restricting
PROSCRIBE – to write rules that forbid or prohibit an action or behavior

26. SEMIN:

- *a Latin root meaning SEED*
DISSEMINATE – to spread widely, as in spreading seeds
SEMINAL – literally an idea that is a seed for an important and
original theory or new intellectual system of thought

27. SPEC AND SPIC:

- *Latin roots meaning to SEE or OBSERVE*
SPECTATOR – someone who sees or watches an event
PERSPECTIVE – how you see something; a point of view
CIRCUMSPECT – literally to see around and thus to be cautious and careful
PERSPICACITY – to see through in the sense of being very perceptive or astute

28. TEN:

- *a Latin root meaning to HOLD*
TENACIOUS– to hold firmly to something; to be very persistent
TENABLE – capable of being held, defensible
TENUOUS – very thin and flimsy; difficult to hold

29. TURB:

- *a Latin root meaning TROUBLED*
TURBULENT – very disturbed; agitated
IMPERTURBABLE– not easily troubled or disturbed
PERTURBED – to be greatly troubled and thus uneasy and anxious

30. VIVERE:

- *a Latin root meaning to LIVE*
VIVACIOUS – full of life and therefore animated
CONVIVIAL – full in life in the sense of enjoying feasting, drinking,
and good company

INDEX

A

WORD	NUMBER	PAGE	APPENDIX
Aberrant	19	9	
Abstemious	412	159	
Acclaim	398	153	
Acerbic	227	85	Root 1
Acolyte	84	36	
Acquiesce	264	100	Root 24
Acrimonious	346	132	Root 1
Acumen		282	Root 1
Acute		282	Root 1
Adamant	145	60	
Adept	435	168	
Adhere	432	167	
Admonish	332	127	
Adroit	156	61	
Adulation	401	155	
Aesthetic	1	3	
Affable	418	161	
Affront	357	137	
Aggregate		283	Root 10
Alleviate	3	4	
Allusion	33	16	
Aloof	373	144	
Altruistic	5	4	
Amalgam	238	89	
Ambiguous	351	135	
Ambivalent	71	31	
Ameliorate	312	119	
Amiable		282	Root 2
Amicable		282	Root 2
Amity		282	Root 2
Amorphous		284	Root 14
Anachronism	212	79	Root 4

WORD	NUMBER	PAGE	APPENDIX
Austere	452	175	
Austerity	319	122	
Autocratic	367	141	
Avarice	240	89	

B

WORD	NUMBER	PAGE	APPENDIX
Baleful	228	85	
Banal	457	177	
Bane	392	151	
Bastion	237	89	
Befuddled	300	114	
Beguile	14	8	
Belie	18	9	
Bellicose	225	84	Root 3
Belligerent		282	Root 3
Bellweather	356	136	
Bemoan	343	132	
Benefactor	87	37	
Bewilder	342	131	
Bias	48	21	
Bland	361	139	
Bohemian	297	113	
Bombastic	203	76	
Boon	393	152	
Boorish	467	181	
Brevity	191	71	
Broad	460	178	
Brooding	486	188	
Brusque	161	63	
Bucolic	339	129	
Burgeon	341	131	

C

WORD	NUMBER	PAGE	APPENDIX
Compassionate	188	71	
Complacent		285	Root 21
Complicity	375	144	
Compromise	476	184	
Compunction	313	120	
Concede	42	19	
Conciliatory	253	96	
Conclusion		282	Root 5
Confident		283	Root 8
Conflate	383	148	
Confluence	255	96	Root 9
Confound	342	131	
Congregate		283	Root 10
Conjecture	50	21	
Connoisseur	93	40	
Conspicuous	425	164	
Consternation	286	108	
Contentious	258	97	
Contrite	484	188	
Conventional	2	3	
Conundrum	245	92	
Conversational	78	33	
Convivial	340	130	Root 30
Copious	215	80	
Cosmopolitan	477	185	
Covet	389	149	
Credible	442	171	Root 6
Credulous	204	76	Root 6
Creed		283	Root 6
Criterion	49	21	
Crystallize	289	109	
Cull	359	137	
Cupidity	240	89	

WORD	NUMBER	PAGE	APPENDIX
Cursory	281	107	
Curt	162	63	
Curtail	319	122	

D

WORD	NUMBER	PAGE	APPENDIX
Dauntless	417	161	
Dearth	384	148	
Debacle	316	121	
Decry	61	27	
Deleterious	101	43	
Demagogue	96	41	Root 7
Demarcate	333	128	
Demise	102	43	
Demography		283	Root 7
Deprecate	370	142	
Deride	497	193	
Despondent	103	44	
Destitute	388	149	
Deter	400	153	
Devour	445	172	
Dexterous	155	61	
Dichotomy	206	77	
Didactic	53	24	
Diffident	6	4	Root 8
Digress	413	160	
Dilatory	268	101	
Dilapidated	494	192	
Dilettante	95	40	
Discerning	17	9	
Disconcerted	252	95	
Discredit	376	144	Root 6
Discriminating	464	180	
Disdain	66	29	

WORD	NUMBER	PAGE	APPENDIX
Disillusion	402	156	
Disingenous	232	87	
Disparate		285	Root 19
Disparity	407	157	Root 19
Dispel	413	167	
Disseminate		286	Root 26
Dissolute	218	81	
Distraught	372	143	
Divisive	443	172	
Doctor	466	181	
Dogmatic	378	145	
Drab	399	153	
Draconian	135	56	
Droll	174	66	
Dubious	64	28	
Duplicitous	314	120	

E

WORD	NUMBER	PAGE	APPENDIX
Earnest	55	24	
Eccentricity	213	80	
Eclectic	202	75	
Economical	454	176	
Ecstatic	315	120	
Edify	226	84	
Effusive	209	77	
Egregious	397	153	Root 10
Egalitarian	194	72	
Elitist	193	72	
Elucidate	244	92	Root 12
Elusive	403	156	
Elude	403	156	
Embellish	436	169	

WORD	NUMBER	PAGE	APPENDIX
Empathy	421	163	Root 20
Empirical	198	73	
Emphatic	54	24	Root 20
Emulate	374	144	
Endemic	320	122	
Enervate	271	103	
Enigma	303	116	
Enmity	143	59	
Enthrall	352	135	
Entrenched	239	89	
Ephemeral	230	85	
Epiphany	349	133	
Epitomize	229	85	
Equanimity	234	88	
Erroneous	331	127	
Erudite	140	57	
Eschew	326	124	
Esoteric	159	62	
Estrange	322	123	
Ethereal	236	88	
Eulogize	39	18	
Euphemism	40	18	
Euphoric	440	170	
Evasive	403	156	
Evenhanded	75	32	
Evocative	302	116	
Exacerbate	438	169	Root 1
Exacting	148	60	
Exasperated	427	165	
Excise	276	104	
Excoriate	154	61	
Execrable	364	140	
Exculpate	104	44	
Exhaustive	471	183	

WORD	NUMBER	PAGE	APPENDIX
Exhilarated	60	25	
Exhort	311	119	
Exonerate	109	44	Root 17
Exorbitant	105	44	
Extemporize	283	108	
Extol	398	153	
Extroverted	472	183	
Exuberant	52	23	
Exultant	292	112	

F

WORD	NUMBER	PAGE	APPENDIX
Fabricate	279	105	
Facetious	299	114	
Fashion	475	184	
Fastidious	357	137	
Feasible	448	173	
Fervent	439	24	
Fiasco	316	121	
Fickle	142	59	
Fidelity		283	Root 8
Figurative Language	24	12	
Flag	470	182	
Flamboyant	491	65	
Fleeting	230	85	
Flippant	63	28	
Florid	335	128	
Flourish	341	131	
Forbearance	270	102	
Forboding	292	112	
Forestall	327	125	
Fortuitous	315	120	
Foster	334	128	
Frank	7	5	

WORD	NUMBER	PAGE	APPENDIX
Frivolous	492	192	
Frugal	291	111	
Fundamental	419	161	
Furnish	469	181	
Furtive	482	187	
Futile	404	156	

G

WORD	NUMBER	PAGE	APPENDIX
Galvanize	282	107	
Garrulous	150	60	
Genial	418	161	
Genteel	237	89	
Gregarious	323	124	Root 10
Gullible	204	76	

H

WORD	NUMBER	PAGE	APPENDIX
Hackneyed	168	64	
Hail	398	153	
Hamper	180	67	
Harbinger	260	97	
Haughty	177	66	
Havoc	381	147	
Headstrong	293	112	
Hedonist	81	35	
Herald	444	172	
Heretic	98	41	
Heyday	423	164	
Hierarchy	426	164	
Hinder	180	67	
Histrionic	157	62	
Hodgepodge	493	192	
Hubris	130	53	
Hyperbole	32	16	

I

WORD	NUMBER	PAGE	APPENDIX
Iconoclast	85	36	
Idealistic	4	4	
Idiosyncrasy	213	80	
Ignominious	231	87	
Immutable		284	Root 15
Impasse	324	124	
Impassioned	439	169	
Imperil	382	147	
Imperious	178	66	
Imperturbable	171	65	Root 29
Impetus	329	125	
Implacable	277	105	Root 21
Implore	484	188	
Impoverished	312	119	
Improvise	283	108	
Impugn	278	105	Root 23
Impulsive	354	136	
Impunity	276	104	
Inadvertent	317	121	
Inane	298	108	
Incongruous	223	84	
Incredulous	247	93	
Indefatigable	262	99	
Indelible	233	88	
Indifferent	72	31	
Indigenous	320	122	
Indignant	61	27	
Indiscriminate	308	117	
Indiscreet	369	141	
Indomitable	133	56	
Indignant	61	27	
Indulgent	294	112	

WORD	NUMBER	PAGE	APPENDIX
Ineffable	241	91	
Inept	165	64	
Infinitesimal	307	117	
Inflame	186	70	
Ingenious	424	164	
Inimical	250	94	
Innocuous	199	73	
Innovator	88	37	Root 16
Innuendo	208	77	
Inscrutable	288	109	
Insidious	200	73	
Insipid	361	139	
Instill	437	169	
Interloper	83	36	
Intractable	146	60	
Intransigent	146	60	
Intrepid	417	161	
Invective	275	104	
Irascible	293	112	
Ire	486	188	
Irony	28	14	
Irreverent	196	72	

J

WORD	NUMBER	PAGE	APPENDIX
Jocular	57	25	
Jovial	57	25	
Juxtaposition	273	104	

L

WORD	NUMBER	PAGE	APPENDIX
Laconic	127	53	
Lament	343	132	
Lampoon	38	17	
Largesse	348	133	

WORD	NUMBER	PAGE	APPENDIX
Latitude	463	180	
Laud	398	153	
Levity	395	152	
Lexicon	100	42	
Liberal	458	177	
Licentious	218	81	
Lighthearted	59	25	
Litany	321	123	
Locution		284	Root 11
Loquacious	149	60	Root 11
Lucid	394	152	Root 12
Lucrative	415	160	
Lugubrious	243	92	
Luminous		284	Root 12

M

WORD	NUMBER	PAGE	APPENDIX
Machinations	363	140	
Magnanimous	181	69	
Maladroit	166	64	
Malaise	109	45	
Malicious	110	45	
Maudlin	139	57	
Mawkish	139	57	
Measured	80	34	
Melancholy	485	188	
Meld	383	148	
Mellifluous	235	88	Root 9
Mendacity	314	120	
Mentor	86	36	
Mercurial	138	57	
Metaphor	24	12	
Meteoric	358	137	
Meticulous	148	60	

O

WORD	NUMBER	PAGE	APPENDIX
Obdurate	146	60	
Objective	79	33	
Obstinate	146	60	
Obsolete	406	157	
Obstreperous	214	80	
Odd	461	179	
Officious	296	113	
Ominous	15	8	
Omnipotent		285	Root 22
Onerous		284	Root 17
Opaque	394	152	
Ornate	451	175	
Orthodox	98	41	
Ostentatious	496	65	
Overbearing	377	145	
Overwrought	158	62	

P

WORD	NUMBER	PAGE	APPENDIX
Pacifism		285	Root 18
Pacifist		285	Root 18
Pacify		285	Root 18
Painstaking	147	60	
Palliate	3	4	
Panoramic	398	153	
Pantheon	248	93	
Paradox	26	13	
Parallel Structure	30	14	
Parenthetical Expression	34	34	
Parity	407	157	Root 19
Parochial	478	185	

WORD	NUMBER	PAGE	APPENDIX
Partisan	152	61	
Pastoral	339	129	
Paucity	384	148	
Pedantic	295	112	
Pedestrian	457	177	
Penchant	175	66	
Peremptory	20	10	
Perfectionist	148	60	
Perfidious	280	105	Root 8
Perfunctory	318	121	
Periphery	450	173	
Pernicious	246	93	
Persevere	490	189	
Personification	25	13	
Perspicacity		286	Root 27
Pertinent	395	152	
Perturbed		286	Root 29
Pervasive	217	81	
Philanthropist	91	39	
Phlegmatic	256	96	
Placate	185	70	Root 21
Placid		285	Root 21
Platitudinous	167	64	
Plausible	422	163	
Plethora	384	148	
Poignant	368	141	
Polar	11	7	
Polarizing	443	172	
Polemic	279	105	
Pompous	70	30	
Portend	287	109	
Posthumous	328	125	
Potentate		285	Root 22

WORD	NUMBER	PAGE	APPENDIX
Restitution	390	150	
Resurgence	108	45	
Reticent	10	5	
Retiring	472	183	
Revere	8	5	
Reverent	195	72	
Revile	449	173	
Revulsion	360	137	
Rough	467	181	
Ruminate	259	97	
Ruse	269	102	
Rustic	339	129	
Ruthless	187	71	

S

WORD	NUMBER	PAGE	APPENDIX
Sacrosanct	85	36	
Saga	22	12	
Sagacity	90	38	
Sage	90	38	
Salient	499	193	
Salutary	266	101	
Sanctuary	485	188	
Sanguine	51	23	
Sardonic	62	28	
Satire	35	17	
Savvy	184	70	
Scathing	154	61	
Scenario	420	161	
Scholarly	58	25	
Scourge	275	104	
Segregate		283	Root 10
Self-deprecation	370	142	

WORD	NUMBER	PAGE	APPENDIX
Superfluous	385	148	Root 9
Surly	243	92	
Surreptitious	482	187	
Synthesis	238	89	

T

WORD	NUMBER	PAGE	APPENDIX
Taciturn	284	108	
Tackle	479	185	
Tactless	369	141	
Tangent	413	160	
Tedious	32	16	
Temper	473	184	
Tenable		286	Root 28
Tenacious	447	173	Root 28
Tendentious	151	61	
Tenuous		286	Root 28
Theatrical	170	65	
Theoretical	197	73	
Thwart	179	67	
Trenchant	493	192	
Trepidation	228	85	
Trite	168	64	
Trivial	128	53	
Trivialize	433	168	
Truncate	261	99	
Turbulent		286	Root 28
Tutelage	86	36	

U

WORD	NUMBER	PAGE	APPENDIX
Ubiquitous	217	81	
Unaffected	118	49	
Unambiguous	285	108	

WORD	NUMBER	PAGE	APPENDIX
Vindictive	182	69	
Virtuosity	379	145	
Visceral	380	145	
Vitriolic	308	117	
Vituperative	207	77	
Vivacious	353	136	Root 30
Volatile	267	101	
Voluminous	215	80	
Voluptuous	124	52	
Voracious	445	172	

W

WORD	NUMBER	PAGE	APPENDIX
Watershed	216	80	
Wary	69	30	
Whimsical	74	32	
Wistful	73	32	
Wry	173	66	

Y

WORD	NUMBER	PAGE	APPENDIX
Yield	480	186	

Z

WORD	NUMBER	PAGE	APPENDIX
Zealot	100	42	
Zealous	473	184	

Made in the USA
San Bernardino, CA
08 April 2014